Merrell's Strong Kids—Grades 6-8

Second Edition

STRONG KIDS™

Other programs in **Strong Kids™:**
A Social & Emotional Learning Curriculum

Merrell's Strong Start—Pre-K:
A Social & Emotional Learning Curriculum,
Second Edition

Merrell's Strong Start—Grades K–2:
A Social & Emotional Learning Curriculum,
Second Edition

Merrell's Strong Kids—Grades 3–5:
A Social & Emotional Learning Curriculum,
Second Edition

Merrell's Strong Teens—Grades 9–12:
A Social & Emotional Learning Curriculum,
Second Edition

Merrell's Strong Kids—Grades 6-8

A Social & Emotional Learning Curriculum

Second Edition

by

Dianna Carrizales-Engelmann, Ph.D.
University of Oregon
Eugene

Laura L. Feuerborn, Ph.D.
University of Washington, Tacoma

Barbara A. Gueldner, Ph.D.
Successful Kids Today
Steamboat Springs, Colorado

and

Oanh K. Tran, Ph.D.
California State University
Hayward

·PAUL·H·
BROOKES
PUBLISHING C°®

Baltimore • London • Sydney

Paul H. Brookes Publishing Co.
Post Office Box 10624
Baltimore, Maryland 21285-0624
USA

www.brookespublishing.com

Typeset by Absolute Service, Inc., Towson, Maryland.
Manufactured in the United States of America by
Sheridan Books, Inc., Chelsea, Michigan.

Cover image © istockphoto/ranplett.
Stock photos and clip art are © istockphoto.com and Jupiterimages Corporation.

Source for Chapter 1 extract: From "Enhancing school-based prevention and youth development through coordinated social, emotional, and academic learning," by M.T. Greenberg, et al., *American Psychologist*, 2003, 58, pp. 466–474.

Library of Congress Cataloging-in-Publication Data

The Library of Congress has cataloged the print edition as follows:

Names: Carrizales-Engelmann, Dianna, author. | Merrell, Kenneth W. Strong start.
Title: Merrell's strong kids, grades 6-8 : a social and emotional learning curriculum / Dianna Carrizales-Engelmann, Ph.D., University of Oregon, Eugene; Laura L. Feuerborn, Ph.D., University of Washington, Tacoma; Barbara A. Gueldner, Ph.D., Successful Kids Today, Steamboat Springs, Colorado and Oanh K. Tran, Ph.D., California State University, East Bay.
Description: Second edition. | Baltimore, Maryland : Brookes Publishing, 2016. | Series: Strong kids | Revised edition of: Strong start / Kenneth W. Merrell. c2007. | Includes bibliographical references and index.
Identifiers: LCCN 2015038553 | ISBN 9781598579543 (paperback)
Subjects: LCSH: Affective education. | Education, Elementary. | Social learning. | Child development. | Emotional intelligence. | Education–Social aspects.
Classification: LCC LB1072 .C366 2016 | DDC 370.15/34--dc23 LC record available at http://lccn.loc.gov/2015038553

British Library Cataloguing in Publication data are available from the British Library.

2020   2019

10   9   8   7   6   5   4   3

Contents

About the Downloadable Material

Purchasers of this book may download, print, and/or photocopy the ancillary material for educational use. These materials are included with the print book and are also available at www.brookespublishing.com/downloads, keycode: 36geDaK4f

CONTENTS OF THE DOWNLOADABLE MATERIAL

Lesson 1

Supplement 1.1: The Limbic System
Supplement 1.2: *Strong Kids* Rules
Supplement 1.3: Comment Slip
Supplement 1.4: *Strong Kids* Lessons
Supplement 1.5: Key Terms and Definitions
Supplement 1.6: List of Emotions
Supplement 1.7: My Emotions

Lesson 2

Supplement 2.1: Picture of a Ferris Wheel
Supplement 2.2: Key Terms and Definitions
Supplement 2.3: Practice Scenarios
Supplement 2.4: Emotions Volume Slider
Supplement 2.5: Identifying and Measuring My Emotions

Lesson 3

Supplement 3.1: Thoughts, Emotions, and Behaviors
Supplement 3.2: Key Terms and Definitions
Supplement 3.3: Cartoon Example
Supplement 3.4: Practice Situations
Supplement 3.5: Ways of Showing Emotions

Lesson 4

Supplement 4.1: Key Terms and Definitions
Supplement 4.2: List of Emotions
Supplement 4.3: Small-Group Student Role-Play Scenarios
Supplement 4.4: Empathy Assignment

Lesson 5

Supplement 5.1: Key Terms and Definitions
Supplement 5.2: What Problem Does My Anger Want Me to Solve?
Supplement 5.3: How Much Does This Bother You?
Supplement 5.4: What Does MY Anger Look Like?
Supplement 5.5: Anger Model
Supplement 5.6: Marcella's Problem
Supplement 5.7: Anger Management Skills and Strategies
Supplement 5.8: Anger Management Worksheet

Lesson 6

Supplement 6.1: Picture of a Snake
Supplement 6.2: Picture of a Herpetologist
Supplement 6.3: Key Terms and Definitions
Supplement 6.4: Picture of a Thought Bubble
Supplement 6.5: Picture of a Man Trapped in a Hole
Supplement 6.6: Common Thinking Traps
Supplement 6.7: Example Situations
Supplement 6.8: Practice Situations Worksheet

Lesson 7

Supplement 7.1: Thinking Traps
Supplement 7.2: Picture of a Snowball
Supplement 7.3: Key Terms and Definitions
Supplement 7.4: Emotions Volume Slider
Supplement 7.5: Picture of Looking for Evidence
Supplement 7.6: Looking for Evidence to Reframe
Supplement 7.7: Evidence for or Against
Supplement 7.8: Reframing Thinking Traps Examples
Supplement 7.9: Reframing Thinking Traps Using Evidence
Supplement 7.10: Reframing Thinking Traps Worksheet

Lesson 8

Supplement 8.1: Pictures of Two Students Arguing
Supplement 8.2: Key Terms and Definitions
Supplement 8.3: Conflict Resolution: What Can I Do?
Supplement 8.4: A Four-Step Problem-Solving Model for Conflict Resolution
Supplement 8.5: Using a Problem-Solving Model to Resolve Conflicts

Lesson 9

Supplement 9.1: Pictures of Stressful Situations
Supplement 9.2: Key Terms and Definitions
Supplement 9.3: Stress Symptoms and Example Situations
Supplement 9.4: Personal Triggers and Stress Identification
Supplement 9.5: Relaxation Techniques
Supplement 9.6: Letting Go of Stress

Lesson 10

Supplement 10.1: Key Terms and Definitions
Supplement 10.2: Feeling Good Activities
Supplement 10.3: Healthy Habits
Supplement 10.4: Weekday Habits and Routines
Supplement 10.5: Weekend Habits and Routines
Supplement 10.6: Example Situation: Helping Marcella Make Healthy Choices
Supplement 10.7: What Did You Do Toward Positive Living This Week?

Lesson 11

Supplement 11.1: Your Younger Self
Supplement 11.2: Key Terms and Definitions
Supplement 11.3: Healthy Living Domains
Supplement 11.4: Examples and Nonexamples of Setting Goals
Supplement 11.5: Setting SMART Goals
Supplement 11.6: Steps to Setting and Attaining Goals
Supplement 11.7: Personal Goal Organizer

Lesson 12

Supplement 12.1: *Strong Kids* Lesson Review and Discussion Questions
Supplement 12.2: Resilience Example Slogans
Supplement 12.3: Helping Resources Handout
Certificate of Achievement

Appendix A

Strong Kids Knowledge Test for Students in Grades 6–8

Appendix B

Basic Fidelity Checklist

About the Authors

Dianna Carrizales-Engelmann, Ph.D., College of Education, 230Q HEDCO, 1215 University of Oregon, Eugene, OR 97403

Dianna Carrizales-Engelmann is currently an instructor at the University of Oregon in Eugene specializing in performance assessment for teacher preparation. Over the course of her career in the field of education, Dr. Carrizales-Engelmann has maintained a consistent focus in the development, research, and troubleshooting of educational assessments. Dr. Carrizales-Engelmann's assessment development experience includes state assessments, nationally standardized assessments, and classroom and curriculum-based assessments. In addition to her role in the field of educational assessment, Dr. Carrizales-Engelmann has had several years of policy-related experience in the areas of education and assessment at the Oregon Department of Education.

Laura L. Feuerborn, Ph.D., Associate Professor, Department of Education, University of Washington, Tacoma, 1900 Commerce Street, Box 35835, Tacoma, Washington 98402

Dr. Feuerborn is Associate Professor at the University of Washington, Tacoma, and is a nationally certified school psychologist. She received her Ph.D. in school psychology with an emphasis in emotional and behavioral supports from the University of Oregon. Since joining the faculty at the University of Washington, Tacoma, in 2006, she has taught graduate-level courses for educators in both general and special education. Her areas of teaching expertise include classroom management, systems of prevention and supports, and collaborative consultation. She developed and now leads a course that focuses on social and emotional learning (SEL) for teachers. Dr. Feuerborn's research centers on the science of implementing systems change. She is an author of the Staff Perceptions of Behavior and Discipline (http://spbdsupport.com), an assessment tool that helps leadership teams understand the needs and perceptions of school staff in the implementation of positive behavior interventions and supports (PBIS). Dr. Feuerborn has been presenting her work in regional, national, and international conferences for more than 15 years. She serves as a reviewer for scholarly journals and publishes peer-reviewed research in the fields of SEL and schoolwide PBIS.

Barbara A. Gueldner, Ph.D., Licensed Psychologist, Successful Kids Today, P.O. Box 772748, Steamboat Springs, Colorado 80477

Dr. Gueldner is a licensed psychologist and nationally certified school psychologist who works with children and families in Steamboat Springs, Colorado. She obtained her doctorate in school psychology from the University of Oregon and has worked in educational, medical, and community settings for 20 years. Dr. Gueldner specializes in promoting wellness and resilience through social and emotional learning (SEL) program development and implementation, parent education and support, integrating mental health care into primary care and schools, and early detection and intervention with developmental, behavioral, social, and emotional problems. She has published in the areas of SEL and general childhood mental health issues, coauthoring journal articles, book chapters, the first editions of *Strong Kids* and *Strong Teens*, and a book on implementing SEL in schools. Dr. Gueldner is involved in a variety of public outreach and educational initiatives in her community.

Oanh K. Tran, Ph.D., Professor, Department of Educational Psychology, California State University, East Bay, 25800 Carlos Bee Boulevard, Hayward, California 94542

Dr. Tran teaches in the Child Clinical/School Psychology (CCSP) Program at California State University, East Bay. The CCSP program is approved by the National Association of School Psychologists (NASP). Dr. Tran also practices as a school psychologist in the San Francisco Bay Area and consults with school districts and mental health agencies. Dr. Tran's direct experience includes working with diverse and at-risk populations in public and nonpublic schools as well as residential, foster care, outpatient, and in-home settings. Her research and professional interests include psychoeducational assessments, special education, social and emotional learning, academic and behavioral consultation, response to intervention, positive behavior supports, cognitive behavioral therapy, and parent training. She has presented locally and nationally and has published articles, chapters, and prevention curricula in the area of children's mental health. Dr. Tran continues her research and mentoring of her graduate students in social-emotional development and learning for students in Grades K–12.

Foreword

This remarkable curricular program is a fitting tribute to Ken Merrell's legacy as one of the foremost scholar–innovators in the realm of emotional literacy and social and emotional learning (SEL). This work, along with its authors, are clearly reflective of the superb contributions that Ken made to our field of practice and research inquiry in teaching our school-age students, from preschool through high school, how to manage their emotions and attitudes in a healthier, more competent manner. I am honored to write this foreword as a means of acknowledging the work that Ken contributed and inspired in a career that was cut short so tragically.

Children and youth today are exposed constantly to so much toxicity in our national discourse about all manner of societal issues, not to mention the potential abuses of pervasive social media use that so dominates their lives. We do not provide them with competent models of interpersonal behavior nor with the tools for evaluating and making sense of what they hear and see. Nor do we model and teach healthy strategies for problem solving difficult social and interpersonal situations. Far too many youth today do not have the means to access material such as that provided in the *Strong Kids*™ curriculum. I can think of no other current innovation deliverable within the schooling context that holds greater importance for our youth's future than this one.

Mastery of the content of this curricular program has so many uses in a student's daily life that are manifested in one's self-management as well as in relating to others. This content holds substantial potential for improving student mental health and social relationships throughout one's social network. This program revision introduces "emotion identification" that allows students to better cope with complex and concurrent emotions, and students are taught how to confront their emotions in a proactive manner rather than as something to simply change or fix. Students are taught about emotional expression in contextual terms that include not only how they are expressed but with whom and where. The scenarios provided as teaching aids are authentic and carefully referenced to the problems and social situations today's students are likely to experience within their respective social networks. In terms of useful content, there seems to be very little that the authors have overlooked. I am especially impressed with the material on selecting smart, achievable goals and strategies for integrating SEL content across social settings and the generalizability–sustainability of key concepts.

The new content added to this revision passes the logic test for me in that it encompasses exactly what I think students of today need to cope effectively with the challenges and stresses of their daily life. These include units on understanding your emotions, understanding the emotions of others, dealing with anger, clear thinking, solving people problems, letting go of stress, positive living, behavior change, and finishing UP. These essential competencies are embedded within five lessons focused respectively on self-awareness, self-management, social awareness, relationship skills, and responsible decision making. Exposure to and mastery of this material through a universal curricular teaching approach would go a long way toward enhancing the socialization process for many of our stressed out and anxious students. I am also impressed with the section on mindfulness and frankly did not expect such a unit in a curriculum of this type. However, as the authors present it, this material appears to fit seamlessly with the other content.

I have long believed that best practices in the SEL domain involve use of the most effective principles of academic instruction to teach this content. There are two types of mastery that should be addressed in this regard: *conceptual and behavioral*. This curriculum addresses both types of mastery and also provides for the universal and small group/individualized teaching of the content for those students who struggle with mastery in a group context. I applaud the authors for their accommodation of this important task in their work.

Over 20 years of research and development have been invested in this program to date. It is also grounded in a strong practitioner feedback loop that has provided invaluable information on the best ways to teach this content in a user-friendly fashion that students find appealing and acceptable. More than anything I can think of, the *Strong Kids* curriculum holds the potential to realize schools' role in promoting the emotional literacy and mental health of today's students. The *Strong Kids* curriculum program is very well designed, meets the best standards of curricular development, is easy to teach, and—best of all— students seem to like it, which, in my view, is the ultimate test of such a product. The *Strong Kids* curriculum is indeed a seminal contribution to our knowledge and practice base on social-emotional development. We owe Ken Merrell and the authors a huge debt!

Hill M. Walker, Ph.D.
Professor Emeritus
College of Education
University of Oregon

Acknowledgments

This second edition of *Strong Kids* and *Strong Teens* is published in memory of and dedication to Dr. Kenneth W. Merrell: teacher, mentor, friend, advisor, and inspiration (1957–2011). These programs would not exist without his vision and commitment to the mission of the Oregon Resiliency Project. Through these revised programs, we aim to honor and extend his legacy of supports for children, adolescents, and school communities. He was on our minds and in our hearts at every step of this process.

We continue to acknowledge the foundational research, development, and support of the Oregon Resiliency Project members (2001–2011): Leah Benazzi, Sara Castro-Olivo, Erin Chaparro, Christine Davis, Keith Herman, Duane Isava, Travis Laxton, Verity Levitt, Kelly McGraw, Kent McIntosh, Jean Mercier, Nicole Nakayama, Christiane Oilar, Kristin Orton, Wendy Reinke, Scott Ross, and Lisa Sterling.

SECTION I

Introduction and Overview

CHAPTER 1

About *Strong Kids*

Strong Kids™: A Social and Emotional Learning Curriculum is a social and emotional learning curriculum that consists of five brief and practical social and emotional learning (SEL) programs designed for the purpose of teaching social and emotional skills and assets that promote resilience and mitigate risk in children and adolescents. These introductory chapters provide information on the following:

- The importance of promoting children's mental health and doing so in the context of SEL

- The design of the *Strong Kids* program

- Evidence of the program's effectiveness

- Tips for using the curriculum effectively and with confidence

- Updates to the second edition.

Strong Kids—Grades 6–8 is designed specifically for use with children in Grades 6–8, or those who are approximately ages 11–14 years. Because *Strong Kids—Grades 6–8* is designed to be both a prevention and an early intervention (EI) program, it has a wide range of applications and may be used effectively with children who are high functioning, typically developing, at risk for social and emotional problems, or struggling with social and emotional difficulties. *Strong Kids—Grades 6–8* can be implemented in a variety of settings: general and special education classrooms, group counseling settings, and youth treatment facilities that have an educational component.

For younger students in the early elementary grades, the *Strong Kids* curriculum also offers *Strong Start—Pre-K*, *Strong Start—Grades K–2*, and *Strong Kids—Grades 3–5*. For older students in higher grades, the curriculum also offers *Strong Teens—Grades 9–12* for use with high school–age students.

Youth in the *Strong Kids—Grades 6–8* age range experience a host of changes during this time in development. Bodies are changing, the complexities of social relationships extend to romantic feelings, friendships may be tenuous at times, navigating relationships through social media becomes increasingly complex, emotional experiences seem more intense, and youth may more openly question parents' and other adults' values and voice their opinions—sometimes in an irritable tone. Youth often become increasingly aware of differences between themselves and the idealized models portrayed in the media. They may also experience difficulties with adjustment and a loss of self-concept in some areas. Beginning at about age 13, rates of depression begin to increase and gender differences begin to become particularly pronounced, with girls reporting depression at a higher rate than boys.

In the middle grades, students also are expected to be more independent with schoolwork and managing themselves in general. Pressures to be organized and responsible for planning ahead and making deadlines, and juggling a more complex extracurricular schedule, can feel overwhelming. Many young people also live in communities or families in which they are exposed to ineffective or inappropriate models for solving conflict and dealing with problems.

Stress increases with these demands, and youth need to cope effectively. *Strong Kids—6–8* is designed to increase their awareness of these issues and offer strategies to manage emotional and social complexities while having fun and engaging in activities that support their academic, social, and emotional learning.

PROMOTING CHILDREN'S MENTAL HEALTH

As many researchers, writers, and public officials have noted, changes in the structure of society and families have resulted in an increasing percentage of children and families who are at risk for developing a variety of behavioral, social, and mental health problems (e.g., Costello & Angold, 2000; Doll & Lyon, 1998; Farmer & Farmer, 1999; Hoagwood & Erwin, 1997; Satcher, 1999). The numbers of children and youth affected by these problems are surprisingly high. Greenberg, Domitrovich, and Bumbarger (2001) asserted that between 12% and 22% of children and adolescents younger than age 18 experience mental health problems of sufficient severity to be in need of mental health services. These percentages represent a staggering figure of up to 1 out of every 5 children and adolescents in some instances. The Centers for Disease Control and Prevention (2013) estimated that among adolescents within a 12-month period, 8% will attempt suicide and 20% of students have been bullied, and during a 30-day period, 41.4% texted or e-mailed while driving a car and 34.9% consumed alcohol. Without question, effective early responses to these problems, including mental health prevention and EI curricula in educational settings, must occur if these challenges are to be stemmed.

Despite sincere and well-meaning attempts to offer real solutions to social, emotional, and mental health problems of students in school settings, many of the programs or interventions that have been implemented are simply ineffective. Walker stated that "educators are notorious for embracing programs that look good but do no actual good" (2001, p. 2). In these educators' defense, we should note that school personnel who work on the front lines of serving children and youth who have significant mental health issues are often overworked and not provided with sufficient resources with which to make the impact they desire. Furthermore, some developers and publishers of mental health prevention programs tend to overwhelm educators and clinicians with claims of effectiveness, even when there is little or no supporting evidence. Worse yet are reactionary school policies, such as the perennial "get tough" approaches that are not only ineffective in the long term but also contribute to the development of systems that are hostile, aversive, socially toxic, and incompatible with optimal development of academic skills and mental health (Hyman & Perone, 1998; Skiba & Peterson, 1999).

Despite these problems and challenges, there is reason for optimism regarding our ability to positively affect the social and emotional health and resilience of children and adolescents, even those from very adverse life circumstances. One reason for this optimism is the accumulation of a large body of scientific evidence regarding what has been termed *developmental resilience* (Doll & Lyon, 1998). This notion of resilience concerns the ability of individuals to cope successfully with adversity, risk factors, and severe life stress and for young people to develop into competent and happy adults despite these problems.

Central to this notion of developmental resilience is the idea that some characteristics of resilience—the cognitive, behavioral, and affective skills that enable one to cope effectively with adversity—may be systematically taught and learned. Although some aspects of resilience or developmental hardiness may be innate or biologically based, the evidence shows that learning plays a crucial role in developing the ability to cope effectively with problems and challenges. Stated simply, the ability to be resilient and to cope effectively in the face of adverse circumstances and challenges in life is something that can be acquired in great measure through systematic and effective instruction in the critical requisite skills involved.

Although the primary mission of public education has traditionally been perceived as promoting the development of academic skills, there is growing support and advocacy for the systematic inclusion of skills that may be considered "nonacademic" but are, in fact, key to supporting students' overall development (Pellegrino & Hilton, 2013). Critical thinking, problem solving, creativity, communication, and responsible thinking are necessary for students to succeed in the 21st century (Partnership for 21st Century Skills, 2008), and a growing body of evidence demonstrates that social and emotional skills are particularly relevant (see Durlak, Dymnicki, Taylor, Weissberg, & Schellinger, 2011, for a meta-analytic review) and believed to be a "missing piece" (Elias, 2006, p. 6). There is no question that most educators, parents, students, and the general public also support and expect a broader mission for schools (Greenberg et al., 2003). Some examples of this expanded agenda include character education, development of good work habits, promotion of good citizenship, development of social and emotional competence, and promotion of a healthy and productive lifestyle. Commenting on the need for this broader agenda, Greenberg and his colleagues stated

> High-quality education should teach young people to interact in socially skilled and respectful ways; to practice positive, safe, and healthy behaviors; to contribute ethically and responsibly to their peer group, family, school, and community; and to possess basic competencies, work habits, and values as a foundation for meaningful employment and. . . . We consequently assert that school-based prevention programming—based on coordinated social, emotional, and academic learning—should be fundamental to preschool through high school education. (2003, pp. 466–467)

We emphatically agree with this statement. In addition, we propose that teaching young people positive social, emotional, and behavioral skills is not only an essential mission for educators and mental health professionals but also one of the most critical challenges facing our society in the 21st century. Students are placed under so many stressors at times during their young development that teaching resilience is critical for academic and life success.

SOCIAL AND EMOTIONAL LEARNING

A framework, aptly named *social and emotional learning*, has guided efforts to effectively teach the social and emotional health and resilience of young people. Drawing from the fields of child and adolescent development, health promotion, principles of instruction, affective neuroscience, positive psychology, cognitive therapy, behavioral theory and application, and prevention science (Zins, Bloodworth, Weissberg, & Walberg, 2004), specific skills are ideally taught over the course of students' academic tenure (i.e., preschool through high school). These skills also should be taught with coordination and strategy in mind (Devaney, O'Brien, Resnik, Keister, & Weissberg, 2006; Greenberg et al., 2003). That is, how will the skills be infused throughout a busy school day? How will we know students are learning and applying the information? What kind of support is needed and is this support feasible? The goal is to provide *all* students with effective instruction and support to mitigate risk behaviors and outcomes and enhance protective factors known to affect positive overall development (Greenberg et al., 2003). Achieving this goal is possible by applying current evidence and continuing to investigate ways in which we can improve.

The efforts of the Collaborative for Academic, Social, and Emotional Learning (CASEL) at supporting SEL in youth have been instrumental in understanding the key areas for social and emotional development and best practices in facilitating this process. CASEL has endorsed five person-centered and interrelated competency areas that are essential to cognitive, social, and emotional development: self-awareness, self-management, social awareness, relationship skills, and responsible decision making (CASEL, 2014; Zins et al., 2004). There is growing evidence that SEL programming, highlighting these competency areas, is effective (e.g., Durlak et al., 2011; Durlak & Wells, 1997; Payton et al., 2008; Sklad, Diekstra, De Ritter, Ben, & Gravesteijn, 2012). Improvements have been measured in areas such as identifying emotions, resolving conflict, self-efficacy, attitudes toward school, positive social behaviors, and academic performance. Conduct problems, as well as emotional distress, have been reduced. In addition to benefits for youth, teachers view SEL to be a priority (Bridgeland, Bruce, & Hariharan, 2013), and school staff are able to implement SEL effectively and without mental health training (Durlak et al., 2011).

Since the early 1990s, many SEL programs have been developed and used in educational and mental health settings. The type of program ultimately selected will depend on a variety of factors such as the needs of the setting, financial considerations, training and resource requirements, and time constraints. *Strong Kids* was designed with these variables in mind and, we believe, offers an affordable and relatively low-resource option, using principles of effective instruction and evidence-based strategies for promoting mental health, to effectively teach SEL skills.

MODEL FOR PREVENTING BEHAVIORAL AND EMOTIONAL PROBLEMS

Education researchers have adapted a public health prevention model for use in school systems (e.g., Merrell & Buchanan, 2006; U.S. Department of Education, 2004; Walker et al., 1996). We believe that this three-tiered model (see Figure 1.1) has great importance for promoting SEL and for school-based promotion of children's mental health in general. Sometimes referred to as the "triangle," this model of prevention and intervention includes service delivery at three levels of prevention: students who currently are not experiencing learning or social/behavior difficulties (*primary prevention*); students who are considered to be at risk for the development of learning or social/behavior difficulties (*secondary prevention*); and students who currently are experiencing significant learning or social/behavior difficulties (*tertiary prevention*).

We can visualize this model and its three levels of prevention as a triangle. The entire triangle represents all students within a school setting, the majority of whom are not experiencing difficulties (i.e., the bottom portion of the triangle),

Figure 1.1. The prevention triangle model, specifically adapted for how to make systems work for assessing, identifying, and serving students with behavioral, social, and emotional problems. (*Key:* IEP, individualized education program.)

some of whom are at risk of developing significant problems (i.e., the middle portion), and an even smaller percentage who are currently experiencing significant difficulties (i.e., the top portion). Typical practice is to focus on those students who are at the top of the triangle—those who are currently experiencing significant learning or social-emotional difficulties. Practitioners tend to spend the majority of their time and effort providing tertiary prevention (i.e., individualized assessment and intervention services) to these students on a case-by-case basis. These students make up the smallest percentage of the school population, but because of the significance of their problems, they often require the majority of time and resources from school personnel (Walker et al., 1996). Figure 1.1 illustrates the prevention triangle model, specifically adapted for how to make systems work for assessing, identifying, and serving students with behavioral, social, and emotional problems.

Shifting to a systemwide prevention model requires looking at the "big picture" by considering the needs of *all* students, not just those who are referred because they are currently experiencing significant difficulties. The foundation of a prevention approach is the use of universal interventions (i.e., primary prevention) designed to enhance the delivery of effective instruction and improved school climate to promote the academic, social, and behavioral resilience of *all* students in the school. This idea requires that educators begin to move some resources and energy toward those children and adolescents who are not currently experiencing significant difficulties in order to promote skills to provide a sort of inoculation for the developmental challenges that may occur. The premise is to reduce the probability that these youth will eventually rise to the "top of the triangle" where more resources are required. More specifically, primary prevention for students who are not currently experiencing learning or social/behavior difficulties is accomplished through schoolwide and classwide efforts that involve the consistent use of research-based effective practices, ongoing monitoring of these practices and student outcomes, staff training, and professional development. The goal of primary prevention is to create school and classroom environments that promote student learning and health and decrease the number of students at risk for learning or social/behavior problems.

As important as it is to focus on primary prevention, we also know that not all students respond similarly to these efforts. Thus, it is important to monitor student progress and to assess whether students are at risk (i.e., in need of secondary prevention efforts) or are experiencing significant difficulties (i.e., in need of tertiary prevention efforts). Identifying students at risk for learning, social-emotional, and behavior difficulties is an important aspect to comprehensive prevention efforts. For students identified as at risk and in need of secondary prevention efforts, the focus is on the delivery of specialized interventions (often at a small-group level) to prevent the worsening of problems and to prevent the development of more significant concerns. The focus on early identification and EI is important.

With respect to mental health and social-emotional problems of children and adolescents, we believe that this prevention model is an ideal way to think about providing SEL programs and other services. Thinking in this way about the challenges faced in promoting social-emotional wellness and mental health among children and adolescents makes these challenges more manageable. Instead of waiting until students have developed severe problems and require extensive time and effort to simply be managed, you can continually focus a portion of your resources on prevention activities that will ultimately reduce the number of students at the "top of the triangle."

DESIGN OF THE *STRONG KIDS* CURRICULUM: BACKGROUND

The *Strong Kids* curriculum was developed by the Oregon Resiliency Project (ORP) at the University of Oregon and under the direction of the late Kenneth W. Merrell, Ph.D. Several goals led the research and development efforts to

1. Target each of the five pathways to wellness advocated by Cowen (1994), a pioneer in the modern science of mental health and wellness promotion:

    *   Forming wholesome early attachments

    *   Acquiring age-appropriate competencies

    *   Having exposure to settings that favor wellness outcomes

    *   Having the empowering sense of being in control of one's fate

    *   Coping effectively with stress

2. Make available a program that was prevention oriented, practical, cost-effective, and feasible for teachers to implement in the classroom and within the course of a typical class period

3. Design the program to be useful across grade levels, thereby providing a means to provide a more cohesive and collaborative approach to SEL programming (Zins, 2004).

As we revised this curriculum, we envisioned *Strong Kids* as a carefully designed SEL program to prevent the development of certain mental health problems and promote social and emotional wellness among young people (see Chapter 4 for more information on the revisions). *Strong Kids* is not the right SEL program for all types of problems. We especially targeted the domain of internalizing behavioral and emotional problems (e.g., depression, anxiety, social withdrawal, somatic problems), using a largely cognitive-behavioral theoretical orientation given its evidence of effectiveness with youth in these areas (Weisz, Hawley, & Doss, 2004), to promote *social and emotional resilience*. *Strong Kids* should not be considered a comprehensive program for preventing school violence or antisocial behavior, even though it may play a role in supporting these aims as part of a comprehensive program of effective behavior support.

The advantage of this programming approach is that *Strong Kids* follows the recommendations outlined by Durlak and DuPre (2008) for skill training by being sequenced, active, focused, and explicit. One disadvantage of this approach is that the program is not designed to be a complete mental health treatment package for children and youth with severe mental health problems. Although our research to date has shown that the curriculum can make a meaningful difference with these populations, it should be used as one component of a comprehensive, intensive intervention program in such cases.

IMPLEMENTATION GUIDELINES AND LESSON STRUCTURE

The *Strong Kids* and *Strong Teens* programs were designed to circumvent common barriers to implementation such as time, resources, and training while upholding criteria for effective instructional design and delivery (Carnine, Silbert, Kame'enui, & Tarver, 2009; Coyne, Kame'enui, & Carnine, 2006). Thus, this curriculum was developed with both time feasibility and ease of implementation as high priorities. Even an exceptionally strong intervention program will fail to make an impact if its time requirements and difficulty of implementation result in few people being able to use it within the time and training constraints of a school system or other youth-serving agency. We recommend teaching the *Strong Kids—Grades 6–8* lessons once per week for 12 weeks, although there is evidence to support implementation at a more accelerated tempo such as two lessons per week for 6 weeks with similar effective outcomes (Tran, 2008). The one lesson per week format may allow students sufficient time to complete any homework that may be assigned, internalize the concepts taught, and practice the new skills they learn, both at school and outside of school.

Each lesson takes between 60 and 80 minutes to complete. All lessons can be shortened by stopping at the end of an activity and finishing up with the Closure activity found at the end of the lesson. When continuing the lesson, teachers simply resume by starting with the Mindfulness-Based Focusing Activity found in the Introduction section, followed by the point in the lesson where the lesson was stopped during the previous instructional period and again ending with the Closure activity. For each lesson, we have suggested a stopping point. Please refer to the Running Short on Time? section, found at the beginning of each lesson, for these suggestions. Lessons also can be lengthened, using additional activities found at the end of each lesson, at the instructor's discretion.

Each lesson includes instructional scaffolding (e.g., optional scripting and explicit directions) to eliminate the need for intensive preparation, a review and introduction of the lesson and key concepts, a range of examples to define the concept, and opportunities to practice and integrate skills through activities such as modeling, guided practice and role play, and independent practice. Generalization and maintenance of skills are promoted by providing strategies for practice throughout the school day, in other academic areas, and across settings.

We specifically designed *Strong Kids* as a low-cost, low-technology program that can be implemented in a school or related educational setting with minimal professional training and resources. It is not necessary to be a licensed mental health professional to learn and implement this curriculum. General and special education teachers, speech-language pathologists, school counselors, social workers, psychologists, and other education or mental health professionals may serve as effective group leaders. The program may be taught in a general education classroom or in selected small-group settings. One of the advantages of the *Strong Kids* curriculum is that it is designed to support academic skills and to be integrated within an instructional program. The activities in this curriculum not only promote SEL and resilience but also support literacy, language arts, social studies, and health.

Strong Kids—Grades 6–8 is highly structured and semiscripted, designed to cover very specific objectives and goals. We developed the objectives and goals for each lesson, as well as the implementation guidelines, based on current research findings in education and psychology, aiming for a prevention and intervention program that is built on a solid base of empirical evidence. Each lesson follows a similar format with the following sections:

Social and Emotional Competency Areas: CASEL (2014) endorsed five key areas necessary in building SEL skills (self-awareness, self-management, social awareness, relationship skills, and responsible decision making); skills categories are assigned to each lesson where content reflects these areas.

Purpose and Objectives: Describes the skills students will learn

Materials Needed: Lists the materials needed for advance preparation

Running Short on Time?: Suggests an optional stopping point to segment the lesson

Instructor Reflection: Provides an opportunity for instructors to reflect on the content of the lesson to increase knowledge and personalize the application

Review: Lists topics covered in the previous lesson

Introduction: Introduces the concepts for the lesson

Mindfulness-Based Focusing Activity: Helps students focus and prepare for the lesson

Key Terms and Definitions: Provides an introduction to any relevant vocabulary

Instructional Content and Practice Activities: Provides content and activities specialized to each lesson's theme

Putting It All Together: Reviews the key concepts practiced in the lesson

Closure: Provides a brief breathing and reflection activity

In addition, each lesson provides optional scripts to aid content delivery, sample situations and examples to better illustrate the content, and opportunities for guided and independent practice. Group leaders can follow the script and examples directly or modify the sample script to present the lesson's main ideas using language that is most appropriate for their group(s). At the end of each of the 12 lessons is a section titled Tips for Transfer Training and Homework. This section includes optional homework assignments and take-home handouts, tactics that are further designed to reinforce learning outside of the *Strong Kids—Grades 6–8* instructional setting. This section also prompts instructors to precorrect (i.e., anticipate students' errors and difficulties in learning the skills), remind (i.e., provide verbal or visual prompts of the steps and actions needed to use the skills), and reinforce (i.e., provide social reinforcement, such as praise, when students use the skills) the lesson objectives. These instructional principles are known to improve skills maintenance over time and generalization across settings (e.g., Langland, Lewis-Palmer, & Sugai, 1998; Sugai, Bullis, & Cumblad, 1997). Ideas for making the content especially relevant to students are included in each lesson, typically within each practice activity. Additional suggestions for activities are listed at the end of each lesson and are provided to encourage practice that is embedded throughout the course of the school day, to make the lesson content relevant to students, and to allow additional opportunities to practice and reinforce the concepts. Lesson 12 can be used as a "booster lesson" to provide an opportunity to reteach and reemphasize critical *Strong Kids* content and skills after a period of time—usually several weeks to a few months—and following the completion of the 12 lessons.

EVIDENCE

The *Strong Kids* curriculum, from *Strong Start—Pre-K* to *Strong Teens*, has been evaluated and continues to be studied within a multitiered model (universal and tertiary prevention and intervention programming), across age and grade levels (elementary through high school–age individuals), and in a variety of settings. The strongest evidence exists for a unilateral increase in knowledge of social and emotional content across studies. Some studies also have found significant decreases in internalizing problem symptoms and increases in social and emotional skills and assets. Teachers and students have found the program worthwhile and feasible, thereby providing evidence for the social validity of the program. A reference section at the end of this chapter provides relevant sources for these studies. If you are conducting research or a program evaluation of the *Strong Kids* curriculum, we would be very interested in hearing from you.

SUMMARY

We are at a pivotal point in history whereby our youths' social and emotional resilience is developing through direct instruction and application, with the use of materials developed from years of research and practice across multiple relevant disciplines. The *Strong Kids* curriculum offers one way of helping our youth develop into socially and emotionally healthy individuals. Together, we can prepare today and tomorrow's global citizens for 21st century stressors and opportunities.

Strong Start, Strong Kids, and *Strong Teens*: Research

Barker, E.S., Marcotte, A.M., & Whitcomb, S.A. (2015). Promoting positive teacher–child interactions through implementation of a social emotional learning curriculum with performance feedback. Manuscript in revision.

Berry-Krazmien, C., & Torres-Fernandez, I. (2007, March 27–31). *Implementation of the Strong Kids curriculum in a residential facility.* Poster presentation at the Annual Convention of the National Association of School Psychologists, New York, NY.

Caldarella, P., Christensen, L., Kramer, T.J., & Kronmiller, K. (2009). Promoting social and emotional learning in second grade students: A study of the *Strong Start* curriculum. *Early Childhood Education Journal, 37,* 51–56. doi:10.1007/s10643–009-0321-4

Castro-Olivo, S. (2014). Promoting social-emotional learning in adolescent Latino ELLs: A study of the culturally adapted Strong Teens program. *School Psychology Quarterly, 29,* 567–577.

Faust, J.J. (2006). *Preventing anxiety and depression: An evaluation of social-emotional curriculum* (Unpublished educational specialist's thesis). University of Wisconsin, Whitewater.

Feuerborn, L.L. (2004). *Promoting emotional resiliency through classroom instruction: The effects of a classroom-based prevention program* (Unpublished doctoral dissertation). University of Oregon, Eugene.

Gueldner, B.A., & Merrell, K.W. (2011). The effectiveness of a social and emotional learning program with middle school students in the general education setting and the effect of consultation on student outcomes. *Journal of Educational and Psychological Consultation, 21,* 1–27. doi:10.1080/10474412.2010.522876

Gunter, L., Caldarella, P., Korth, B. B., & Young, K. R. (2012). Promoting social and emotional learning in preschool students: A study of Strong Start Pre-K. *Early Childhood Education, 40,* 151–159.

Harlacher, J.E., & Merrell, K.W. (2009). Social and emotional learning as a universal level of support: Evaluating the follow-up effect of Strong Kids on social and emotional outcomes. *Journal of Applied School Psychology, 26*(3), 212–229. doi:10.1080/15377903.2010.495903

Isava, D.M. (2006). *An investigation of the impact of a social emotional learning curriculum on problem symptoms and knowledge gains among adolescents in a residential treatment center* (Unpublished doctoral dissertation). University of Oregon, Eugene.

Kramer, T.J., Caldarella, P., Christensen, L., & Shatzer, R.H. (2010). Social and emotional learning in the kindergarten classroom: Evaluation of the *Strong Start* curriculum. *Early Childhood Education Journal, 37,* 303–309. doi:10.1007/s10643-009-0354-8

Kramer, T.J., Caldarella, P., Young, R., Fischer, L., & Warren, J.S. (2014). Implementing *Strong Kids* school-wide to reduce internalizing behaviors and increase prosocial behaviors. *Education and Treatment of Children, 37,* 659–680.

Levitt, V. (2009). *Promoting social-emotional competency through quality teaching practices: The impact of consultation on a multidimensional treatment integrity model of the Strong Kids Program* (Unpublished doctoral dissertation). University of Oregon, Eugene.

Marchant, M., Brown, M., Caldarella, P., & Young, E. (2010). Effects of Strong Kids curriculum on students at risk for internalizing disorders: A pilot study. *Journal of Empirically Based Practices in Schools, 11*(2), 123–143.

Merrell, K.W., Juskelis, M.P., Tran, O.K., & Buchanan, R. (2008). Social and emotional learning in the classroom: Impact of *Strong Kids* and *Strong Teens* on students' social-emotional knowledge and symptoms. *Journal of Applied School Psychology, 24,* 209–224. doi:10.1080/15377900802089981

Meyer, K.M. (2014). *Program evaluation of the Strong Start curriculum as a selected intervention for early elementary students* (Unpublished doctoral dissertation). University of Massachusetts, Amherst.

Nakayama, N.J. (2008). *An investigation of the impact of the Strong Kids curriculum on social-emotional knowledge and symptoms of elementary aged students in a self-contained special education setting* (Unpublished doctoral dissertation). University of Oregon, Eugene.

Sicotte, J.L. (2013). *Effects of Strong Start curriculum on internalizing, externalizing behaviors, and emotion knowledge among kindergarten and first grade students* (Unpublished doctoral dissertation). University of Massachusetts, Amherst.

Tran, O.K. (2008). *Promoting social and emotional learning in schools: An investigation of massed versus distributed practice schedules and social validity of the Strong Kids curriculum in late elementary aged students* (Unpublished doctoral dissertation). University of Oregon, Eugene.

Whitcomb, S.A., & Merrell, K.W. (2012). Understanding implementation and effectiveness of Strong Start K–2 on social-emotional behavior. *Early Childhood Education Journal, 40,* 63–71. doi:10.1007/s10643-011-0490-9

White, N.J., & Rayle, A.D. (2007). Strong Teens: A school-based small group experience for African American males. *The Journal for Specialists in Group Work, 32,* 178–189. doi:10.1080/01933920701227224

REFERENCES

Bridgeland, J., Bruce, M., & Hariharan, A. (2013). *The missing piece: A national survey on how social and emotional learning can empower children and transform schools.* Washington, DC: Civic Enterprises.

Carnine, D.W., Silbert, J., Kame'enui, E.J., & Tarver, S.G. (2009). *Direct instruction reading* (5th ed.). Upper Saddle River, NJ: Pearson/Prentice Hall.

Centers for Disease Control and Prevention. (2013). Youth risk behavior surveillance—United States, 2013. *Surveillance Summaries, 63*, 1–168. Retrieved from http://stacks.cdc.gov/view/cdc/23483

Collaborative for Academic, Social, and Emotional Learning. (2014). *What is SEL? Skills and competencies.* Chicago, IL: Author. Retrieved from http://www.casel.org/social-and-emotional-learning/core-competencies

Costello, E.J., & Angold, A. (2000). Developmental psychopathology and public health: Past, present, and future. *Development and Psychopathology, 12*, 599–618.

Cowen, E.L. (1994). The enhancement of psychological wellness: Challenges and opportunities. *American Journal of Community Psychology, 22*, 149–179.

Coyne, M.D., Kame'enui, E.J., & Carnine, D.W. (2006). *Effective teaching strategies that accommodate diverse learners* (3rd ed.). Upper Saddle River, NJ: Pearson/Prentice Hall.

Devaney, E., O'Brien, M.U., Resnik, H., Keister, S., & Weissberg, R.P. (2006). *Sustainable schoolwide social and emotional learning: Implementation guide and toolkit.* Chicago, IL: Collaborative for Academic, Social, and Emotional Learning.

Doll, B., & Lyon, M.A. (1998). Risk and resilience: Implications for the delivery of educational and mental health services in schools. *School Psychology Review, 27*, 348–363.

Durlak, J.A., & DuPre, E.P. (2008). Implementation matters: A review of research on the influence of implementation on program outcomes and the factors affecting implementation. *American Journal of Community Psychology, 41*(3–4):327–350.

Durlak, J.A., Dymnicki, A.B., Taylor, R.D., Weissberg, R.P., & Schellinger, K.B. (2011). The impact of enhancing students' social and emotional learning: A meta-analysis of school-based universal interventions. *Child Development, 82*, 405–432. doi:10.1111/j.1467-8624.2010.01564.x

Durlak, J.A., & Wells, A.M. (1997). Primary prevention mental health programs for children and adolescents: A meta-analytic review. *American Journal of Community Psychology, 25*, 115–152. Retrieved from http://hmprg.org/assets/root/PDFs/2012/07/prevention_meta_analysis_durlak_wells_1997.pdf

Elias, M.J. (2006). The connection between academic and social-emotional learning. In M.J. Elias & H. Arnold (Eds.), *The educator's guide to emotional intelligence and academic achievement* (pp. 4–14). Thousand Oaks, CA: Corwin Press.

Farmer, E.M.Z., & Farmer, T.W. (1999). The role of schools in outcomes for youth: Implications for children's mental health services research. *Journal of Child and Family Studies, 8*, 377–396.

Greenberg, M.T., Domitrovich, C., & Bumbarger, B. (2001, March 30). The prevention of mental health disorders in school-aged children: Current state of the field. *Prevention and Treatment, 4*(Article 1). Retrieved from http://www.researchgate.net/profile/Brian_Bumbarger/publication/216458565_The_prevention_of_mental_disorders_in_school-aged_children_Current_state_of_the_field/links/0fcfd50d20aaf66cf7000000.pdf

Greenberg, M.T., Weissberg, R.P., O'Brien, M.U., Zins, J.E., Fredericks, L., Resnick, H., et al. (2003). Enhancing school-based prevention and youth development through coordinated social, emotional, and academic learning. *American Psychologist, 58*, 466–474. doi:10.1037/0003-066X.58.6-7.466.

Hoagwood, K., & Erwin, H. (1997). Effectiveness of school-based mental health services for children: A 10-year research review. *Journal of Child and Family Studies, 6*, 435–451.

Hyman, I.A., & Perone, D.C. (1998). The other side of school violence: Educator policies and practices that may contribute to student misbehavior. *Journal of School Psychology, 36*, 7–27. Retrieved from http://youthjusticenc.org/download/education-justice/suspension-and-expulsion/The%20Other%20Side%20of%20School%20Violence:%20Educator%20Policies%20and%20Practices%20That%20May%20Contribute%20to%20Student%20Misbehavior.pdf

Langland, S., Lewis-Palmer, T., & Sugai, G. (1998). Teaching respect in the classroom: An instructional approach. *Journal of Behavioral Education, 8*, 245–262.

Merrell, K.W., & Buchanan, R.S. (2006). Intervention selection in school-based practice: Using public health models to enhance systems capacity of schools. *School Psychology Review, 35*, 167–180.

Partnership for 21st Century Skills. (2008). *21st century skills, education, and competitiveness: A resource and policy guide.* Washington, DC: Author. Retrieved from http://www.p21 .org/storage/documents/21st_century_skills_education_and_competitiveness_guide.pdf

Payton, J., Weissberg, R.P., Durlak, J.A., Dymnicki, A.B., Taylor, R.D., Schellinger, K.B., & Pachan, M. (2008). *The positive impact of social and emotional learning for kindergarten to eighth-grade students: Findings from three scientific reviews (Technical report).* Chicago, IL: Collaborative for Academic, Social, and Emotional Learning.

Pellegrino, J.W., & Hilton, M.L. (Eds.). (2013). *Education for life and work: Developing transferable knowledge and skills in the 21st century.* Washington, DC: National Academies Press. Retrieved from http://www.leg.state.vt.us/WorkGroups/EdOp/Education%20for%20Life%20 and%20Work-%20National%20Academy%20of%20Sciences.pdf

Satcher, D. (1999). *Mental health: A report of the Surgeon General, 1999.* Washington, DC: U.S. Department of Health and Human Services. Retrieved from http://dx.doi.org/10.1037/ 0735-7028.31.1.5

Skiba, R., & Peterson, R. (1999). The dark side of zero tolerance: Can punishment lead to safe schools? *Phi Delta Kappan, 80,* 372–376, 381–382. Retrieved from http://curry.virginia.edu/ uploads/resourceLibrary/dark_zero_tolerance.pdf

Sklad, M., Diekstra, R., De Ritter, M., Ben, J., & Gravesteijn, C. (2012). Effectiveness of school-based universal social, emotional, and behavioral programs: Do they enhance students' development in the area of skill, behavior, and adjustment? *Psychology in the Schools, 49*(9), 892–909. doi:10.1002/pits.21641

Sugai, G., Bullis, M., & Cumblad, C. (1997). Provide ongoing skill development and support. *Journal of Emotional and Behavioral Disorders, 5,* 55–64.

Tran, O.K. (2008). *Promoting social and emotional learning in schools: An investigation of massed versus distributed practice schedules and social validity of the Strong Kids curriculum in late elementary aged students* (Unpublished doctoral dissertation). University of Oregon, Eugene.

U.S. Department of Education, Office of Special Education Programs (OSEP), Center on Positive Behavioral Interventions and Supports. (2004). *School-wide PBIS.* Retrieved from http://www .pbis.org/school

Walker, H.M. (2001). "Preventing mental disorders in school-aged children: Current state of the field": Commentary. *Prevention and Treatment 4*(1).

Walker, H.M., Horner, R.H., Sugai, G., Bullis, M., et al. (1996). Integrated approaches to preventing antisocial behavior patterns among school-age children and youth. *Journal of Emotional and Behavioral Disorders, 4,* 194–209. Retrieved from http://idahotc.com/Portals/6/Docs/ Tier%20Training/Preventing%20Antisocial%20Behavior%20Patterns.pdf

Weisz, J.R., Hawley, K.M., & Doss, A.J. (2004). Empirically tested psychotherapies for youth internalizing and externalizing problems and disorders. *Child and Adolescent Psychiatric Clinics of North America, 13*(4), 729–815. Retrieved from http://web.missouri.edu/~hawleyk/pdfs/ WeiszHawleyJensenDoss2004.pdf

Zins, J.E., Bloodworth, M.R., Weissberg, R.P., & Walberg, H.J. (2004). The scientific base linking social and emotional learning to school success. In J. Zins, M. Wang, & H. Walberg (Eds.), *Building academic success and social-emotional learning: What does the research say?* New York, NY: Teachers College Press.

CHAPTER 2

Preparing Your Lessons and Your Students

To implement *Strong Kids—Grades 6–8*, you should have access to a projector, a copy machine, chart paper, chalk, color markers, or a marker board and a means of showing occasional Internet videos or images when the lesson requires. Many of the lessons also include reproducible templates for in-class handouts or worksheets for students, also available for download (refer to About the Downloadable Material for download information). Materials are made easily accessible via download, so you can project lesson supplements, handouts, and other images from a laptop or desktop computer or share the hard copy material directly. However, if a computer with an accompanying projector is not available for implementation, you can choose another option available at your site where materials can be projected or shown on the board (e.g., overhead projector) for the lesson materials. Although it is not essential to project the images or other materials, we have found that doing so provides the advantage of being able to go over a graphic illustration or chart in front of the class while you introduce the critical concepts that are connected to them. Alternatively, some teachers and group leaders have found that they prefer to make paper copies of the supplements and provide each student with a copy of these materials rather than presenting the materials with a projector.

SUPPLEMENTARY MATERIALS

Each *Strong Kids—Grades 6–8* lesson includes supplementary materials needed for each lesson. The supplementary materials can be found at the end of the lesson and are available for download. These materials are labeled throughout the text with a "reminder" symbol (a finger with a string tied to it) in the margin. For the sake of consistency, we refer to these materials as "supplements" and have titled them that way. These supplements are available as online downloads for use as in-class handouts, worksheets, and homework handouts. Each supplement is labeled with its intended use and indicates whether it should be used as a handout for students, as a visual aid for you to display as you discuss a section, or both. Prior to teaching the lesson, review the Materials Needed section at the beginning of each lesson and make copies of downloads or handouts before lesson implementation as needed. These supplements are all reproducible for users of the curriculum. Although we have made suggestions regarding how to use the supplementary materials, you should feel free to adapt them to your own needs and situation. In addition, some lessons require the use of online videos or images to help illustrate the content. When a video or image is recommended, a description is provided to help in locating these videos or images online. More supplemental materials and resources can be found by visiting our companion web site: www.strongkidsresources.com.

PROVIDING AN AGENDA

During the course of teaching *Strong Kids—Grades 6–8*, we recommend that you make use of a visual schedule to provide students with some predictability regarding the lesson for the day. It may be helpful to outline the lesson agenda briefly in a bulleted list or flow chart format before the class begins in order to establish a visual reference that you can refer to with your students. In this case, an outline of the topics included in the curriculum may be useful as well as an agenda for each individual lesson.

STATING EXPECTED BEHAVIORS

Because of the nature of the lessons in *Strong Kids—Grades 6–8*, behavior expectations for students or group members must be very clear and discussed at the very start of *Strong Kids*. Some of the units revolve around sensitive issues, and every opportunity should be taken to provide instruction and subsequent reinforcement for appropriate behavior. Students should feel free to share their beliefs and feelings on the targeted topics but must not feel pressured into revealing anything that makes them feel uncomfortable or makes others in the group feel uncomfortable. You should state expected behaviors before instruction, before modeling examples, and before the practice sections of lessons. In some cases, you may need to teach and reinforce behavioral expectations more frequently than these suggested times, or you may remind students before each lesson.

As a general recommendation for promoting appropriate behavior in school and related settings, we recommend that teachers and group leaders develop and teach a few simple rules for appropriate behavior. There are three guidelines in Lesson 1 that you may use as examples. When making rules, be sure to state expectations clearly and positively. For example, if it is necessary to make a rule around fighting, instead of saying "no fighting," we might say "respect your classmates, which means being friendly, keeping hands to self, looking for nice things to say, and no arguing or fighting." Rules should be simple and appropriate to the developmental level of the children for whom they are intended. In addition, the list of rules should be kept to a minimum. Usually, no more than five general rules are needed. You will find that rules are more effective when you teach them to students and then find frequent opportunities to reinforce them through reminders, examples, and so forth. In addition, the literature suggests giving positive praise to any negative statement in a five-to-one ratio (Fredrickson & Losada, 2005). This way, students feel more supported and encouraged to engage in the prosocial behaviors. You also may want to post these rules in your classroom as a reminder for students and to offer opportunities for practice.

PLANNING FOR SMOOTH TRANSITIONS

Time is one of the most precious commodities in your classroom or center. In a brief curriculum such as *Strong Kids—Grades 6–8*, the element of time is especially critical. To make the best use of your limited time in teaching the curriculum, use your transition time wisely before and during the lessons. We recommend that you have all materials prepared and organized for easy distribution to students. Make sure that equipment is in working order before you start the lessons. *Explicitly state directions before and during transitions.* If possible, precorrect for any possible behavioral difficulties. If, due to student discussion or other scheduling restraints, you find you need to end the lesson before it is complete, we recommend completing at a natural transition such as the end of an activity and then concluding the lesson with the Closure activity.

PHYSICAL ARRANGEMENTS

For the lessons in this curriculum, all students must have a clear view of you, the group leader. It is recommended that students are situated in forward-facing seats or a horseshoe shape. You may want to preassign students to groups of two or three because some activities in certain lessons will require small-group discussion or a mini-project. This practice not only will save time but also will give you control of how your students are grouped. Always use movement around the classroom and around the student groups, voice level, and voice intonation to increase the interest of your students and, consequently, increase active participation.

ADAPTATIONS FOR UNIQUE NEEDS AND DISABILITIES

In many of the lessons, you will be encouraged to create scenarios pertaining to a certain topic. To facilitate and encourage student participation, think of situations that would best reflect the interests, abilities, and level of understanding of the students in your class or group. You may choose to use current situations relevant to your classroom and school or global current events to illustrate the concepts. The situations provided in the units are to be considered examples and can be modified extensively to best fit the unique needs of your students. Making appropriate adaptations for the needs of your students not only will make the delivery of lessons go more smoothly but also will aid with generalization and maintenance of new skills. Before starting the program, it is important to consider if there are behavioral needs in your group, learning difficulties, or developmental disabilities so you can prepare for any adaptations or modifications. Also, many of the Mindfulness-Based Focusing Activities include engaging the senses, such as touch and hearing. If students use wheelchairs or have sensory impairments, these activities will need to be adapted according to their needs. For low-functioning groups, adapt lessons by creating simpler examples and by breaking the lessons into shorter sessions.

For high-functioning groups, introduce complexity in the form of concurrent emotions and involved situations. For mixed groups, be sure to provide opportunities for questions, and allow peer interaction when appropriate so that students with a stronger grasp of the emotions can stay engaged by participating in explanations and/or skits for students who need extra support. The following are suggested modifications and adaptations:

- Work with fewer items per page or line and/or materials in a larger print size.

- Have a designated reader or group leader.

- Use a larger desk for group work, if available.

- Set up a buddy system to identify students who may be higher functioning.

- If assistive technology is used, identify key words/concepts to be programmed into the device.

- Use various and combinations of sensory modalities.

In the second edition of *Strong Kids—6–8*, an Instructor Reflection section is included to encourage the group leader to consider the lesson topic from a personal perspective. Use this opportunity for reflection to come up with appropriate examples from your own experiences and/or to generate empathy for how your students may experience the subject matter.

ADAPTATIONS FOR CULTURALLY AND LINGUISTICALLY DIVERSE LEARNERS

As our society becomes increasingly diverse, researchers and practitioners are recognizing the need to address cultural issues in curriculum development and implementation. Efforts to address cultural issues have ranged from ignoring or dismissing the need for cultural adaptations to arguing the need for culture-specific research and curricula tailored for each cultural subgroup. Between these two extreme positions has emerged a set of criteria and recommendations for making cultural adaptations to existing curricula. The cultural adaptation approach retains the core assumptions and skill domains of the existing curriculum but recommends tailoring the teaching of these concepts to the specific needs of particular groups of interest. Research supports the success of making cultural adaptations to existing social and emotional curricula for specific groups (see Castro-Olivo, 2014; Muñoz et al., 2002; Yu & Seligman, 2002).

We began the development of *Strong Kids* with the assumption that no single curriculum could meet the learning needs of all students. By focusing on teaching a set of key ideas related to SEL and resilience, however, we believe that the curriculum can successfully meet the needs of a wide range of students when appropriate adaptations are made. Some particular cultural variables that may require attention in curriculum adaptation processes include language, race/ethnicity, acculturation, socioeconomic status, sexual orientation, religion, gender, disability status, and nationality.

GENERALIZATION AND MAINTENANCE OF SKILLS

Instructors often find it difficult to help students generalize social and emotional skills to different settings and to ensure that these skills are maintained over time. To increase sustainability and generalizability of skills learned in the *Strong Kids* and *Strong Teens* programs, look for opportunities to use the Tips for Transfer Training and Homework and the supplemental activities that are found at the end of each lesson. We have included prompts for precorrecting errors in learning the expected skills, reminding students of the concepts being learned, and reinforcing students for demonstrating the skills that have been introduced and taught in the program. Reinforce *Strong Kids* and *Strong Teens* skills both within and outside the teaching setting as much as possible. Make sure that parents, teachers, administrators, and other staff are aware of the skills you are instructing, because your students will require frequent feedback in several settings in order for the skills to be durable and generalized. After the program has been completed, Lesson 12, Finishing UP!, can be adapted and used as a "booster lesson" to reteach and reinforce the major objectives from all the lessons. Also, specific lessons may be chosen to target skills in need of reteaching. For example, after completing the *Strong Kids* or *Strong Teens* program, if you notice that your students are having increasing difficulty resolving conflicts, you might choose to reteach Lesson 8, Solving People Problems, and implement the supplemental activities offered at the end of that lesson.

SUGGESTIONS FOR SUCCESS

As you teach the lessons in *Strong Kids—Grades 6–8*, you will increase your likelihood of success by observing and following a few additional suggestions for successful implementation of the curriculum. We have developed these suggestions through piloting the program in numerous settings and through the feedback we have received from our associates who have used it in their schools and treatment centers.

- *Practice your lessons* before implementing them. Each lesson is slightly different and will require advance preparation in the form of photocopying and generating examples, grouping, and in some cases considering actors for a skit. Each lesson also will require your own personal involvement and understanding of the subject matter. Each lesson builds on the previous, so the more prepared you are, the more successful and efficient the lesson instruction will be.

- Be sure to give the students an *overview* of each lesson's purpose. Explain that a different topic/unit will be taught each week (or as frequently as possible), because students may come to expect a continuation of a certain topic as opposed to a new topic each lesson.

- In our experience, folders that are specifically designated for students to store their handouts, notes, and homework assignment sheets will help *keep materials organized* and will reduce the amount of time needed by the teacher or group leader to start the weekly lessons. We suggest that you consider having all of your students keep a special *Strong Kids* folder for this purpose. However, use the system that works best for your students to organize their *Strong Kids* handouts.

- Ensure that you allow sufficient time to *review the topics* from prior lessons and integrate concepts when at all possible.

- Introduce or reintroduce a *behavior management technique,* such as a token economy, to reinforce prosocial behaviors during the unit. Remind students of your school and classroom rules as well as the rules associated with this curriculum.

- This curriculum involves teaching a wide range of skills in a relatively short period of time. In order to use your time most effectively, *directly teach these skills.* Place your priority on instruction and allowing your students to ask questions. During the lessons, you may need to keep discussion and activity time to a minimum. However, we encourage you to have in-depth discussions with your students as much as possible during class meetings or as you integrate the concepts in other settings or in other classes.

- *Reinforce* any *Strong Kids—Grades 6–8 skills* that you might observe, both within and outside the teaching setting. Make sure that parents, teachers, administrators, and other staff are aware of the skills you are instructing, because your students will require frequent feedback in several settings in order for the skills to be durable and generalized.

- Be prepared to *include a "twist"* to a scenario from your own experience or something the class may recognize from recent experiences. Many lessons include references to twists in which a scenario is presented from a different perspective or with additional context. Understand your students and determine how much complexity you can add to the lessons to strengthen their interaction with the content.

- *Complete at least one homework example* with the entire class or group to help them understand the assignment and be prepared to complete it. It is recommended to complete the homework handouts from the beginning lessons as a way to provide a model early on.

- As a general practice, we suggest that you *do not add new students to the group once the program has already started.* Particularly when the program is taught to small groups of students rather than entire classrooms, we have found that having new students join the group once it has started can be disruptive to the group process and may result in a slowing of the flow of training as well as a reduction in the willingness of group members to participate. If you do find that you need to add students, look for an opportunity to brief the new student or students separately in advance, and bring them up to speed on the topics presented so far and how your group interacts and shares information. It may be important for you to also brief the existing group so they are aware of the change and aware of how the new student(s) will be incorporated into grouping and other activities.

- Look for opportunities to *use the Tips for Transfer Training and Homework* and the supplemental activities that are found at the end of each lesson. These suggestions have been designed to facilitate the transfer of skills learned through the program across different settings and to help students maintain what they have learned over time. Again, we have included prompts for precorrecting errors in learning the expected skills, reminding students of the concepts being learned, and commending students for demonstrating the skills that have been introduced and taught in the program.

- Be on the lookout for signals from your students that they may need more support than the curriculum can provide. Check the comment box regularly; students in immediate social and emotional need may seek indirect routes to request help. Remember that these lessons are not intended for students in crisis or for students who have more significant mental health needs. Lessons 1 and 12 include reminders about connecting students to their larger network of supports for specific needs. Be prepared to provide these contacts to students throughout the curriculum. Prior to starting *Strong Kids*, it is recommended that you talk to your school psychologist or counselor about your implementation plans and learn more about the mental health resources available at your school or site. As applicable, consider inviting your school's primary mental health practitioner (school psychologist, counselor, or other affiliated mental health provider) into your class to introduce him- or herself to your students.

The Big Ideas of *Strong Kids—Grades 6–8*

As noted previously, a successful curriculum adaptation process requires particular innovations and modifications to meet the needs of specific individuals and groups. At the same time, these adaptations must retain the general concepts, or big ideas, on which the curriculum is based. With this notion in mind, we list the most important features of *Strong Kids—Grades 6–8* with the hope that these ideas will be taken into account when making any type of adaptation to the curriculum. With the underlying goals of improving SEL curriculum and resilience in children and adolescents; preventing and reducing depression, anxiety, and other internalizing disorders; and promoting awareness of moods and symptoms of internalizing disorders, these big ideas include the following:

- To teach children and youth to understand their own and other people's feelings

- To teach children and youth to understand the link between thoughts and emotions and to learn to monitor and modulate them appropriately

- To teach children and youth to identify thinking traps that may interfere with healthy decision making

- To help students learn strategies for increasing habits for positive living

- To help children and youth learn to learn identify stress and cognitive and behavioral strategies to manage stress

- To teach children and youth problem-solving skills, effective communication skills, and the anger model to be more successful in social contexts (e.g., listening, being assertive)

- To teach children and youth to set appropriate and realistic goals based on their own values and to monitor their behavior in order to reach their goals using SMART goals (specific, measurable, attainable, relevant, and timely)

- To help students identify comfortable and uncomfortable feelings and distinguish healthy and unhealthy ways to express emotions

Specific Strategies for Making Cultural Adaptations

Keeping these big ideas in mind, *Strong Kids—Grades 6–8* may be adapted to better fit the needs of diverse children. It is critical to be culturally sensitive because often there are cultural differences in expressing emotions. For this purpose, we propose a few guidelines for making cross-cultural adaptations. These suggestions are based on our own experiences in attempting to adapt the *Strong Kids* curriculum with specific cultural groups. They are also based in great measure on the premises of the American Psychological Association's Guidelines for Providers of Psychological Services to Ethnic, Linguistic, and Culturally Diverse Populations (available at http://www.apa.org/pi/oema/resources/policy/provider-guidelines.aspx).

1. Get to know your students.

   - Ask students about their cultural identities, activities, and rituals.

   - Reflect on the dominant cultural variables in your classroom and how these aspects of culture affect the way your students behave and think.

   - Identify common success and failure experiences, problem situations, and challenging life circumstances confronted by your students.

   - Encourage students to share aspects of their culture with the larger group.

2. Get to know your students' communities.

   - Visit the families and, as appropriate, the homes of students in your class or group.

   - Identify a cultural liaison to help you with your research about your students' culture.

   - Ask the cultural liaison to assist with the cultural adaptation process.

3. Deliver the curriculum in a manner that your students can understand.

   - Modify the language of each lesson so that your students can easily understand the key ideas.

   - Use examples and situations that match the lives of your students (e.g., change characters' names, include extended family, include children who use wheelchairs, use problem examples that your students have experienced).

4. Encourage tolerance and establish a climate in which differences are viewed as resources, not deficits.

   • Teach students ways to show respect for different cultural groups.

   • Encourage and reinforce students for respecting the examples and comments made by their peers.

   • Establish and enforce a classroom rule that teasing and name calling are not allowed.

5. Adapt assessment tools.

   • Adapt the assessment materials so that students can understand (e.g., language, context).

   • Pilot test some of the assessment materials with small groups of students prior to implementing the curriculum to ensure that students understand the questions.

6. Become aware of variations within cultures. For example, some cultures tend to be more expressive and value the discussion of individual emotions and beliefs, whereas others tend to be more reserved and value privacy.

   • Do not assume too much about a student's culture or ethnicity.

   • Avoid making overgeneralizations about cultural groups. Not all members of a culture act the same way.

   • Examine your own values, assumptions, and worldviews and how these are the same and different from those of your students.

   • Continually examine the accuracy and fairness of your assumptions about the beliefs and behaviors of different cultural groups.

7. Seek feedback.

   • View the adaptation process as an ongoing process.

   • Consult with students, your colleagues, and community members about the relevance and accuracy of the adaptation efforts.

   • Ask the students how well the curriculum is matching their needs and life experiences (see Castro-Olivo, 2010).

In sum, adapting *Strong Kids—Grades 6–8* or any other SEL curriculum for use with culturally and linguistically diverse learners may be challenging, but it is essential if the curriculum is to have the most meaningful impact on the learners. The suggestions we have offered in this section may be useful as a guide to making the flexible *Strong Kids—Grades 6–8* program appropriate for children and youth from a variety of cultural backgrounds.

REFERENCES

Castro Olivo, S. (2010). One size does not fit all: Adapting SEL programs for use in our multicultural world. In K.W. Merrell & B.A. Gueldner (Eds.), *Social and emotional learning in the classroom: Promoting mental health and academic success*. New York, NY: Guilford.

Castro-Olivo, S. (2014). Promoting social-emotional learning in adolescent Latino ELLs: A study of the culturally adapted Strong Teens program. *School Psychology Quarterly, 29*, 567–577.

Fredrickson, B., & Losada, F. (2005). Positive affect and the complex aspects of human flourishing. *American Psychologist, 60*(7), 678–686.

Muñoz, R.F., Penilla, C., & Urizar, G. (2002). Expanding depression prevention research with children of diverse cultures. *Prevention and Treatment, 5*. doi:10.1037/1522-3736.5.1.513c

Yu, D.L., & Seligman, M.E.P. (2002). Preventing depressive symptoms in Chinese children. *Prevention and Treatment, 5*. doi.org/10.1037/1522-3736.5.1.59a

CHAPTER 3

Overview of the Lessons

The *Strong Kids* programs consist of 12 carefully sequenced lessons that are designed for maximum impact on cognitive, affective, and social functioning within a relatively brief period of time. This chapter provides an overview of each lesson. Read the descriptions carefully prior to preparing your first lesson so that you will understand the lesson sequencing and the big ideas behind the *Strong Kids* programs.

LESSON 1: ABOUT *STRONG KIDS:* EMOTIONAL STRENGTH TRAINING

In the first lesson, About *Strong Kids:* Emotional Strength Training, students are introduced to the program. Behavioral expectations—including respectful listening of others, participation, and maintaining confidentiality—are reviewed and discussed. A general overview of the overall curriculum and individual lessons is presented, providing students with information regarding what they can expect over the course of the program. Emotions and critical terms such as *resilience, adversity,* and *perseverance* are defined for the first time, and students are encouraged to seek adult assistance if they are experiencing difficulties. If optional student assessments are administered as part of the curriculum, they should be given to students for completion during this first lesson.

LESSONS 2 AND 3: UNDERSTANDING YOUR EMOTIONS

The second and third lessons, Understanding Your Emotions (1 and 2), are intended to improve students' emotional vocabulary and awareness. Being able to understand and recognize one's emotions is an important skill for all individuals during all stages of their lives because people experience emotions at school, at home, at work, and at play. Being able to recognize one's emotions and react in a helpful way, even when the feeling is uncomfortable, will allow students to create and sustain positive relationships in school and throughout their lives.

In Understanding Your Emotions 1, students learn to identify different emotions and the physical feelings that occur with emotions and to distinguish feelings as being comfortable or uncomfortable. Students also learn to measure the intensity of emotions and begin to identify what the emotion may be communicating about themselves or the situation they are experiencing. The goal of this lesson is to apply the skills learned to different situations at different times and in different settings. In Understanding Your Emotions 2, students learn that thoughts and behaviors are linked to emotions, and by identifying thoughts and behaviors, one can better understand emotions and learn how to express oneself in a way that is helpful. Students also learn that emotions are expressed differently, depending on the situation. Students then have the opportunity to use their new skills in application exercises, making it more likely that they will be able to generalize the new skills to other situations.

LESSON 4: UNDERSTANDING OTHER PEOPLE'S EMOTIONS

The purpose of the fourth lesson, Understanding Other People's Emotions, is to introduce students to the concept and practice of empathy and thus help them better understand other people's feelings. Although the previous three lessons have focused on students' own feelings, Lesson 4 covers the ability to recognize the emotions of others and share their perspectives, an essential skill in conflict resolution and compassion. Students who can identify the feelings of others are more likely to be tolerant of people with different views. Students will learn to see clearly how their actions can affect the emotions of other people.

Children with antisocial tendencies often experience what is called *hostile attribution*, in which they misperceive others' emotions as anger. This misperception can lead to aggression and violence. Students who practice empathy skills are more able to see a variety of emotions other than anger. By learning to look for physical cues (sometimes referred to as *clues*), they may be more likely to discern the true feelings of others.

Lesson 4 first explains key concepts and then moves into identifying clues about the emotions other people are feeling. Once students are able to identify the potential clues and what they might mean, the lesson progresses to a role play in which students will experience how people may perceive the same situation differently. The children will be asked to take the perspectives of others in order to gain a greater understanding of empathy. Finally, the homework handout provides opportunities for students to apply these skills to their own life experiences.

LESSON 5: DEALING WITH ANGER

The fifth lesson, Dealing with Anger, teaches students that everyone experiences anger in his or her life. Many students, however, are not able to appropriately understand and effectively deal with their anger. Misunderstanding anger, and an inability to appropriately manage it, can often manifest itself in inappropriate behaviors such as arguments and fights, depression, and severe frustration, each of which can have unfortunate consequences.

This lesson teaches students to understand their anger through a multistep anger model and teaches skills for helping them manage their anger. Anger is introduced as one of many normal emotions that serve a purpose in helping people understand and adapt to the world. It is important that students understand two basic concepts: 1) that anger is a normal emotion and 2) that anger serves the important function of protection and motivation in our lives. Students are taught to understand anger using the sequential anger model to improve their ability to recognize what anger looks like in action. In this lesson, students learn that anger does not "just happen." It is triggered by predictable events and progresses through a series of steps within which individuals can play an active role. Students are taught to understand their active roles in the anger process and the fact that they are not helpless "victims" of their anger but are active participants in choosing how to respond to anger.

LESSONS 6 AND 7: CLEAR THINKING

Individuals who are depressed and anxious are very likely to develop or have previously developed patterns of unrealistic, distorted, and otherwise maladaptive cognitions or thoughts. The Clear Thinking lessons are designed to help students to be more aware of their thought patterns and recognize how the students themselves can contribute to their moods, choices, and actions. The lesson is divided into two parts: Clear Thinking 1 and Clear Thinking 2. Clear Thinking 1 teaches students strategies that are helpful in recognizing unhelpful or maladaptive thought patterns by providing descriptions of some of the more common "thinking traps" that individuals use. When possible, the thought patterns such as "binocular vision," "dark glasses," and "black-and-white thinking" are depicted both as visual icons and in simplified language to facilitate comprehension and retention. Clear Thinking 2 uses the information provided in Clear Thinking 1 to teach students techniques such as how to use evidence to proactively identify thinking traps and applying strategies to reframe unhelpful thoughts and attributions. Practice exercises and vignettes are used for discussion.

LESSON 8: SOLVING PEOPLE PROBLEMS

The eighth lesson, Solving People Problems, is designed to promote awareness of useful strategies for resolving social conflict. Interpersonal conflict provides one of the most fertile breeding grounds for depression, anxiety, and negative thinking. Thus, learning appropriate and effective ways to resolve these conflicts may be a strong preventive factor for deterring emotional problems as well as social problems.

Because conflicts may occur daily and can be a source of stress and frustration for students, step-by-step outlines for resolving conflicts are presented. This lesson details the use of a problem-solving model for managing day-to-day social conflicts and presents techniques for its use and application. The lesson is predominantly organized to address conflicts with peers; however, application of various strategies—such as deal-making, compromising, discussion, and brainstorming—are presented in situations that involve hierarchical relationships as well. Students will learn from this lesson that conflict is often a natural part of social interaction and that, with the tools to address conflict, more social interactions can be approached with awareness, respect, openness, sensitivity, and confidence. Practice exercises and role-play situations also are used as examples and teaching tools.

LESSON 9: LETTING GO OF STRESS

Using appropriate techniques to manage stress is an important strategy to promote emotional resilience and prevent physical and emotional problems. Lesson 9, Letting Go of Stress, provides the foundation for teaching students about stress and relaxation. Through the lesson and activities, the students will learn how to identify stress in their lives. An opportunity is provided for students to learn a few relaxation techniques that have been proven to be effective with many people as well as to generate their own ways of coping with stress. The homework assignment allows students to apply the discussed techniques.

Students begin to learn about themselves and how to deal with stress in an effective and healthy manner. Stress is a fact of every person's life. Stress can be healthy to some degree; however, too much stress or not dealing with it effectively can lead to long-term problems. The sooner students learn how to identify it and deal with this aspect of being human, the better their chances are for a healthy existence. Learning how to let go of stress is an integral skill in the development of a strong and resilient kid.

LESSON 10: POSITIVE LIVING

Lesson 10, Positive Living, is new to the second edition of *Strong Kids—Grades 6–8*. It provides students with strategies to incorporate positive habits into day-to-day life to offset negative habits that can affect health and emotion. For students prone to negative thinking, positive feelings are promoted through a discussion of lifestyle choices that involve physical health (eating and sleeping), emotional and mental health (TV time vs. productive time), community connections (helping others and being involved), and family and social connections (maintaining healthy relationships). Encouraging positive choices and thoughts about looking for healthy options in our daily activities is intended to generate habits toward long-term well-being.

The Positive Living lesson is designed to arm all students, not just those who may be prone to pessimism and spirals of negativity, with ways to think about day-to-day behaviors with intention so that healthy choices can be made. The method includes training students to spot the difficult situations that may be changed by altering areas of their lives in which they have more control.

LESSON 11: CREATING STRONG AND SMART GOALS

Throughout life, people are asked to achieve many goals. Frequently, they are not taught the steps that are necessary to achieve these goals. Research supports the idea that students who are able to set and achieve goals independently perform better than students who are told what goals to achieve. This evidence also confirms that learning how to engage more consistently in appropriate positive activities can help to reduce symptoms of depression and anxiety. The steps outlined in this lesson are all necessary in order for students to attain their goals as well as to identify values in the different domains of their lives. Learning these steps and having immediate success by implementing them is crucial to the success of this lesson. If students set a short-term goal first and are successful in the goal-attainment process, then they will be more likely to use the process again in other applications. These steps are beneficial for students' academic achievement, and when individuals set realistic and attainable goals, they begin taking control of their lives, which leads to an increase in the number of positive activities in which they participate. This lesson teaches students the skills necessary to set realistic short- and long-term goals, to identify the key steps in attaining their goals, and to apply the procedures to their own lives by increasing the amount of positive activities in which they are engaged. Developing skills for increasing positive activities through setting and attaining positive goals is of critical importance in sustaining positive mental health.

To this end, in this lesson students learn the skill of goal setting and increasing positive activity as a means to a healthy life. This lesson addresses the importance of increasing and maintaining positive activities and helps students develop an awareness of their own strengths and limitations across major life domains such as physical, mental, and emotional health and engagement in school, family, and community. Students also set SMART goals (those that are specific, measurable, attainable, relevant, and timely), develop action plans for goal attainment, and learn strategies for monitoring their progress and persevering after setbacks.

LESSON 12: FINISHING UP!

The title of the final lesson, Finishing UP!, has a double meaning. It implies that this lesson is the final one in the curriculum, but also it shows how we are striving to end on a positive or upbeat note, integrating the learned concepts, and celebrating the accomplishments that have been made through involvement with the *Strong Kids* curriculum. This lesson provides the opportunity for students to review key points and terms from the lessons presented throughout the program. Issues of confidentiality are revisited, and information for handling more critical emotional issues (using appropriate resources) is covered. The Finishing UP! lesson also provides an opportunity for teachers to assess students using follow-up measures. These results can be compared with the information gained from the optional preassessments that may be administered at the time the first lesson is presented.

CHAPTER 4

What's New

Updates to *Strong Kids* and *Strong Teens*

We have made some exciting and progressive changes to the *Strong Kids* and *Strong Teens* programs in light of recent advances in the field of SEL and in response to user feedback. The following section describes the major changes in content within the programs, changes across the levels of programs, and changes to the lesson components.

CHANGES TO THE CONTENT

In the revised versions of *Strong Kids* and *Strong Teens*, you will find substantive improvements to the content. These changes are delineated as follows and in Table 4.1. First, the revisions better reflect the dynamic nature of emotions and interpersonal relationships and promote cognitive flexibility and problem solving. Because emotions are not always easy to identify, and they may not fall neatly into simple categories such as *happy, sad,* or *mad,* we introduce emotion identification, including complex and concurrent emotions, earlier in the program in order to develop more advanced emotional literacy. We have deemphasized the use of judgmental terms such as *appropriate* and reduced the amount of dichotomies such as *okay-not okay* and *positive-negative,* also allowing for the experience of emotions on a continuum of intensity. We use "twists" in examples, which change a small aspect of the example, thereby altering the way students perceive the situation and the outcome. We also include more modern graphics to pique the interest of students and help ground the more abstract ideas. The updated scenarios better capture the more challenging and realistic situations that students experience.

The experience of distressing emotions such as anger or sadness is discussed in this edition using a slightly different orientation. Rather than conveying only the message that uncomfortable feelings are something to change or fix, we emphasize the value of simply listening to what our bodies are communicating through these emotions. The intention is to build a tolerance for discomfort and thereby reduce reactivity. Also, in keeping with a major impetus of the original programs—to address SEL issues associated with students who internalize their emotions—we discuss both the potential negative consequences of acting out *and* withdrawing, hiding, and repressing emotions.

Table 4.1. New content by lesson

Lesson and topic	Summary of new content
1. About *Strong Kids: Emotional Strength Training*	The concept of emotions is introduced in Lesson 1 rather than in Lesson 2. Introduces emotion names, including a broader scope of emotional vocabulary and images of children modeling emotions Introduces the concept of concurrent emotions Introduces mindfulness-based focusing activities
2. Understanding Your Emotions 1	Lesson 2 introduces the concept of physical feelings associated with emotions. Normalizes feelings of discomfort Includes strategies to promote mindfulness of emotions, thoughts, and physical feelings
3. Understanding Your Emotions 2	Lesson 3 introduces the concept of emotions, thoughts, and behaviors interacting. Includes discussion of the ways in which behaviors communicate emotions, including helpful and unhelpful behaviors Includes discussion of avoidance or repression of feelings Considers the context in the expression of emotions: The way we show how we're feeling depends on where we are, who we are with, what we want/need in the situation.
4. Understanding Other People's Emotions	In the revised programs, this lesson is sequenced before the lesson on anger to provide more instruction on empathy and alternative perspectives first. Introduces enhanced distinctions between empathy and sympathy Includes enhanced discussion and role play regarding perspective taking
5. Dealing with Anger	Lesson 5 frames the reaction to anger as a range of choices. Introduces the option of not reacting when experiencing anger Includes concepts pertaining to complex and concurrent emotions: Anger can be experienced along with emotions like sadness or jealousy.
6. Clear Thinking 1	"Thinking errors" are now defined as "thinking traps." Introduces two new cognitive distortions or thinking traps: "All alone," the feeling that one's experiences are so unique that no one else could possibly understand, and "broad brush," overgeneralizing from one experience, often at play in the development of stereotypes Addresses another cognitive distortion, a belief that one's feelings and thoughts are reality; in this lesson and in Clear Thinking 2
7. Clear Thinking 2	Lesson 7 introduces the new concept of "snowball effect"; that is, one thinking trap can lead to more thinking traps or an accumulation of pessimistic thinking. Includes scenarios that address perfectionistic thinking; an example pertains to perfectionistic thoughts about body image Includes discussion about identifying patterns or habits of thought, in addition to intensity, as a way to identify distorted perceptions Includes new, more concrete analogies and images to help students understand the concept of reframing
8. Solving People Problems	Lesson 8 emphasizes respectful and responsible choices about personal behavior based on social norms, realistic evaluation of consequences of various actions, and the well-being of self and others. Includes expanded options to resolving conflicts using a problem-solving model Includes gray areas or less clear-cut examples
9. Letting Go of Stress	Lesson 9 reframes stress, shifting from a perception that the stressor is harmful to one that stress can pose a healthy challenge. Illustrates how to evaluate expectations as realistic or unrealistic Includes procrastination and avoidance Includes more activities to help students cope with stress (e.g., nature, physical activity, deep breathing, diet)
10. Positive Living	Lesson 10 replaces the previous edition's Positive Thinking lesson. Includes ways to promote a sense of personal control and facilitate the development of healthy habits and activities across school, home, and community settings. Provides students with the opportunity to assess their daily routines and whether or not they are helpful Introduces the concepts of balance and evaluating actions that may have short- and/or long-term benefits

11. Creating Strong and SMART Goals	Lesson 11 introduces setting SMART (specific, measurable, attainable, relevant, and timely) goals (Doran, 1981).
	Promotes self-assessment in areas of physical and emotional health and school, family, and community connections; identification of personal strengths and areas for growth
	Emphasizes effort and a growth mindset (e.g., Dweck, 2006) and perseverance after setbacks
12. Finishing UP!	Lesson 12 provides more integration of critical concepts found across all lessons.
	Promotes more awareness of when help may be needed
	Includes a section on accessing community resources and where to go for help
	Emphasizes resilience and persistence

We address issues that students increasingly experience in global society. We integrate sociocultural issues in discussions of emotional awareness, expression, and empathy. Because *with whom* and *where* we express our emotions can be just as important as *how* we express our emotions, we discuss emotional expression in terms of not just actions but also the context or setting. Throughout the programs, we use more current and authentic examples and reference problems that students today are likely to experience, such as social networking dilemmas, stereotypes, and other complex social situations. We also have anticipated the developmental changes that students experience with age and peer groups.

Because many of the main concepts of the Positive Thinking lesson (e.g., optimism and resilience) are now infused throughout many of the lessons, we have added a new lesson, Positive Living, to replace the Positive Thinking lesson. This new lesson promotes a sense of personal control over daily behaviors and actions and promotes the development of healthy habits across school, home, and community settings. To build on these concepts, the next lesson incorporates SMART (specific, measurable, attainable, relevant, and timely) goals (Doran, 1981). Setting SMART goals helps to ensure that goals are realistic and achievable.

In the new edition, we have worked to improve issues often experienced in the promotion of SEL, such as sustainability and generalizability. We now offer a diverse menu of activities to promote the integration of content across settings and the maintenance of skills over time. Whereas Chapter 12, Finishing UP!, was primarily a review of the lessons in the original version of the programs, this lesson now better promotes the integration of critical concepts. Last, to reinforce the concepts introduced previously, we draw more explicit connections across the lessons.

In addition to the new content, we also incorporate more methods to promote student engagement and involvement. Many of the lessons include an introductory activity to highlight the relevance of the content, stimulate thought, and/or pique the students' interest in the material. Also, several lessons include a menu of activities so that instructors can select the application activity that best suits his or her students.

SOCIAL AND EMOTIONAL COMPETENCIES

CASEL, the leader in SEL research, policy, and implementation efforts, promotes five person-centered and interrelated competency areas that are essential to

Table 4.2. Lessons and social and emotional competencies

Strong Kids lesson and topic	Self-awareness	Self-management	Social awareness	Relationship skills	Responsible decision making
1. About *Strong Kids*: Emotional Strength Training	●				●
2. Understanding Your Emotions 1	●		●		
3. Understanding Your Emotions 2	●	●	●		●
4. Understanding Other People's Emotions			●	●	
5. Dealing with Anger	●	●	●	●	●
6. Clear Thinking 1	●	●			
7. Clear Thinking 2	●	●	●		●
8. Solving People Problems	●	●	●	●	●
9. Letting Go of Stress	●	●			●
10. Positive Living	●	●			●
11. Creating Strong and SMART Goals	●	●			●
12. Finishing UP!	●	●	●	●	●

cognitive, social, and emotional development: self-awareness, self-management, social awareness, relationship skills, and responsible decision making (CASEL, 2014; Zins et al., 2004). The new versions of *Strong Kids* and *Strong Teens* have stronger, more explicit connections to the five SEL competencies as defined by CASEL. At the beginning of each lesson, the connection to the SEL competencies is explicitly illustrated by a user-friendly graphic. This helps support planning and documentations of the alignment of SEL instruction with these well-established competencies. The connections between the competencies and the corresponding lesson are depicted in Table 4.2.

MINDFULNESS-BASED PRACTICES

In preparation for the second edition of the curriculum, our review of the literature indicated that the use of mindfulness-based practices (MBPs) has grown in its application with youth and in schools (Burke, 2010; Harnett & Dawe, 2012; Meiklejohn et al., 2012; Zenner et al., 2014). MBPs such as breathing exercises, sitting meditation, and yoga have been used for many years. Secularized versions of these practices have been scientifically studied over the past 30 years, most notably through the Mindfulness Based Stress Reduction (MBSR) program (Kabat-Zinn, 2013). MBPs that are used for children and adolescents have been adapted from many of the MBSR practices and rendered developmentally appropriate for use in schools and mental health care settings. Research is in the early stages with youth, yet MBPs show promising evidence for yielding positive benefits in such areas as awareness and acceptance, emotion and behavioral regulation, attention, academic engagement and performance, and social competence (see Burke, 2010; Harnett, & Dawe, 2012; Meiklejohn et al., 2012; Zenner et al., 2014, for reviews of this literature).

In conceptualizing the infusion of brief MBPs into *Strong Kids—Grades 6–8*, we reviewed literature pertinent to applying MBPs with clinical and nonclinical populations, the use of MBPs in schools and other settings, the hypothesized mechanisms for how MBPs may work to produce their effects (e.g., Teper, Segal, & Inzlicht, 2013), how MBPs may build resilience (e.g., Coholic, Eys, & Lougheed, 2012), and issues relevant to feasibility and acceptability by youth and school personnel. We also drew from the literature describing evidence-based therapies that have cognitive-behavioral roots, which infused principles of mindfulness and practice, such as mindfulness-based cognitive therapy (MBCT), dialectic behavioral therapy, and acceptance and commitment therapy (ACT). Because of the time constraints involved in adding another activity to an existing program, we reviewed examples of practices that were brief (e.g., Flook, Goldberg, Pinger, Bonus, & Davidson, 2014; Schonert-Reichl & Hymel, 2007) and complemented cognitive-behavioral therapy–oriented approaches to teaching students about emotions and self-regulation (e.g., Broderick & Metz, 2009).

Our intention is to preserve the wellness promotion and cognitive-behavioral theoretical orientation that was the basis of the first edition of *Strong Kids—Grades 6–8*. *Strong Kids* is not a mindfulness-centered curriculum. We aimed for a transformative approach whereby an existing program may be enhanced through the use of a variety of brief MBPs and by infusing general concepts of a mindfulness perspective throughout the lessons. Instruction and examples use a tone of acceptance and openness to experience that may range from comfortable to uncomfortable. The use of terms perceived as judgmental (e.g., "good" and "bad," "appropriate" and "inappropriate") were reframed as "helpful" and "unhelpful" whenever the context supported such a change. Furthermore, emotional experience is reframed to include the notion that emotions, and associated thoughts and feelings, also can be experienced and investigated rather than automatically pushed away or changed.

The MBPs in the 12 lessons are adapted from the foundational elements of MBSR (Kabat-Zinn, 2013) and other evidence-based sources. In designing each exercise, we drew inspiration from resources such as Hooker and Fodor's (2008) overview of activities that have been tested with children, Saltzman's (2014) approach to teaching these concepts to youth, and Semple and Lee's (2011) application of mindfulness within a cognitive therapy orientation with children with internalizing problems.

Each activity is found in the Introduction section and is referred to as a Mindfulness-Based Focusing Activity in the lesson. Students are given an explanation for the activity in Lesson 1, along with some ideas to explain what they can expect in starting the activities. A script is provided for convenience and efficiency and, in keeping with the spirit of *Strong Kids*, to decrease the amount of preparation time for instructors. Please note that these activities are optional. If your institution chooses, simply omit it and continue with the Introduction to the lesson.

Some instructors may wish to have more background information and additional training in MBPs to better understand and implement these ideas. For additional information on mindfulness you may wish to visit our companion web site www.strongkidsresources.com and the following Internet resources:

- Association for Mindfulness in Education (AME): A collaborative association of organizations and individuals working together to provide support for mindfulness training as a component of K–12 education; http://www.mindfuleducation.org/

- Garrison Institute's Initiative on Contemplation and Education: Working to develop the field of contemplative education for K–12 educators and classrooms; https://www.garrisoninstitute.org

- Mindfulness-Based Stress Reduction (MBSR) and the Center for Mindfulness at University of Massachusetts Medical School; http://www.umassmed.edu/cfm/

CHANGES ACROSS THE PROGRAM LEVELS

We were often asked how the programs differ across the developmental levels of the programs; that is, how does *Strong Kids—Grades 3–5* differ from *Strong Kids—Grades 6–8*, and how does *Strong Kids—Grades 6–8* differ from *Strong Teens?* The new programs have been revised to better target, differentiate, and address developmental considerations of SEL.

The *Strong Kids* and *Strong Teens* lesson topics were selected to reflect the most critical components of resilience and align to the five competencies of SEL, lending well to the implementation of the program as a universal or schoolwide SEL program. The programs are based on theory and research that indicates that each SEL competence can be taught effectively to children of all ages. Children and adolescents alike can benefit from learning how to identify and manage their emotions, take the perspectives of others, and make responsible decisions. For these reasons, the lesson topics and objectives remain stable across all three levels of the programs. Therefore, although it is beneficial to implement the programs to students each year, *Strong Kids— Grades 3–5* is not a prerequisite to *Strong Kids—Grades 6–8*, and *Strong Kids—Grades 6–8* is not a prerequisite to *Strong Teens*. Students can benefit from the programs regardless of the level at which they first receive instruction. However, the SEL topics bring different contexts and different meanings for students as they age. Making a responsible decision can present more complex considerations for an adolescent than for a student in third grade. Thus, although the major objectives remain unchanged across the levels, the ways in which the lessons approach the objectives are adjusted to fit the development of the student. As the levels advance, the instruction and examples become increasingly sophisticated and abstract. Whereas *Strong Kids* focuses on more concrete concepts and issues relevant to elementary and middle school, *Strong Teens* addresses more abstract concepts and uses examples with more complex social situations and issues that are more relevant to teens, such as postsecondary planning.

NEW LESSON COMPONENTS

Although the lessons continue to follow a standardized format, we have added several elements to all the lessons: 1) SEL competencies, 2) suggestions for when instructors are running short on time, 3) instructor reflection, 4) introductory mindfulness-based focusing activity, 5) putting it all together, 6) closing breathing activity, and 7) additional activities. These changes were made in response to the most progressive advancements in research, theory, and science of implementation in the field of SEL.

Running Short on Time?

Time is one of our scarcest resources, particularly in modern, busy schools. This section includes recommended ways instructors can segment lessons when the full amount of time needed to implement a single lesson is not available. Guidance for segmenting lessons is found in Chapter 1 and at the beginning of each lesson. These are only suggested recommendations, and we understand that the implementation will vary for every user or setting.

Instructor Reflection

In keeping with the original intent of the *Strong Kids* programs, we are continuously considering ways in which we might help busy practitioners feel better prepared to teach SEL programs such as *Strong Kids* and *Strong Teens*. This section provides a few helpful suggestions for instructors to get acquainted with the concepts in each lesson and to have the opportunity to practice skills prior to teaching the lesson. Also, it allows users to reflect on their personal experiences with the skills taught in each lesson. Understanding how one has coped can help facilitate a more successful implementation of the lesson.

Optional Mindfulness-Based Focusing Activity

A brief, 2- to 3-minute, scripted mindfulness activity is placed at the beginning of each lesson to promote calm, focus, and enhanced awareness of experience in preparation for the lesson content. The mindfulness activities at the start of each lesson begin with a standard activity that promotes nonjudgmental observation of the present moment by instructing students to become aware of their body positioning (hands and feet resting in place) and the sensation of their natural breath. Beginning in the second lesson and onto the last lesson (12), the standard activity is followed by more content-specific practice. For example, in the lesson teaching awareness of thoughts, students are asked to become aware of thoughts as they arrive, to watch them, and to let them pass. In the lesson that focuses on perspective-taking, students participate in an activity that promotes awareness of sounds; in the lesson on managing stress, a loving-kindness exercise toward one's self is applied. In a lesson focusing on awareness of thoughts and attributions, students practice noticing thoughts and labeling them in categories such as "planning," and they practice loving-kindness toward others in a lesson on coping with social conflict. Other activities include noticing the breath and how the body moves during breathing, an exercise modeled after the body scan used in MBSR, a whole-body movement exercise, and imagining success or accomplishment and the thoughts and physical sensations that correspond. A culminating activity for the last lesson incorporates elements of the previous activities into one. We selected language intentionally to promote a sense of curiosity, kindness, and nonjudgment.

Putting It All Together

This section serves the purpose of the former "integrating key concepts" section and further encourages active application of the key skills within the lesson as a whole concept.

Closing Breathing Activity

At the end of each lesson, a 1-minute diaphragmatic breathing exercise, also scripted, is used to promote relaxation (e.g., Larson, El Ramahi, Conn, Estes, & Ghibellini, 2010) and reflection and assimilation of the lesson content.

Additional Activities and Homework

This section offers additional innovative ways to teach the content outside of the lesson and may bolster skills maintenance and generalization. For teachers who are unable to make use of homework assignments with their groups, we no longer "require" homework but list it as optional. Extra practice is always best, but whether or not homework is completed should not hinder the next lesson.

SUMMARY

Our efforts to create an effective, user-friendly, and practical mental health promotion program, coupled with the real-world experience and feedback we gained over nearly 20 years of research and development and use, have convinced us that the *Strong Kids* curriculum has much to offer and can be a valuable tool for facilitating SEL and promoting resilience. It is our hope that the changes that have been made to the *Strong Kids* programs are positive and helpful, not only in the lives of the students who will be receiving the program but also in the lives of the adults who will be spending time teaching it. We hope that users who were acquainted with the first edition of the *Strong Kids* programs find the updated versions familiar, but with new twists and fresh angles, and that new users of the *Strong Kids* programs find the second edition intuitive, cohesive, and timely. As you use the program and its examples to support your students, we encourage you to consider your own experiences. We hope that not only will you make important connections for and with your students, but you may also stumble onto new ways to look at old problems of your own.

REFERENCES

Broderick, P.C., & Metz, S. (2009). Learning to BREATHE: A pilot trial of a mindfulness curriculum for adolescents. *Advances in School Mental Health Promotion, 2*, 35–46.

Burke, C.A. (2010). Mindfulness-based approaches with children and adolescents: A preliminary review of current research in an emergent field. *Journal of Child and Family Studies, 19*(2), 133–144. doi:10.1007/s10826-009-9282-x

Coholic, D., Eys, M., & Lougheed, S. (2012). Investigating the effectiveness of an arts-based and mindfulness-based group program for the improvement of resilience in children in need. *Journal of Child and Family Studies, 21*(5), 833–844. doi:10.1007/s10826-011-9544-2

Collaborative for Academic, Social, and Emotional Learning. (2014). *What is SEL? Skills and competencies.* Retrieved from http://www.casel.org/social-and-emotional-learning/core-competencies

Doran, G.T. (1981). There's a S.M.A.R.T. way to write management's goals and objectives. *Management Review, 11*, 35–36.

Dweck, C.S. (2006). *Mindset: The new psychology of success.* New York, NY: Random House.

Flook, L., Goldberg, S.B., Pinger, L., Bonus, K., & Davidson, R.J. (2013). Mindfulness for teachers: A pilot study to assess effects on stress, burnout, and teaching efficacy. *Mind, Brain, and Education, 7*, 182–195. doi:10.1111/mbe.12026

Harnett, P.H., & Dawe, S. (2012). The contribution of mindfulness-based therapies for children and families and proposed conceptual integration. *Child and Adolescent Mental Health, 17*(4), 195–208. doi:10.1111/j.1475-3588.2011.00643.x

Hooker, K.E., & Fodor, I.E. (2008). Teaching mindfulness to children. *Gestalt Review, 12*, 75–91. Retrieved from http://www.gisc.orgwww.gisc.org/gestaltreview/documents/Teaching MindfulnesstoChildren.pdf

Kabat-Zinn, J. (2013). *Full catastrophe living* (Rev. ed.). New York, NY: Bantam.

Larson, H., El Ramahi, M., Conn, S., Estes, L., & Ghibellini, A. (2010). Reducing test anxiety among third grade students through the implementation of relaxation techniques, *Journal of School Counseling, 8*, 1–19.

Meiklejohn, J., Phillips, C., Freedman, M.L., Griffin, M.L., Biegel, G., Roach, A., . . . Saltzman, A. (2012). Integrating mindfulness training into K–12 education: Fostering the resilience of teachers and students. *Mindfulness, 3*(4), 291–307. doi:10.1007/s12671-012-0094-5

Saltzman, A. (2014). *A still quiet place: A mindfulness program for teaching children and adolescents to ease stress and difficult emotions.* Oakland, CA: New Harbinger Publications.

Schonert-Reichl, K.A., & Hymel, S. (2007). Educating the heart as well as the mind social and emotional learning for school and life success. *Education Canada, 47*, 20–25. Retrieved from http://www.jcsh-cces.ca/upload/Educating_Heart_Spring07-1.pdf

Semple, R., & Lee, J. (2011). *Mindfulness-based cognitive therapy for anxious children. A manual for treating childhood anxiety.* Oakland, CA: New Harbinger Publications.

Teper, R., Segal, Z., & Inzlicht, M. (2013). Inside the mindful mind: How mindfulness enhances emotion regulation through improvements in executive control. *Current Directions in Psychological Science, 22*, 449–454. doi:10.1177/0963721413495869

Zenner, C., Herrnleben-Kurz, S., & Walach, H. (2014). Mindfulness-based interventions in schools—A systematic review and meta-analysis. *Frontiers in Psychology, 5*, 603. Retrieved from http://www.ncbi.nlm.nih.gov/pmc/articles/PMC4075476/

Zins, J.E., Bloodworth, M.R., Weissberg, R.P., & Walberg, H.J. (2004). The scientific base linking social and emotional learning to school success. In J. Zins, M. Wang, & H. Walberg (Eds.), *Building academic success and social-emotional learning: What does the research say?* New York, NY: Teachers College Press.

SECTION II

The *Strong Kids—Grades 6–8* Curriculum

LESSON 1

About *Strong Kids*: Emotional Strength Training

SEL Competencies Addressed in This Lesson

Teacher Notes

_____

_____

_____

_____

_____

_____

_____

_____

_____

_____

Purpose and Objectives

This lesson orients students to the curriculum and introduces emotional vocabulary. In this lesson, students will

- Be introduced to the curriculum and the plan for regular instruction

- Learn the expected behaviors for participation in the curriculum

- Begin to identify emotions

Materials Needed

☐ Supplements 1.1–1.2 (online download)

☐ Supplement 1.3 (online download and preprint)

☐ Supplement 1.4–1.6 (online download)

☐ Supplement 1.7 (homework handout)

☐ Comment Box

Running Short on Time?

Suggested stopping points: end of Optional Pretest Assessments or end of the Awareness Statement to Instructor and Students section and the Closure section. See Chapter 1 for more information on segmenting lessons.

Instructor Reflection

You and your students are embarking on a 12-lesson journey that explores our social and emotional lives. Research demonstrates that learning about our social and emotional world helps build resilience and can offset the negative effects of the fast-paced and stressful society in which we live. Before you lead your students through each lesson, you may feel more comfortable with the materials if you take some time to reflect on each lesson's content as it relates to you, your understanding of the information, and your own experiences. An Instructor Reflection exercise is provided at the beginning of each lesson to allow you time to reflect on the content you are about to present. Also, you may find it helpful to review the introductory material in Chapters 1 through 4 before beginning the lessons. The star icon (see margin), used throughout all lessons, signifies that these chapters offer additional explanation or information pertinent to the lesson content or administrative guidelines, which can help you implement the lesson.

For this lesson, consider how the behavioral expectations for participating in the curriculum align with your classroom behavior expectations. Note that special consideration is given to the fact that students will share personal information and thus it will be treated as confidential within the group. Consider how you might remind students to be respectful to one another when they share. You also may wish to review the list of emotions in Supplement 1.6 and consider how you experience and perceive emotions. Are there some emotions with which you feel more, or less, comfortable? Consider potential roadblocks you may face in presenting this information, or concerns that may arise, and identify colleagues with whom you can collaborate and any resources available to you at your site.

Introduction

🕐 1 MIN.

In this section and the sections that follow, sample scripts are provided. You may use the scripts, or your own words, during instruction. For this first section, talk to students about the fact that they are starting a new program called *Strong Kids*. Give examples on the topics that will be covered, and indicate that the skills they learn will help them be socially and emotionally stronger in their lives. Ask students what they think they might need to be socially and emotionally strong.

Sample Script

Today, we will begin a new program called Strong Kids. Strong Kids is about learning ways we can be strong and healthy with our minds and bodies and in our relationships with other people. We'll learn how to understand our emotions and other people's emotions. We'll talk about how to solve problems, how to set goals, and how to think in a way that helps us and makes us stronger. We will meet [e.g., once per week] for [e.g., 45 minutes]. This program will help you learn skills that you will practice in order to be socially and emotionally healthy throughout your life. What do you think is needed to be socially and emotionally strong?

Optional Pretest Assessments

10–20 MINS. If you are using assessment measures to evaluate student growth during the *Strong Kids* curriculum, have your students complete the pretests at this time. Administer the same assessment measures again after Lesson 12, Finishing UP! We suggest using the *Strong Kids* Knowledge Test (see Appendix A) to measure students' knowledge of the concepts covered in the lessons. You also may use other assessment tools of your choosing. Visit http://www.strongkidsresources. com to review measures that have been useful. Tell students it is okay if they don't know the answers to the questions on the measurement tools. The tests are used to evaluate what they know now. When all students have a copy of the pretest, provide them with the appropriate instructions. The amount of time it will take to complete these assessments will depend on the number of assessment measures and the length of each. Ten to 20 minutes is an estimate. See Chapter 2 for more information on adjusting the curriculum to fit the needs of your students.

Sample Script

First, I'm going to ask you to answer some questions that will help me understand what you know about emotions. There are no right or wrong answers, and you may not have heard some of the words before, but do your best work and answer all of the questions. Raise your hand if you need help understanding any of the questions. I'll start by reading the directions, then you can begin answering the questions.

Introduce the Mindfulness-Based Focusing Activity

3 MINS. Discuss with students that they will participate in a mindfulness, or focusing, activity at the start of every lesson. Discuss that they may feel awkward or restless at first and they have the option to keep their eyes open. These brief activities are intended to teach students a skill that can help them focus at the beginning of each lesson and concentrate on the lesson. Use Supplement 1.1 as a download to illustrate the limbic system in the brain. For background and implementation information on these activities, please see Chapter 4.

Sample Script

At the start of each lesson, we will begin with an activity to settle our bodies and focus our minds. This focusing, or mindfulness, activity will help to train your brain to pay attention, learn new information, understand how you feel, and make positive choices. In the middle of our brains, we have an information processing center called the limbic system. This system processes emotions and communicates with the front part of our brain, right where our foreheads are, that helps us think clearly and make decisions. When we are feeling stressed, anxious, or upset, the limbic system sends an alert signal to our bodies, making us feel uncomfortable. Sometimes, this feels like we want to fight or get away from something, or stay put. When this happens, the front part of our brain doesn't work as well and we may react very quickly without thinking things through. It's like pouring water into a bowl that's turned upside down—the water that is needed won't go into the bowl. When our limbic system sends strong signals throughout our body, we might have a harder time remembering information and making positive choices. When we are more focused and calm or feeling creative, hopeful, and compassionate, our brains work more efficiently and can work with information in a logical, helpful way. In this case, this is like pouring water straight into an upturned bowl. We remember the information and think about it more deeply.

I will ask you to close your eyes or look at a point on the floor in front of you, breathe, and pay attention to what I'm saying. If you choose to keep your eyes open, please look only at the space in front of you, not at your neighbor. You want to focus on what you feel, not what your neighbor is doing. You may feel a little uncomfortable, awkward, or restless at first, but it gets easier the more we practice.

Mindfulness-Based Focusing Activity

🕐 2 MINS. **Sample Script**

Let's begin. Close your eyes, or leave your eyes open and look at a point in front of you on the floor or on your desk. Now, rest your hands comfortably on your desk or in your lap. Feel your feet on the floor or your hands as they rest. Just like scientists are curious, or interested in things around them, we are going to start each lesson by exploring, in a kind and curious way, what it feels like to pay attention to some of the messages our bodies send us and to some of the things around us. Let's start by taking three breaths together and paying attention to our breath. Just breathe as you normally do. [Pause.] Now, pay attention to what it feels like taking a breath in and a breath out. Maybe you feel air going in through your nose or mouth and going out your nose or mouth. [Pause.] Maybe you feel your stomach moving. Let's spend about a minute just noticing what breathing feels like in our bodies. [Allow 1 minute to practice awareness.] Now, let's take two breaths together. [Pause. Model two slow breaths.] When you finish letting out your breath, slowly open your eyes. Now that we've practiced becoming aware of our breathing, we are ready to move on to our lesson.

Defining Behavior Expectations and Participation

🕐 5 MINS.

Use Supplement 1.2 to introduce and review the expectations for being in the group and their definitions. These expectations are important to follow so that everyone feels safe in sharing and participating in the discussion. Students will be asked to share personal information but are never obligated to do this, especially if they feel too uncomfortable. See below (after the Sample Script) for an optional idea for a way in which students can communicate if they feel uncomfortable sharing or have questions or concerns. If you choose to include this option, include it as part of your introduction and before reviewing the guidelines in detail.

Sample Script

You are now a part of a group with some important expectations or rules. During the Strong Kids lessons, you may be asked to share personal stories. When someone is sharing a story, we will listen quietly. Sharing this information outside of the group is not allowed. Your classmates are trusting you to keep the information private. If someone outside of our group asks you to share information about something someone in our group shared during these lessons, just say: "I can't tell you that; those discussions are private" or "What's said in the group stays in the group." If you feel uncomfortable sharing, you can stop at any time. If you want to talk about your situation in private, please talk to me personally. It's important to remain respectful toward one another as we are learning these skills. Here are the expectations:

Respect others: Listen quietly when someone is speaking. Pay attention.

Come prepared and do your best work: Complete any activities assigned from the last lesson. Participate in activities to the best of your ability.

Personal information stays in the group: What is talked about in the group stays with the group. Do not gossip about what other people have shared. [Consider explaining what gossip is; e.g., saying things about other people that might hurt their feelings.]

Optional: There may be students who may feel uncomfortable speaking to you about a particular concern. To encourage these students to share or obtain your assistance privately, you may wish to consider a comment box, with preprinted comment slips, whereby students can write a question or concern and drop it in the box. Use Supplement 1.3 as a download and preprint to show students an example of the comment slip. Please see Chapter 2 for ways in which you can address comments that may be concerning.

Sample Script

You can also fill out a comment slip [show Supplement 1.3] and put it in this Comment Box. On the slip, you will write your name and your concern/question or comments if you are uncomfortable sharing with the group. If I talk about something I read in the Comment Box, I will be careful not to say who wrote it and I will leave out any parts that could give clues about who wrote it. All comments and questions are important.

Activity A: Practicing the Expectations

 3 MINS.

Use Supplement 1.2 to review the expectations and discuss examples and non-examples of following the expectations. You also can ask the class to share their own examples and nonexamples. *Note:* An "example" reflects the appropriate or intended use of a term or concept (to do). A "nonexample" illustrates the opposite of the concept (not to do). It is helpful to include examples and nonexamples that are not quite so obvious—those that define ambiguous or gray areas. This could include a nonexample of the "personal information stays in the group" rule, which describes a vague post to social media or other electronic communication (e.g., text).

Sample Script

Let's discuss some examples of following the expectations and some nonexamples of following the expectations. Examples mean those choices that you want to or are expected to make. Nonexamples are those choices that you don't want to or shouldn't make. Here are the rules:

Respect others.

- *Example: You listen quietly while someone is speaking and until they finish what they are saying.*

- *Nonexamples: You talk to your neighbor while someone is speaking. You "tune out" or begin working on something else.*

Come prepared and do your best work.

- *Example: You complete the work you were asked to do.*

- *Nonexamples: You didn't do the worksheet that was assigned. You complete the worksheet in a rushed way right before class or in another class.*

Personal information stays in the group.

- *Example: Someone who's not in the group asks you what someone shared during the class. You tell this person, "What's said in the group stays in the group!"*

- *Nonexample: You either say what happened or you say, "Wow, I can't tell you what she said, but Shanna was really weird today in class."*

Awareness Statement to Instructor and Students

 2 MINS. Explain to students that *Strong Kids* will focus on talking about situations and emotions. Discuss that if anyone feels uncomfortable, it is important to seek additional support. Identify people with whom students can talk (e.g., teacher, parent, school counselor, principal) and brainstorm ways that students can communicate their concerns. At the end of the program, students will have another opportunity to identify whether additional support is needed and where they may go to obtain support. As the lessons progress, remain vigilant for students who appear to be experiencing difficulty or having an uncomfortable response to the content. See Chapter 2 for ideas on how to identify and address these issues.

Sample Script

During the next several weeks, we will talk about different situations and emotions. If you find that you are feeling worried or upset and aren't sure what to do about it, it's important that you talk to an adult. Let's talk about whom you can talk to if you feel this way. [Invite some discussion on this topic.]

Review the Lesson Topics

 1–2 MINS. Use Supplement 1.4 to introduce the lesson topics that will be discussed.

Sample Script

During this program, we will be discussing these topics that are covered in 12 lessons. As part of each topic, there will be activities that involve partners or small-group discussions, role plays, scenarios, handouts, and video clips that will help you learn the concepts.

Key Terms and Definitions

 2 MINS. Use Supplement 1.5 as a handout to define the key terms that will be used in this lesson.

Sample Script

Here are some important terms that will help us understand the information we'll talk about in Strong Kids. We'll define the words and discuss examples to understand what they mean.

Introduction to Emotions

🕒 5–10 MINS. Everyone has emotions. Emotions are like signals that tell us something about our situation.

Sample Script

Traffic lights are signals that tell you to slow down, stop, or go. Emotions are like signals too. Emotions say, "Hey! Pay attention! You're experiencing something you like, don't like, or aren't sure about." We can feel one emotion, like anger, or several emotions at the same time, like disappointment, irritation, and anger. Emotions are our body's way of telling us about a situation. Everyone has emotions, every day, and everywhere!

Activity B: Identifying Emotions

🕒 4–9 MINS. Use Supplement 1.6 as a visual aid to show students a variety of emotions they may experience. This activity can be done with a large group or in small groups. Students also can identify and discuss emotions not on this list.

Sample Script

Let's talk about emotions that you might feel now or have felt in the past. This could be one emotion or a couple that you feel at the same time. We'll also talk about how the emotions acted as signals about a situation. Understanding our emotions helps us to persevere and be resilient, or to work hard to meet our goals and bounce back when things are difficult.

Ask students to do the following

1. Identify a single emotion or combination of emotions they are feeling now or that they felt during a specific event such as the school's last team game, the last assembly, or a car trip with their family.

Sample Script

Look at the list of names and pictures of emotions. Taking turns, let's discuss emotions that you are feeling now or that you have felt recently. For example, if my best friend got a new phone, I might feel happy for her and also envious of her.

2. Draw lines to the emotions that they might feel at the same time.

Sample Script

Often, you will experience more than one emotion at the same time. Look at the list again and think about the emotions you might experience together. You can draw a line that connects the emotions.

3. Discuss how the emotion was acting like a signal.

Sample Script

Next, let's talk about how these emotions act like a signal and give us information. For example, if my friend got a new phone, I might feel some emotions about that. My emotions might be telling me that I feel envious, because I want the same phone too. I might use this signal to motivate me to do something about the situation. I might start to think of a way to earn the money to get it or how to talk to my parents about getting a phone.

Putting It All Together

 ⏱ 2–3 MINS. Use the following activity to practice the concepts discussed in this lesson.

Sample Script

Let's practice what we've learned by putting it all together.

Using Supplement 1.2, ask students to recall the expectations for being in the group. Then, ask students to name a few emotions they felt during the class period. You can also use this time to discuss students' observations and experiences of the focusing activity at the beginning of the lesson.

Sample Script

What are the expectations for being in the group? What are some emotions you felt during this class? What did you notice during the focusing activity?

Closure

 ⏱ 2 MINS. Close the lesson using a short breathing activity and a reflection on the lesson content. Students may find it helpful to place their hands on their stomachs, just under their ribs, to feel the expansion and retraction when doing this exercise properly. For background information on this activity, refer to Chapter 4.

Sample Script

Let's take a moment to regroup. At the end of every lesson, we'll do a short breathing exercise. This exercise is just a little different than the one we did in the beginning and will help us end the lesson in a calm place. We'll also take a moment to think about what we learned today.

Close your eyes or look a point in front of you, and rest your hands in your lap. Feel your feet on the floor. Relax the muscles in your body and face. Relax and soften your stomach muscles. Counting to 3, take a deep breath in slowly. Inhale the air down into your lungs. Feel your chest and stomach expand like a balloon. [Pause.] *Now, exhale, counting to 4. Feel your chest and stomach collapse as all the air exits your body.* [Pause.] *Again, inhale deep into your lungs so that your stomach expands* [Pause.] *and exhale.* [Pause.] *Take a moment to think about something you learned today that was important to you or that you really liked.* [Note to instructor: Pause for a moment to allow time for reflection.] *Counting to 3, take one more deep breath in slowly* [Pause.] *and exhale counting to 4.* [Pause.]

Tips for Transfer Training and Homework

Use the ideas and activities in the following section to practice this lesson's content with your students at other times during the day. Also, remember to precorrect, remind, and reinforce concepts from this lesson in activities throughout the school week across settings including home, the bus, the cafeteria, and the community.

Additional Activities

- Using handheld mirrors or other technology (e.g., photo booth applications), whereby students can look at their own faces or the faces of others, ask students to model what their faces look like when they experience an emotion and then look at the face in the mirror or other technology. You can suggest to students that they do this at home also.

- During the school day, prompt students to identify emotions they are feeling and write them down. Ask students to think about how the emotion may be acting like a signal.

- Ask students to keep a journal, and prompt them to write in the journal after each lesson or daily. Students can use the journal for general reflection or for additional skills practice.

Homework Handout

Pass out the homework handout, Supplement 1.7, My Emotions. This homework asks student to identify and reflect upon emotions. Ask students to answer the questions as best as they can.

The Limbic System

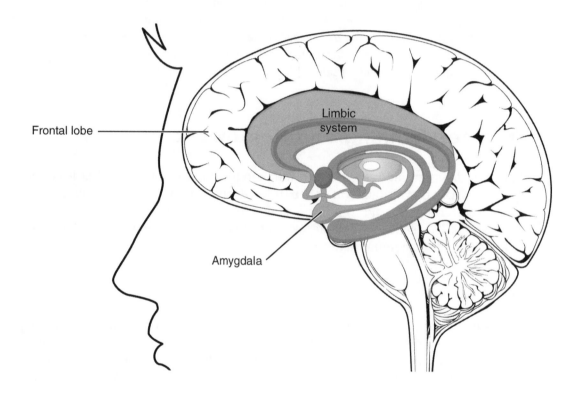

Frontal lobe

Limbic system

Amygdala

Strong Kids Rules

1. **Respect others:** Listen quietly while someone else is speaking.

2. **Come prepared and do your best work:** Complete any activities assigned from the last lesson. Participate in activities as you feel comfortable.

3. **Personal information stays in the group:** What is talked about in the group stays in the group. Do not gossip about what other people have shared.

Comment Slip

Name _____   **Date** _____

Question/Comment/Concern _____

_____

_____

_____

_____

_____

_____

_____

_____

Strong Kids Lessons

Lesson 1: We are introduced to the program, learn the rules of the group, and begin to learn about emotions.

Lesson 2: There are physical feelings that go along with our emotions.

Lesson 3: There are thoughts and behaviors or actions that go along with our emotions.

Lesson 4: We can learn about other people's emotions and ways to show empathy.

Lesson 5: We can learn to identify and manage angry emotions.

Lesson 6: We can identify when our thoughts get stuck in thinking traps.

Lesson 7: There are strategies we can use to think about other perspectives in a situation.

Lesson 8: We can learn ways to solve problems and get along with others.

Lesson 9: There are strategies we can use to deal with stress in our lives.

Lesson 10: There are things we can do to live a positive and healthy life.

Lesson 11: We can set goals and do things that will help us lead a healthy life.

Lesson 12: We review the information and skills we've learned.

Key Terms and Definitions

Adversity, troubles, and failure

This is a situation or experience that is difficult for you or in which you feel as if you have done poorly.

Examples: Your parents get divorced, your family is having a hard time paying the bills, you're not doing as well in school as you'd like to, you wish you had better friendships, or you made a mistake.

Resilience

Bouncing back from difficulties in your life shows resilience.

Example: Something is difficult in your life and you feel sad, upset, or angry. You use some strategies from *Strong Kids* and you notice you feel better and know you can get through a difficult time and bounce back.

Perseverance

This is when you work hard, keeping at it, to reach a goal.

Example: Something in school is a lot of work, but it's important to you to do your best so you keep trying. Or maybe you want to play a sport but you make a lot of mistakes. You keep practicing.

Emotion

A feeling that acts like a signal, an emotion gives us information about our situation and ourselves.

Example: Some emotions we may feel are happiness, sadness, fear, disgust, surprise, and anger.

List of Emotions

Afraid

Angry

Bored

Frustrated

Confused

Disappointed

Embarrassed

Excited

Happy

Sad

Surprised

Disgusted

Irritated

Joyful

Stressed

Worried

Other emotions: annoyed, ashamed, brave, calm, cautious, curious, doubtful, ecstatic, guilty, hopeful, ignored, impulsive, inspired, jealous, lonely, optimistic, peaceful, rejected, relaxed, relieved, scared, shocked, shy, sorrowful, startled, sympathetic, thankful, upset, withdrawn

My Emotions

Directions: Think of a time when you felt one emotion or several all at once. Use this memory to answer the next few questions.

1. What was the emotion, or what were the emotions that happened at the same time?

    _____

    _____

    _____

    _____

2. Using the circle below, indicate how much of the emotion or emotions you felt. An example is provided.

3. Where were you? What was the situation?

    _____

    _____

    _____

    _____

4. How did you know you felt the emotion or the emotions?

    _____

    _____

    _____

    _____

5. How did the emotion or emotions act like a signal? What did it tell you about your situation or yourself?

    _____

    _____

    _____

    _____

LESSON 2

Understanding Your Emotions 1

Teacher Notes

_____

_____

_____

_____

_____

_____

_____

_____

Purpose and Objectives

This lesson provides students with the knowledge and skills to identify physical feelings that occur concurrently with emotions. In this lesson, students will

- Develop the ability to identify physical feelings that occur with emotions

- Identify emotions on a continuum from comfortable to uncomfortable

- Measure the intensity of emotions

Materials Needed

☐ Supplements 1.6, 2.1 (online download)

☐ Supplements 2.2–2.4 (online download and handout)

☐ Supplement 2.5 (homework handout)

☐ Optional video of a Ferris wheel

Running Short on Time?

Suggested stopping points: end of Activity C and Closure activity.

Instructor Reflection

Emotions can be experienced in our bodies and may range in feeling from comfortable to uncomfortable. Emotions also vary in intensity and can change according to context (e.g., If you tripped and fell and there was no one around, you might feel startled and perhaps a little concerned. But if there were several people around, you might feel startled and embarrassed). It is valuable for people to get to know their own personal experience with emotions—there are similarities and differences among us all. To do this, simply notice your emotional experiences throughout the day, however slight or intense, and consider: What is the emotion? Are you experiencing several emotions at once? Are there physical sensations occurring at the same time? Is there comfort, discomfort, or both, and how intense does the emotion feel?

Review

 2–3 MINS. Review the ideas (listed below) that were discussed in Lesson 1: About *Strong Kids*.

- These are the rules of the group: respect others, come prepared, do your best work, and maintain confidentiality.

- Identify a person you could talk to if you are having a difficult time.

- We experience a lot of emotions. They act like signals and give us information about our situations, thoughts, and choices.

Sample Script

During our last meeting, we started the Strong Kids program. We talked about what we will be learning in these lessons and the expectations for being in the group, and we identified a range of emotions. We also talked about identifying someone you could talk to and how emotions act like signals.

Introduction

 2–3 MINS. Introduce the lesson. Lead students in a focusing activity. Then, show students Supplement 2.1 and share, via discussion, that 1) physical feelings are associated with emotions; 2) they can be experienced on a continuum of comfortable and uncomfortable or both; and 3) they can be measured by their intensity. Allow students time to respond to the prompt questions.

Sample Script

Today we're going to learn about how we experience physical feelings when we have an emotion.

Mindfulness-Based Focusing Activity

 2 MINS.　**Sample Script**

Like last time, let's begin with an activity to settle our bodies and focus our minds. Close your eyes or look at a point in front of you on the floor or on your desk. Now, rest your hands comfortably on your desk or in your lap. Feel your feet on the floor or your hands as they rest. Let's begin by taking three breaths together, just breathing as we normally do. [Pause.] Now, like last time, focus your attention on how the breath

feels going in and going out. You might feel your chest or stomach move. Maybe you feel like your stomach is filling up like a balloon and then the air is going out. Just notice what you are feeling. Whatever you feel is okay. We are simply noticing our breath. [Pause.] Describe to yourself what you notice. You might say to yourself, "I feel cool air going into my nose" or "I feel my stomach moving." Continue breathing as you normally do, for about a minute. [Allow students about a minute to practice.] You probably notice that you have thoughts that take your attention away from noticing your breath. That's normal. When you notice this, just focus again on your breath. [Pause for three to five breaths.] Now, let's take two breaths together. [Pause.] When you finish letting out the second breath, slowly open your eyes. Now that we've observed what we feel when we breathe, we are ready to move on to our lesson.

Introduction (Continued)

 1 MIN. Show students Supplement 2.1 as a visual example, or a video of a Ferris wheel.

Sample Script

Look at this picture [or video] of a Ferris wheel. Maybe you've been on this ride at a fair, or maybe you've just looked at it. Some people want to go on this ride because they enjoy the physical feelings they have when they're on it—they may be relaxed or energized. They might feel the emotion "excited" or "happy." Other people feel sick to their stomach or their bodies feel very tense, either when they're on the ride or even just looking at it. They might also feel afraid. Today, we're going to talk about how our bodies experience or feel emotions and how paying attention to these feelings can help us.

Key Terms and Definitions

5 MINS. Use Supplement 2.2 as a handout to define the key terms that will be used in this lesson.

Sample Script

Here are some important terms that will help us understand the information we'll talk about today. We'll define the words and discuss examples to understand what they mean.

Physiological Feelings Associated with Emotions

5–10 MINS. When we experience emotions, our bodies can feel them too.

Sample Script

When we experience emotions, our bodies can feel them. You might feel the same physical feelings as other people or they might be different. Either is okay.

For example, if your shoulders and arms feel tense, you're breathing faster, your jaw is clenched, and you feel like yelling, those might be physical signals that you're feeling irritated. If your stomach is hurting, your body is shaking, your breathing is more shallow, and your heart is beating fast, you might be feeling scared. Different people can feel different things, but we all have physical feelings with our emotions. Let's do an activity so you can see how your body experiences emotions.

Activity A: Identifying Physical Feelings

🕐 **4–9 MINS.** Use Supplement 1.6 (List of Emotions, Lesson 1) as a guide. Choose *one* activity below to give students an opportunity to practice identifying physical sensations associated with emotions. Examples of emotions and corresponding physical sensations are listed below the activities.

Sample Script

Let's practice noticing any physical feelings we may experience when we have an emotion.

1. Play songs or sounds that can evoke emotions (e.g., "Happy" by Pharrell Williams, "Don't Worry Be Happy" by Bobby McFerrin). Discuss the emotions students felt and what their bodies were experiencing.

2. Ask students to close their eyes and take three breaths. Instruct them to recall a situation, perhaps being on the beach, going to a party, or being at their favorite place. Instruct them to imagine where they were and what they were doing, saying, or thinking. Ask them to notice any physical sensations they detected related to the emotion and ask them to describe it.

3. Using art supplies, make cue cards with the name of an emotion on one side. Students will write down or draw the physical feelings on the other side of the card.

Below are example emotions with possible corresponding physical feelings. Students can also suggest other physical sensations. It can be helpful to prompt students to use creative or less common language to describe the way their bodies feel in response to emotions, such as "skin feels prickly" as a reaction to irritation or impatience or "heart feels fluttery and buoyant" in response to excitement or joy.

- Worry: Stomach discomfort, headache, muscles feel stiff, shallow breathing, restless, tired

- Stress: Aches and pains, stomach aches/upset, tense muscles, heart beats fast, shallow breathing, clenched jaw and face

- Regret and sadness: Tired/fatigued, ache in the chest or heart, lump in throat, stomach upset, general pain

- Fear: Heart beats fast, breath is rapid, dry mouth, tingling

- Confusion and irritation: Dizzy, head feels fuzzy, body tense and jumpy

- Embarrassment or awkwardness: Face feels warm, body feels warm, heart pounding or beating fast

Experiencing Emotions on a Continuum from Comfortable to Uncomfortable

🕐 5–10 MINS. Emotions are felt on a continuum from uncomfortable to neutral to comfortable.

Sample Script

Emotions can feel really comfortable, really uncomfortable, and somewhere in between. Really comfortable might feel like, "I love this feeling and I want to feel this way all the time!" Really uncomfortable might feel like, "Yikes, make it stop! I don't want to feel this way anymore!" If it's somewhere in between, we might not even notice the emotion. One way is not better or more normal than the other way to feel. Depending on the situation and the circumstances, it can be totally normal to feel comfortable in some situations and uncomfortable in others. Some situations can even make us feel both comfortable and uncomfortable at the same time. Understanding how we feel gives us more information about ourselves and our experience.

Activity B: Identifying Emotions on the Continuum of Comfortable and Uncomfortable

🕐 4–9 MINS. Use Supplement 2.3 as a handout to practice identifying and exploring emotions in large or small groups.

Sample Script

Now let's practice not only identifying emotions and the physical feelings we have, but also whether we feel comfortable, uncomfortable, somewhere in between, or both comfortable and uncomfortable.

For each example, ask students the following questions:

- What physical sensations give you clues about how you feel?

- What emotions might you be experiencing? (*Hint:* We can experience more than one emotion at the same time, and different people can have different experiences.)

- Do you feel comfortable, uncomfortable, or both? (e.g., *comfortable:* I like feeling that way; *uncomfortable:* I don't like feeling that way; *both:* I felt uncomfortable but noticed that I felt better after a while.)

Physical feelings and possible emotions experienced for each scenario:

Scenario	Physical feelings	Possible emotions
1	Heart beating fast, eyes widen, feel frozen	Afraid, worried, confused, comforted
2	Tired, stomach is queasy	Sad, concerned, worried
3	Breathing faster, sweating	Excited, afraid, energized
4	Jump a little, look around, body relaxes	Surprised, confused, relieved
5	Restless (getting out of seat), hard to focus	Overwhelmed, worried, irritated
6	Calm, excited	Happy, confident, relieved, embarrassed

It's Normal to Feel Discomfort

🕐 1 MIN.   Although we'd like to experience the comfortable emotions all the time, it is not realistic or always helpful.

Sample Script

We may want to feel comfortable emotions all the time, but it's just not possible. Occasionally, we may actually be in a situation that feels uncomfortable and that feeling can help keep us safe. Dealing with uncomfortable emotions can be difficult, but we learn a little bit about ourselves every time we feel and pay attention to an emotion, even when it feels uncomfortable. The more we learn about how we react to or handle our emotions, the stronger we are the next time we feel that emotion. Emotions come and go. If you're on the Ferris wheel, maybe you feel excited or scared while you're on the ride. When it's over, you might feel disappointed or relieved. The way we feel can change moment by moment, every day, and that's okay. In the next lessons, we will learn how to identify ways of feeling and how to manage when we are feeling uncomfortable emotions.

Measure the Intensity of Emotions

🕐 5 MINS.   Emotions are experienced in levels of intensity; some are barely noticeable, whereas others are very apparent. Use Supplement 2.4 to illustrate this idea.

Sample Script

The intensity of an emotion, or how much of an emotion we are feeling, can be measured by thinking about a volume slider, like on your phone, computer, or music player. A volume slider tells us if the volume is off, so you can't hear anything; somewhere in the middle; or really loud. We can think this way about our emotions too. Sometimes, we barely feel an emotion and sometimes we feel a whole lot of it! Sometimes, it's in between. It's normal to feel a range of emotion and for that emotion to go up or down over time. Thinking about the intensity of an emotion can give us more information about our situation and how much or little we are feeling.

Activity C: Measuring Intensity

 4 MINS.

Use Supplement 2.4 as a handout for this activity. First, model your own example. Then, use the examples listed after the sample script to begin a discussion on how to rate emotional intensity. Direct students to the supplement, and ask them to point to a location on the slider that reflects this measurement. You can also opt to have students use an object, such as a paperclip or pencil, and move it from side to side or make a mark on the paper. Finally, ask several students to volunteer to identify situations where they experienced an emotion. Have the students select a level of emotional intensity for that situation.

Sample Script

Let's use the slider to describe how much emotion we feel. For example, if you felt only a little irritated, you might point to a spot on the far left. If you felt extremely irritated, you might point to a spot on the far right. If you think it was in between, you'd point to a place in the middle of the slider. I'll go first: I'm thinking of a time when I felt [insert emotion]. I was [insert the situation]. I think my experience of [insert emotion] was medium on the slider, but I noticed that the intensity of my emotion dropped over time. I noticed in the beginning it felt uncomfortable, but then it faded and gradually went away. Now, let's go through a few examples and rate our emotional intensity on the slider. Notice how you might feel over time. Then, I'll ask for volunteers to share their own examples.

Here are some example scenarios:

- *Taking a test*
- *Giving a speech*
- *Passing a test*
- *Getting a present*
- *Being ignored by a friend*
- *Starting winter break*

Raise your hand if you'd like to share your own examples.

Putting It All Together

5 MINS. Use the following activity to practice the concepts discussed in this lesson.

Sample Script

Let's practice what we've learned by putting it all together.

Use the scenarios from Supplement 2.3 and in your own words, lead students in a discussion on the following talking points:

- What is (are) the emotion(s)?

- Does the emotion feel comfortable, uncomfortable, or both?

- Think about your emotions as if they were on a volume slider like on your music player or TV. How intense did the emotions feel?

- What is the emotion telling you about yourself? (e.g., Some emotions I enjoy, others I don't; I feel it a lot or a little.)

- What is the emotion telling you about your situation? (e.g., I like/don't like it. Other people get upset when I feel that way. I feel like I want to flee/fight/freeze.)

- *Twist*: If you were in a different situation, would you feel differently? For example, does it matter if you are alone or with other people? Would you have a different feeling if you were with friends, a teacher, or a parent? Would your feeling be more intense or less intense?

Closure

⏱ 2 MINS. Close the lesson using a short breathing activity and a reflection on the lesson content.

Sample Script

Let's take a moment to regroup. Close your eyes and rest your hands in your lap. Feel your feet on the floor. Relax the muscles in your body and face. Relax and soften your stomach muscles. Counting to 3, take a deep breath in slowly. Inhale the air down into your lungs. Feel your chest and stomach expand like a balloon. [Pause.] *Now, exhale, counting to 4. Feel your chest and stomach collapse as all the air exits your body.* [Pause.] *Again, inhale deep into your lungs so that your stomach expands* [Pause.] *and exhale.* [Pause.] *Take a moment to think about something you learned today that was important to you or you really liked.* [Note to instructor: Pause for a moment to allow time for reflection.] *Counting to 3, take one more deep breath in slowly* [Pause.] *and exhale counting to 4.* [Pause.]

Tips for Transfer Training and Homework

Use the ideas and activities in the following section to practice this lesson's content with your students at other times during the day. Also remember to precorrect, remind, and reinforce concepts from this lesson in activities throughout the school week and to encourage students to use the skills taught in this lesson across settings including home, the bus, the cafeteria, and the community.

Additional Activities

- During class content that includes literature, history, or current events, infuse a discussion about the emotions that literary characters, historical figures, or modern-day individuals may have experienced. Ask students to identify whether the person described emotions by physical feelings, whether the reader could guess the intensity of the emotion, and whether the emotions were experienced as comfortable, uncomfortable, or both.

- Ask students to participate in a journaling activity to identify the emotions they experience throughout the day, the physical feeling associated with these emotions, and their level of intensity. Use the Homework activity as a guide.

- If your students talk about emotions during class discussions, ask them to describe the physical feelings that occurred, along with a description of the intensity and their comfort level.

Homework Handout

Pass out Supplement 2.5, Identifying and Measuring My Emotions. Students are asked to identify situations in which they feel certain emotions, describe the physical sensations that gave them clues, and estimate the intensity of the emotion.

Picture of a Ferris Wheel

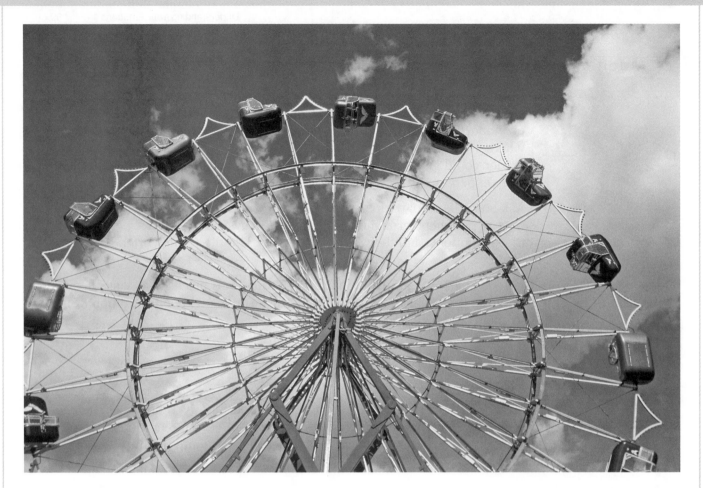

Key Terms and Definitions

Emotion

A feeling that acts like a signal, an emotion gives us information about our situation and ourselves.

Examples: Irritated, frustrated, angry, content, anxious

Physical feelings

We can have physical feelings when we have an emotion.

Example: If I feel embarrassed, I might feel dizzy and my face might get red and feel warm.

Comfortable

Comfortable feels good or not bad. You might feel like you want to hold on to the feeling.

Example: Spending time with a good friend and listening to music feels comfortable.

Uncomfortable

Uncomfortable feels not good or even bad. You might feel like you want to get rid of the feeling.

Example: You were ignored by a friend who does not return your texts.

Emotional intensity

This is how much or how little of an emotion we feel.

Example: Sometimes we feel a little bit of an emotion, sometimes a lot, and sometimes in between.

Practice Scenarios

Scenario 1: In the hallway, a student starts calling you names in a loud voice. Your heart starts beating fast, your eyes get wider, and you feel frozen. You wonder if this is a signal to do something about it or stay quiet. *Twist:* Your best friend is standing next to you and looks at you.	**Scenario 2:** You just found out your friend went home sick from school. You're not sure what's wrong, but she said she hadn't been feeling well for a couple of days. You feel tired and your stomach feels a little queasy.
Scenario 3: You're at a friend's house playing video games. The video game is getting pretty intense and there are some parts that seem even scary. You are breathing faster and starting to sweat. *Twist:* You enjoy spending time with this friend and know that a trusted adult is home that you can talk to if you want to about feeling scared.	**Scenario 4:** You are in front of the school and you hear someone shouting. You jump a little and look around, trying to find where the shouting came from. You notice that the bus driver is shouting someone's name and has a backpack in his hands. You feel your body relax.
Scenario 5: You are working on a project that's due tomorrow and you just got started on it at 5 p.m. You're not sure where to start and are pretty sure you don't have all the information you need. You keep getting up out of your chair and you say something mean to your sister. It's hard to focus.	**Scenario 6:** Your math teacher tells you that you did better on a test than last time. Your body feels calm and excited. It's important to you that the teacher noticed how you did. *Twist:* On the other hand, your teacher said this in front of other people and you wonder what they think because they did not get a compliment.

Really comfortable   Really uncomfortable

Emotions Volume Slider

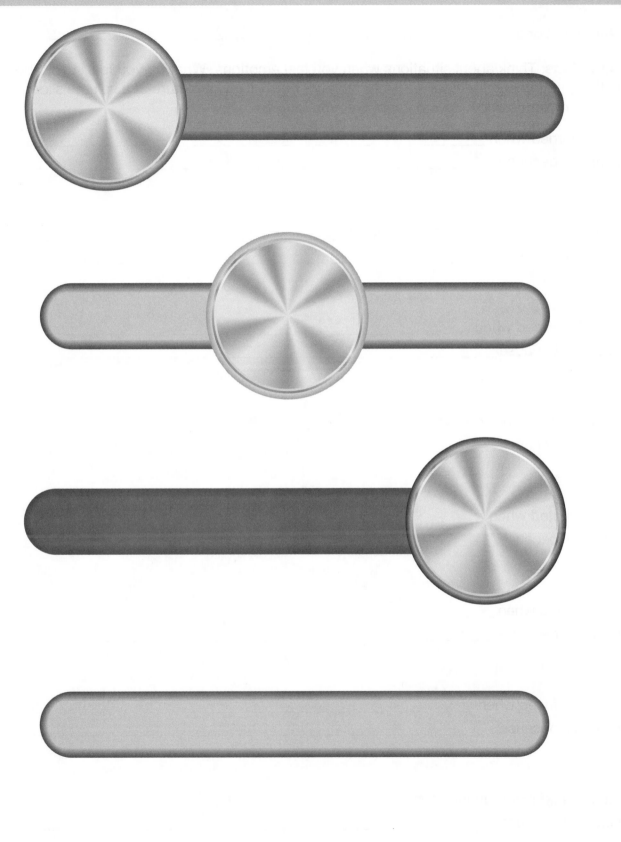

Identifying and Measuring My Emotions

Name (optional) _____

Directions: Think about situations when you feel emotions. What do you feel in your body? Is the emotion comfortable, uncomfortable, or both? Draw a picture of a volume slider next to each emotion to show how much of the emotion you feel.

I feel worried when _____.

I can tell because _____.

I feel lonely when _____.

I can tell because _____.

I feel frustrated when _____.

I can tell because _____.

I feel jealous or envious when _____.

I can tell because _____.

I feel irritated when _____.

I can tell because _____.

I feel strong when _____.

I can tell because _____.

I feel confused when _____.

I can tell because _____.

I feel thankful or grateful when _____.

I can tell because _____.

LESSON 3

Understanding Your Emotions 2

SEL Competencies Addressed in This Lesson

Responsible decision making, Self-awareness, Self-management, Social awareness, Relationship skills

Teacher Notes

Purpose and Objectives

This lesson teaches students to identify thoughts, emotions, and behaviors; understand the relationships among them; and increase awareness that people have choices in how they think and act, which can promote resilience. In this lesson, students will

- Identify thoughts and behaviors that occur with emotions

- Identify behaviors that communicate emotions in helpful and unhelpful ways and understand that the way we communicate with others may affect our relationships

- Recognize that the way in which emotions are expressed depends on our backgrounds and the context in which we experience emotions

Materials Needed

☐ Supplement 3.1 (online download)

☐ Supplements 3.2–3.4 (online download and handout)

☐ Supplement 3.5 (homework handout)

☐ Video clips or advertisements (e.g., from magazines) with age-appropriate content, illustrating people or characters showing emotions, for Activity A

Running Short on Time?

Suggested stopping points: end of Activity B and Closure activity.

Instructor Reflection

Emotions are connected to physical feelings, as discussed in the last lesson, as well as thoughts and behaviors or actions. For example, if you find yourself thinking, "I'll never get everything done" (thought) and rushing to complete tasks or procrastinating (behavior/action), you might suspect that you are feeling "overwhelmed" (emotion). You might also notice that you are experiencing fatigue or a headache (physical feelings). To prepare for this lesson, reflect on particular thoughts and behaviors and how these may be connected to emotions and the physical feelings that may accompany them. What did you feel like doing during these times? What did you do to express the emotion and cope with it? Consider the emotions that feel difficult or particularly uncomfortable. Do you tend to hold your emotions inside or let them out? How do you do this? Under what circumstances would you express the emotions in one way in one situation and in another way in a different situation? Often, this exercise is best done in the moment—write down your experiences so you can relate to these ideas and your students' responses.

Review

🕐 **2–3 MINS.** Review the ideas (listed below) that were discussed in Lesson 2: Understanding Your Emotions 1.

- Physiological feelings are associated with emotions.

- Emotions can be experienced as comfortable, uncomfortable, in between, or both.

- It is to be expected that we will feel uncomfortable at times, and that is okay; paying attention to this can help us learn and make us stronger.

- Emotional intensity can be compared to a volume slider on our music player, computer, or TV to help us understand the strength of our feelings.

Sample Script

During our last meeting, we learned that we experience all kinds of feelings when we have emotions. Sometimes we feel comfortable, uncomfortable, in between, or both. We also learned that we can measure how intense emotions feel by thinking about a slider on a volume control to show how much or how little of the emotion we feel.

Introduction

🕐 **1–2 MINS.** Using Supplement 3.1, introduce the lesson, which focuses on how our emotions can be linked with our thoughts and behaviors. Then, lead students in a focusing activity.

Sample Script

Today, we're going to talk about how we have thoughts and behaviors when we feel emotions. This picture shows how they all can go together and how one may affect another. We have choices in how we think and act when we feel emotions, especially when we feel them intensely, like when we feel really angry, worried, or upset. Understanding these better will help us act respectfully to ourselves and others, no matter what we are feeling.

Mindfulness-Based Focusing Activity

🕐 2 MINS. **Sample Script**

Let's begin with an activity to settle our bodies and practice focusing our minds. Close your eyes or look at a point in front of you on the floor or on your desk. Rest your hands comfortably on your desk or in your lap. Feel your feet on the floor or your hands as they rest. First, pay attention to your breathing for three breaths. [Pause.] Today, we will focus on the emotions we are experiencing this very moment. Maybe you feel excited, worried, sad, awkward, or calm. Any emotion is okay and normal to experience. We can sometimes find clues to emotions in our bodies—maybe in our stomachs, our shoulders, or even our jaws. When you notice an emotion, you can say to yourself, "Hello, worry" or "Hello, happiness" and pay attention to what it feels like. You can put your hand over your heart to help you connect with your emotions. Let's take another minute or two to pay attention to the emotions you are feeling. Remember, if you discover your thoughts wandering, simply bring your attention back to noticing your emotions. [Allow students about a minute to practice.] Now, let's take two breaths together. [Pause.] When you finish letting out the second breath, slowly open your eyes. Now that we've observed our emotions, we are ready to move on to our lesson.

Key Terms and Definitions

🕐 5 MINS. Use Supplement 3.2 as a handout to define the key terms that will be used in this lesson.

Sample Script

Here are some important terms that will help us understand how emotions are linked to our thoughts and behaviors. We'll define the words and discuss examples to understand what they mean.

Thoughts Are Linked with Emotions

🕐 10-15 MINS. Use Supplement 3.3 as a handout to teach how identifying thoughts can be helpful to understanding emotions. Use the two examples listed below to teach the concepts. For Activity A, use Supplements 3.3 and 3.4. Instead of Supplement 3.4, you may opt to use appropriate video clips or advertisements that show people or animated characters having emotional experiences.

Sample Script

Did you know that our thoughts can happen at the same time, before, or after we have emotions? Identifying and watching our thoughts can be helpful in understanding our emotions. If you've ever been trying to focus on something and someone keeps talking loudly, you might think to yourself, "Stop talking! I can't think about what I'm supposed to do!" Those thoughts might give you clues that you are feeling irritated and annoyed.

Example 1: Use the first cartoon in Supplement 3.3 to illustrate thoughts occurring with emotions.

Sample Script

This cartoon shows a person and his or her thoughts, which are written in the thought bubble overhead. Raise your hand and tell me what the person is thinking. What emotion do you think the person is experiencing based on what he or she is thinking?

Example 2: Using the blank cartoon in Supplement 3.3, write in the "thoughts," ask students to guess at possible emotions the person is experiencing, and draw facial expressions to correspond to the emotion(s).

Sample Script

Let's try another example. Let's pretend that tonight you have math homework, a science test to study for, and a basketball game. You might be thinking, "How am I going to get all of this done?" or "I just want to do something fun for a change." You might say these things to yourself or to a friend. What emotion or emotions do you think you're feeling? [Possible responses are stressed, overwhelmed, worried, and discouraged.]

Activity A: Identifying Thoughts and Emotions

 5–10 MINS. Use Supplements 3.3 and 3.4 as handouts. Instead of Supplement 3.4, you can ask students to generate their own examples or use appropriate video clips or advertisements that show people or characters showing emotional experiences. You might find videos online or in movies/TV shows. Ensure that content is appropriate for students' ages. Choose *one* activity below to give students an opportunity to practice identifying thoughts associated with emotions.

Sample Script

Let's practice identifying our thoughts and emotions with more examples.

1. Students break into pairs or small groups. Students can use the blank cartoon from Supplement 3.3 or draw their own cartoon. Use Supplement 3.4 as examples or ask students to generate their own examples. Ask students to imagine and generate ideas regarding the thoughts and emotions the person may be experiencing. Instruct students to write words in the bubble that reflect what the person may be thinking.

2. Using brief video clips or advertisements that show people or characters displaying various emotional behaviors that are appropriate to this age group, instruct students to imagine and generate ideas regarding the thoughts and emotions the character(s) may be experiencing. Students may also role play the thoughts that they guess the characters are having.

Behaviors and Actions Can Communicate Emotions

🕐 5–10 MINS. Behaviors or actions can tell us or other people that we are experiencing an emotion.

Sample Script

Sometimes, our behaviors or actions can tell us or other people that we are experiencing an emotion. Sometimes, it's obvious what we're feeling by what we say. Sometimes, our body language expresses how we're feeling. For example, if you sigh really loudly, roll your eyes, raise your voice, or feel like you want to be alone, you might be feeling irritated or overwhelmed. If you scrunch up your face and say, "Eew! Gross!" you might be experiencing disgust. If you stand up straight, speak clearly, and say, "No problem. I've got it," you might be feeling confident. All these actions can be linked to emotions. We can look for clues as to how we're feeling by how we act.

Activity B: Identifying Behaviors and Emotions

 🕐 4–9 MINS. Use Supplement 3.4 as a handout, students' own examples, or the video clips or advertisements you used in Activity A. For continuity, it is recommended to use the same examples that were used in Activity A. Choose *one* of the following activities to demonstrate the ways words and body language communicate emotion.

Sample Script

Now, we'll practice identifying the behaviors or actions that can go along with emotions. You'll use the same examples from the last activity and describe or act out the words, behaviors, actions, or other body language that the person in the example used to convey emotions. Then, talk about or act out the actions you would use to demonstrate that same emotion or emotions if you were in that situation.

1. Have students break into the same groups as in Activity A. Use Supplement 3.4 or other examples the students generated from Activity A. For each scenario, instruct students to 1) describe or act out the words, behaviors, or actions the person may be experiencing that are associated with the emotions and thoughts in the scenario; and 2) describe or act out the behaviors they would personally show to communicate the emotions if they were in that situation.

2. Using the video clips or advertisements from the last activity, ask students to 1) identify the verbal and nonverbal language that conveys the emotion(s) depicted (e.g., the words the person uses, the person's activity level, facial expressions, tone of voice) and 2) describe or act out the behaviors they would personally show to communicate that emotion.

Expressing Emotions with Helpful and Unhelpful Behaviors

🕒 5–10 MINS. Emotions can be expressed in a variety of ways. Some ways of expressing emotion can be helpful to the situation, whereas others can be less helpful or even hurtful.

Sample Script

Have you ever been in a situation where someone yelled at you, gave you the "silent treatment" by ignoring you, or said something that really hurt your feelings? Or maybe you showed one of these behaviors to someone else. We can do these things when we feel emotions such as anger, frustration, worry, and hurt or when we don't know how to communicate how we feel. Yelling, saying mean things, or giving the silent treatment can be hurtful to other people and to ourselves. There are a few times when it may be okay to yell at someone—for example, if you are in danger. But in most cases it's important to do something else with an intense emotion. We want to have good relationships with other people and we also want to respect ourselves. We can choose to act in a way that is helpful or respectful or in a way that is unhelpful and disrespectful. With practice, we can be in charge of how we express our emotions.

Activity C: Identifying Helpful and Responsible Actions

🕒 4–9 MINS. Use Supplement 3.4 as a handout, students' own examples, or the video clips or advertisements you used in Activity A. For continuity, it is recommended to use the same examples that were used in Activity A. Choose *one* of the following activities to demonstrate the ways in which verbal and nonverbal behaviors communicate emotion. For the activity chosen, ask students to imagine and identify 1) whether the behaviors were helpful or unhelpful and respectful or disrespectful to others and/or themselves and the reasons why, and 2) what could have been done differently to be helpful or respectful and communicate what was wanted or needed?

Sample Script

Now, let's practice figuring out whether behaviors and actions are helpful or unhelpful and respectful or disrespectful. You will also talk about anything that might have been done differently to communicate what was needed or wanted in the situation.

1. Use the scenarios from Supplement 3.4 or students' examples.

2. Use the scenarios from the video clips or advertisements.

Responding to Emotions to Match the Situation

5-10 MINS. The ways we show emotions can be affected by where we are, who we are with, and what we want or need to get out of a situation. How we show emotions can also be affected by the way we are raised and our cultural norms.

Sample Script

The ways we show how we're feeling often depend on where we are and who we're with. Take, for example, feeling sad. If you're at home with a family member or with a friend you trust and you feel sad about something, you might cry or talk about why you feel sad. But if you're in science class, you might try hard to not cry and you might keep your thoughts and feelings to yourself. It might feel more comfortable to express yourself in one place or with certain people. You also might think about what you need or what you want to get from expressing yourself. Do you want to be listened to? Do you want to keep some privacy? Do you need some support? You might think about how expressing yourself might affect others. Also, different families express emotions differently—some families talk about their feelings a lot, and others don't. How you express your emotions is sometimes related to how your family expresses their emotions.

Activity D: Responding to Emotions to Match the Situation

4-9 MINS. Use Supplement 3.4 as a handout, students' own examples, or the video clips or advertisements you used in Activity A. For continuity, it is recommended to use the same examples that were used in Activity A. Choose *one* of the following activities. Ask students to consider how they might express themselves 1) if they were at home, in the classroom, at the mall, in a restaurant, and/or in other environments that are applicable to the group; and 2) if they were with friends, teachers, strangers, or their families. Also, ask students for reasons why they would act the way they would, depending on the situation or who they are with. What do they want or need in each situation (e.g., to be heard, to be respectful, to hear what others are saying or doing first)? Please note that different cultures have different norms and expectations for expressing emotion. It may be beneficial to discuss these differences with your students. Please refer to Chapter 2 for additional guidance and information on this topic.

Sample Script

Now we'll think about the ways we express ourselves, depending on where we are, whom we're with, and what we need or want in the situation.

1. Use the scenarios from Supplement 3.4 or students' examples.

2. Use the scenarios from the video clips.

Putting It All Together

🕐 5 MINS.　Use the following activity to practice the concepts discussed in this lesson.

Sample Script

Let's practice what we've learned by putting it all together.

Choose one or more examples that were discussed in which students might need a little extra practice or review. Ask students to discuss the talking points listed below.

Sample Script

We're going to review a couple of the examples we discussed and talk about them in more depth.

- Identify the situation, emotion, thoughts, and behaviors.

- Guess the physical feeling(s) the person may have been experiencing.

- Evaluate whether the behaviors were helpful or unhelpful to the individual or in their relationship with another person.

- Discuss how the person may have considered contextual or cultural norms.

Closure

🕐 2 MINS.　Close the lesson using a short breathing activity and a reflection on the lesson content.

Sample Script

Let's take a moment to regroup. Close your eyes and rest your hands in your lap. Feel your feet on the floor. Relax the muscles in your body and face. Relax and soften your stomach muscles. Counting to 3, take a deep breath in slowly. Inhale the air down into your lungs. Feel your chest and stomach expand like a balloon. [Pause.] *Now, exhale, counting to 4. Feel your chest and stomach collapse as all the air exits your body.* [Pause.] *Again, inhale deep into your lungs so that your stomach expands* [Pause.] *and exhale.* [Pause.] *Take a moment to think about something you learned today that was important to you or you really liked.* [Note to instructor: pause for a moment to allow time for reflection.] *Counting to 3, take one more deep breath in slowly* [Pause.] *and exhale counting to 4.* [Pause.]

Tips for Transfer Training and Homework

Use the ideas and activities in the following section to practice this lesson's content with your students at other times during the day. Also remember to precorrect, remind, and reinforce concepts from this lesson in activities throughout the school week and to encourage students to use the skills taught in this lesson across settings including home, the bus, the cafeteria, and the community.

Additional Activities

- During the day, you will notice students responding to their emotions in helpful and unhelpful ways. Provide specific praise when you notice helpful responses. When you notice students engaging in unhelpful behaviors, ask them, "What do you think you are feeling?" "How can you tell?" "What thoughts are you having?" and "What do you want out of this situation?" Then, brainstorm alternative behaviors or actions that are helpful and respectful.

- Encourage students to use their journals to record their emotions, thoughts, and behaviors. Students can reflect on what they needed or wanted in that situation, whether their behaviors were helpful and respectful, and what they may consider doing differently, if anything.

- During class content that includes literature, history, or current events, infuse a discussion about the emotional experiences, thoughts, and actions of literary characters, historical figures, or modern-day individuals. Ask students to speculate what the individuals may have been communicating with their behaviors. Would they have acted differently in another environment, at another time, or with other people? Were their behaviors helpful or unhelpful to themselves and others in the short term or the long term?

Homework Handout

Pass out Supplement 3.5, Ways of Showing Emotions. Instruct students to evaluate the situations and indicate whether the responses were helpful or unhelpful.

Thoughts, Emotions, and Behaviors

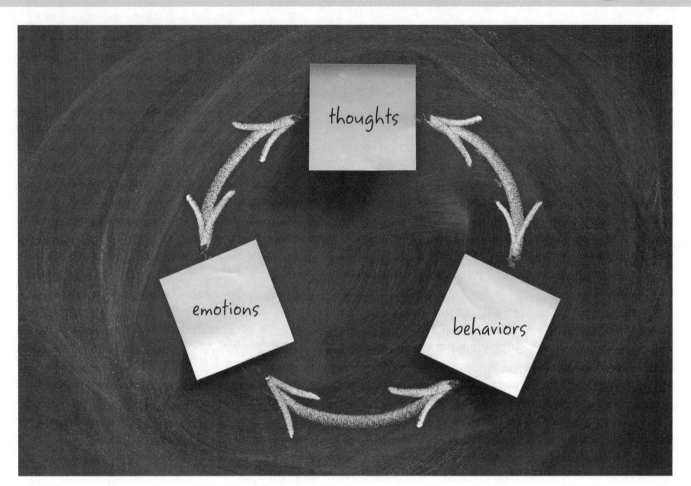

Key Terms and Definitions

Emotions

A feeling that acts like a signal, an emotion gives us information about our situation and ourselves.

Examples: Sad, happy, worried, excited, embarrassed, angry

Thoughts

What we think: We have lots of thoughts during the day. You can have thoughts before, after, or during emotions.

Examples: "I can't believe she said that!" "I'm not sure what to do about this situation." "What if I fail this class?"

Behaviors or actions

What we do or say: We have lots of choices regarding what we do or say when we feel emotions.

Example: Ahmed feels really irritated. He can yell, refuse to talk, or take deep breaths and let the emotion pass.

Respect/respectful

This is a way of behaving toward yourself or others that shows consideration, thoughtfulness, and courtesy.

Example: Michael disagreed with what his friend was saying and felt angry. He decided to take a few breaths and said, "I hear what you are saying. Maybe we should talk about this a little later."

Disrespect/disrespectful

This is a way of behaving toward yourself or others that shows a lack of courtesy or consideration.

Example: Farah's room was a mess. It had been a couple weeks since she last cleaned it. There were clothes on the floor and the trash was overflowing. During dinner, Farah's mother asked her to clean up her room that evening. Hours went by and before she went to bed, her mother asked if she'd cleaned up. Farah hadn't. Farah snapped at her mother and said, "I'll just do it tomorrow" and slammed her door.

Merrell's Strong Kids—Grade 6–8: A Social and Emotional Learning Curriculum, Second Edition,
by Dianna Carrizales-Engelmann, Laura L. Feuerborn, Barbara A. Gueldner, and Oanh K. Tran.
85

Cartoon Example

Practice Situations

Situation 1: Your best friend is sitting at the lunch table with someone you don't get along with. You're not sure what to do.

Situation 2: You see a group of your friends at your favorite restaurant. You wonder why you weren't asked to go, too.

Situation 3: You are in band and playing a new song. You lose your place in the music, stop playing, then start again in the wrong place. Someone behind you laughs.

Situation 4: The person sitting next to you in science class asks to see your homework.

Situation 5: Your coach compliments you on the game you played today. This is the first time she's given you a compliment.

Situation 6: You were planning on going over to a friend's house, but when you get home from school, you find out you can't go because you have to help clean up the house.

Ways of Showing Emotions

Name (optional) _____

Read each sentence and decide whether the student's response was helpful or unhelpful.

😊 This is a helpful or respectful way to show emotions.

☹️ This is an unhelpful or hurtful way to show emotions.

_____1. Latisha feels overwhelmed and stressed. She talks to her teacher about how to get started on her project and what she needs to finish by the end of the week.

_____2. Michael is hungry and really tired from being at school all day. He feels irritable. When he gets home, he yells at his mom when she asks how his day went.

_____3. Ling was surprised to find out she didn't make the soccer team this year. When her friend asks her if she made it, she snaps, "It's none of your business!" and walks away.

_____4. Eli is having a hard time thinking of what to write about for the language arts assignment that's due tomorrow, and he's feeling stressed. As he's writing, his pen leaks ink all over his paper. He bangs his fist on the desk, hurting his hand, and other people look at him.

_____5. Marcella saw her best friend talking to the new girl at school. She's worried her friend isn't going to hang out with her anymore. She takes a couple of deep breaths and decides she could be friends with the new girl, too.

_____6. Ahmed has a stomachache and hasn't been feeling well all day. He feels a little sad, too. He thinks he'll talk to his grandmother tonight and go to bed a little early.

LESSON 4

Understanding Other People's Emotions

Teacher Notes

_____

_____

_____

_____

_____

_____

_____

_____

Purpose and Objectives

This lesson teaches students to cultivate empathy by identifying with and considering others' emotions. In this lesson, students will

- Use context to consider how someone else may be feeling

- Practice taking the perspective of others to develop a better understanding of others' motivations and actions

Materials Needed

☐ Videos of people experiencing an emotion or sharing a personal story

☐ Photocopy of volunteer script for the skit in Activity C

☐ Supplements 4.1–4.3 (online download and handout)

☐ Supplement 4.4 (homework handout)

Running Short on Time?

Suggested stopping points: end of Activity B and Closure activity.

Instructor Reflection

Understanding other people's feelings can be difficult. With current technology providing an easy alternative to human interaction, there are lots of ways to avoid interacting with people and lots more mistakes that can be made when we do! Have you ever had an interaction with another person in which you were not certain exactly how to read his or her emotion and/or how to react as a result? How did you find out what he or she was feeling? Once you knew, did you know what to do to support this person in a way that felt right for both of you? What about the other way around? Have you ever found yourself in a situation in which you were in need of support but the person you turned to was unable to provide a supportive voice when you needed one? Think about times you were successful in supporting a friend through a crisis (or when you were supported) and how the interaction played out. Use those experiences as you support your students while keeping in mind that in the 21st century, interactions can occur across a variety of platforms.

Review

🕒 2–3 MINS. Review the ideas that were discussed in Lesson 3: Understanding Your Emotions 2.

- Communicate emotions in helpful ways.
- Different people show emotions in different ways and in different situations.
- Thoughts and behaviors are linked to emotions and vice versa.

Sample Script

During our last meeting, we talked about different ways of showing emotions— some helpful and some not so helpful. We talked about how different people can show emotions in different ways and that where you are, or who you are with, might change the way you choose to show your emotions. We also said that thoughts can affect how you feel. Well, today we are going to think more about what emotion looks like so we can notice when other people are feeling certain emotions. This will help us communicate with others in a helpful way.

Introduction

🕒 2–3 MINS. Introduce the lesson. Lead the students in a focusing activity. Then, introduce the concept of empathy and the intent to understand and better identify other people's emotions. Allow students time to respond to any prompted questions you may raise.

Sample Script

Today, we'll be talking about empathy, which is the ability to understand and share in the feelings of another person. We will talk about noticing other people's feelings, about seeing a situation from another person's perspective, and about what we can do when someone is going through something.

Mindfulness-Based Focusing Activity

🕒 2–3 MINS. **Sample Script**

Before we get started with today's lesson, let's practice settling our bodies and focusing our minds. Like before, close your eyes or leave your eyes open and look at a point on the floor or on your desk. Rest your hands comfortably on your desk or in your lap. First, notice your breathing, the feeling of the air going in through your nose and out through your mouth. [Pause for three to five breaths.] Today, we will act like detectives and take a few moments to listen with attention and curiosity to the sounds around us. There are all kinds of sounds that we can hear right now. Pay attention to what you hear. Notice what it is and where it's coming from, far and near. Let's listen. [Allow students about 1 minute.] If your thoughts start to wander, gently bring your attention back to the sounds you hear. [Allow another minute of practice.] Now, let's take two breaths together. [Pause.] When you finish letting out the second breath, slowly open your eyes. Now that we've listened to the sounds around us, we are ready to move on to our lesson.

Key Terms and Definitions

5 MINS. Use Supplement 4.1 as a handout to define the key terms that will be used in this lesson. Use short video clips or your own examples to illustrate the terms.

Sample Script

Here are some important terms related to understanding other people's emotions and actions. Let's talk through these.

Recognizing Other People's Emotions

20 MINS. Emphasize to students that making an effort to understand people's feelings is an important skill that influences how we interact with others and the relationships we have with others.

Sample Script

The first part of empathy is thinking about how someone might be seeing the situation. Sometimes, that is not obvious. If you're not sure how someone sees something or what their perspective is, the best way to find out is to ask, because sometimes people can act and feel differently than you might expect. Sometimes it's not possible or appropriate to ask someone how they see a situation, so we look for clues in other places—such as their behavior, things they say or don't say, things they've told us before, and information we know about the situation in general.

Note: In working through Activities A and B, identify and discuss the behaviors each individual is showing. Ask, "How can you tell?" or "What did you see?" to encourage students to focus in on the specific cues they are using to make their identification. If the students are consistently guessing correctly, advance the discussion by asking students to speculate, "What sort of things could make a person feel that way?" Write down the students' examples to use in discussions throughout the remainder of the lesson. If students are not consistently guessing correctly, reveal the intended emotion and ask, "Would anyone show it in a very different way?"

Activity A: Identifying and Modeling Emotions

🕐 8–10 MINS. Use Supplement 4.2 to identify emotions using visual cues. Some students are asked to share physical emotions and others are asked to identify clues.

Sample Script

Let's think some more about how some emotions look by using this list like we did in Lesson 2. We've discussed some of these already. Some of the emotions on this list are simple emotions that you might feel any day. But some of them are more complicated and might only occur under certain circumstances.

Read through the emotions listed on Supplement 4.2, including the terms below the pictures, or ask your students to take a minute and read through them.

Now I want some volunteers to select an emotion to display. When you have an emotion in mind, put your hand up, and when I call on you, I want you to name your emotion and show me an example of how it could look if someone felt that way. It doesn't matter if someone does the same one as you.

Sample Script

Now, see if you can tell what emotion I am feeling. [Model the emotion "skeptical" (raised eyebrows, smirk, slight head-shake) or another emotion of your choice.] *What emotion do you think that was?* [After the emotion has been identified, ask] *What kind of things could have happened to make me feel that way? It may help to think of times you have felt skeptical.* [If students come up with another emotion that matches your expression, be sure to acknowledge how similar some emotions can look, but let them know the exact emotion you had in mind.]

That was a good discussion about [Skepticism.]. *Now, let's talk about some other emotions using some different scenarios; show me what you would look like if you experienced:* [Use your own example or one of the suggestions below.]

- You put your hand out for a high five, but the person turned away.
- You won an award that you weren't expecting.
- A favorite actor or actress died.
- You unexpectedly got concert tickets from your parents.
- Someone unfriended you online.
- You found ants all over your bed.

Activity B: Guessing Emotions

🕐 5–7 MINS. Instruct individual students to choose an emotion without telling their class-mates what they have chosen and to model the body language that reflects that emotion. Ask other students to look for clues to help guess the emotion that is being modeled. Remind students that this is to get them to practice thinking about other people's feelings and that it may not be easy to get it right every time. Reiterate that not everyone experiences or shows emotions the same way.

Sample Script

Now, I need two brave volunteers to show a couple more emotions. You can show us an emotion from this list or you can show us a completely different emotion. Don't tell us what the emotion is right away. We are going to try to guess. We're not always going to get it right—that's why we're practicing how to do this. After we've guessed, I would like you to tell us what the emotion was and the reason that caused you to feel that way. [Ask the volunteers to whisper quietly to tell you, or write down the emotions they are portraying in advance.]

Taking Someone Else's Perspective

🕒 30 MINS. Students identify physical cues of others and understand someone else's perspective through role play. A student volunteer will be needed for a role-play demonstration. Allow time to prepare with the volunteer student before presenting this activity.

Sample Script

For this next activity, I need one volunteer to pretend to be the corner store cashier. [Allow for a transparent selection process to get a volunteer for the skit. Step aside briefly to chat with your volunteer about his or her role. Consider conducting this selection and discussion process in the minutes prior to class.]

Activity C: How Does He or She Feel?

🕒 15 MINS. Role-play the following situation. You (the teacher) will pretend to be a student called Marcella (if female) or Michael (if male). Choose a student to play the part of a cashier. Identify any other roles that might supplement the scenario for your students. Use physical cues such as frowning, an irritated voice, disappointed words, or an annoyed look to demonstrate the physical cues that go with emotions.

Sample Script:

Watch as [volunteer student] *and I show you a brief skit about a girl called Marcella* [boy called Michael]. *I want you to think about Marcella's* [Michael's] *emotions during this skit and see if you can guess how she* [he] *is feeling.* [Volunteer student] *is role-playing the cashier and I will be playing the part of Marcella* [Michael]. *Afterward, I'm going to ask you some questions about it.*

THE CORNER STORE: ROLE PLAY

Background for the Actors: Michael (Marcella) finally has lunch privileges and can go to the corner store to buy lunch and treats at lunch time. On his (her) first day in the store, he (she) picks up several small snacks and presents them to the cashier. The cashier rings it up and announces loudly, "$11.74"! Michael (Marcella) only has $7.13. There's a line of older students behind him (her).

Sample Script (Teacher as Michael/Marcella)
[Chatting, laughing, and giggling with the person next to him (her). Feel free to ad lib to demonstrate how happy you are to be shopping alone!] *I can finally buy my own snacks! I'm getting king-sized candy bars. This is great. Don't worry, I'll share with you. Yes, I can afford it. It's not that much.* [etc.]

Cashier Sample Script (Volunteer student acting as a cashier)
[Option: write an alternate version of this script for the volunteer student ahead of class.) *$11.74, please.*

Sample Script (Teacher as Michael/Marcella)
Using body language only, pull out all of your money from your various pockets and then react to the price as Michael (Marcella) might. Allow the students to discuss your reaction. [Possible body language for Michael/Marcella: Look at the snacks and the cashier in silent confusion and disbelief, touch the money again as if to count it. Look at your friend.]

Cashier Sample Script *Do you have it or not? Next.*

Next, discuss the following questions with the class:

- What do you think Michael (Marcella) is feeling?

- What did he (she) say or do that led you to that conclusion?

- Why is it important to understand someone else's perspective?

- What could you do or say if you were Michael's/Marcella's friend?

  Have you ever felt like Michael/Marcella? If you understood how he/she might feel, and if you felt a bit embarrassed just by watching this skit, you were taking Michael's/Marcella's perspective. You were feeling empathy!

Activity D: Active Listening and Showing Empathy

15 MINS. Use Supplement 4.3 as a handout to practice active listening skills. In this activity, students will practice active listening and responding skills. Have students get into three groups. Once the groups are organized and ready to present their scenario to the whole class, start by reading each situation out loud to the class and then having the designated individual(s) from the group

act out the emotion as they choose. In each situation, encourage discussion around how the students would support that friend. Indicate that action is not always necessary and that "active listening" is sometimes all that is necessary.

Consider enhancing this activity by introducing the "twist" to allow additional interpretations to unfold. Or, if time allows, ask if anyone in the rest of the class would have displayed the same emotion in a different way.

Sample Script

There are two kinds of support we can offer—sympathy or empathy. In both cases, we can show that we are listening to someone by leaning our body slightly forward and toward the person, by looking at the person's face and giving them our full attention while they are talking, and by nodding occasionally. We can also keep a kind expression on our face and repeat to the person what we heard them say when the time is right. For example, we can say, "So you didn't have enough money and all your friends were there to see it!" You can also say things like, "I'm so sorry."

Empathy takes sympathy a little further by showing how deeply you understand. Usually, this means that something very similar has happened to you and you really do feel what the person feels when you realize the situation they're in. You could say, "That happened to me once, and it was really awkward." Even if we haven't been in a similar situation, we can still feel and show empathy by taking another's perspective, by imagining what we would feel if we were in their shoes. Let's practice with more examples. Each of your groups is going to get a different story. I'd like you to choose one person from your group to be the main character and the rest of you will be acting together as the director to help him or her to act out the emotion the person might have in that situation. The rest of the class is going to guess the emotion and offer support.

After each group shows their depiction, ask the students the following questions:

- What do you think the main character is feeling?

- What physical cues led you to that conclusion?

- Why is it important to know someone else's perspective?

- What could you do or say if you were a friend of the main character?

- Were you able to empathize with their situation? Did you feel what they might be feeling?

Twists

Feel free to incorporate the following twists into each situation to add dimension when appropriate.

Situation 1

- *Twist 1:* How might Farah be feeling if she could tell that the package contained a small trampoline that she had been asking for?

- *Twist 2:* How might Farah be feeling if she had just received a lecture from her parents about accepting gifts from strangers?

Situation 2

- *Twist 1:* How might Michael feel if his parents had just told him that his messy room could have consequences and he had laughed?
- *Twist 2:* How might Michael feel if the deadline for repaying or finding the book is tomorrow?

Situation 3

- *Twist:* How might Latisha feel if Ahmed encourages her to share the ownership of the proposal?
- *Twist:* How might Latisha feel if Ahmed told her she could not share in the ownership of the proposal?

Putting It All Together

🕐 5 MINS.   Use the following discussion to practice the concepts discussed in this lesson.

Sample Script

Let's practice what we've learned by putting it all together.

Use the following talking points to reemphasize the concepts discussed in this lesson.

Sample Script

Let's review a couple of the examples we discussed and talk about them.

- What is empathy and what is perspective taking?
- Why do you think empathy is important?
- What is the best way to figure out a person's perspective?
- How would you show empathy differently from sympathy?
- How can we practice developing empathy?

Closure

🕐 2 MINS.   Close the lesson using a short breathing activity and a reflection on the lesson content.

Sample Script

Let's take a moment to regroup. Close your eyes. Feel your feet on the floor. Counting to 3, take a breath in slowly. Inhale [Pause.] and exhale, counting to 4.

[Pause.] *One more time, inhale* [Pause.] *and exhale* [Pause.] *Take a moment to think about something you talked about today that was important to you and you really liked.* [Note to instructor: pause for a moment to allow time for reflection.] *Counting to 3, take one more deep breath in slowly* [Pause.] *and exhale counting to 4.* [Pause.]

Tips for Transfer Training and Homework

Use the ideas and activities in the following section to practice this lesson's content with your students at other times during the day. Also, remember to pre-correct, remind, and reinforce concepts from this lesson in activity throughout the school week.

Additional Activities

- During class breaks or free times, encourage students to look out for students who may need support. This might be a good time to discuss how empathy relates to bullying. Empathy can act as an antidote to bullying and spur bystanders to help.

- During moments of sharing in class, encourage other students to listen actively and reflectively and offer empathetic statements to the person who has shared something personal. Remind students that this skill takes practice for it to feel authentic and more automatic.

- Prior to receiving a new student in your group or classroom, encourage existing students to reflect on their first day in a new group and decide on positive and welcoming approaches to share with the new student.

Homework Handout

Pass out Supplement 4.4, Empathy Assignment. Students are asked to respond to questions about times when they could tell how someone was feeling, the cues they noticed, and what they did to help that person. They are asked to think of ways they can understand the feelings of someone who they know is having a hard time.

Key Terms and Definitions

Empathy

Empathy is understanding another person's emotions enough to truly identify with them or even feel how he or she might be feeling in a situation. Empathy is different from sympathy.

Example: If you have lost a pet, it may be easier to find words from your own experience to say to that person so he or she knows that you understand the experience.

Sympathy

Realizing that another person is having an unpleasant experience and being willing to comfort or assist him or her in some way is showing sympathy.

Example: If you haven't lost a pet, you can still find words to let that person know how sorry you are that he or she has lost a pet and that you are feeling sad for him or her and are there to help.

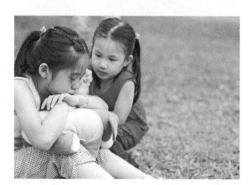

Perspective/point of view

This is the feelings and opinions each person has about an experience or during an experience. Taking someone's perspective is looking at something from his or her point of view.

Example: If someone tells you a story about times he or she used to spend with a pet, you can visualize more clearly what he or she will be losing now that the pet is gone.

Social cues

Things a person may do or say give us clues about what he or she may be feeling or thinking during an experience.

List of Emotions

Happy

Scared

Bored

Angry

Sad

Surprised

Worried

Excited

Confused

Irritated

Embarrassed

Joyful

Frustrated

Disgusted

Jealous

Disappointed

Other emotions: apathetic, grieving, dreading, horrified, confident, hopeful, shy, annoyed, guilty, proud, calm, content, awestruck, empathetic, relieved, anxious, nervous, vulnerable, ignored, rejected, neglected, ashamed, infatuated, barely tolerant, reluctantly accepting, horrified but interested, desperate, mildly interested, lonely, awkward, amused, unsympathetic, judgmental, impatient, proud of yourself, proud of someone else, invincible, unimportant, invisible, hyper, focused, upset, cranky, optimistic, pessimistic, pessimistic but hopeful, unfocused

Small-Group Student Role-Play Scenarios

Situation 1: You are Farah. Today is Friday. You just received a package in the mail from a name and address you don't recognize! Your parents won't be home until later. Act out how you think Farah might feel.

Situation 2: You are Michael. Your parents have been asking you to clean out your room for a long time but you haven't. Your room is a disorganized mess and you can't find anything. You just found out that you have to pay for a library book that you borrowed a very long time ago. If you don't find it, your parents will be charged $55 for the cost of the book. Act out how you think Michael might feel.

Situation 3: You are Latisha. You are working with Ahmed on a social studies project. The teacher told you to think of a project that will impact the environment in a positive way for a long time and develop a proposal for your class to be engaged. The winning team will get the honor of being named as the founders. You have some great ideas, but Ahmed proposes a superb idea that would be wonderful for the environment. You really want to be named as co-founder, but you can't think of a way to contribute to the proposal. Act out how you think Latisha might feel.

Empathy Assignment

Name (optional) _____

Think of two times when you could tell how someone else was feeling.

1. _____
   _____
   _____

2. _____
   _____
   _____

How could you tell? (What were the cues that you noticed?)

1. _____
   _____
   _____

2. _____
   _____
   _____

What did you do, or what could you do or say to help that person?

1. _____
   _____
   _____

2. _____
   _____
   _____

Think of someone who you think might be having a hard time now (do not use his or her real name). Think of some ways you can understand this person's feelings and show empathy using the skills you have learned in this lesson.

1. _____
   _____
   _____

2. _____
   _____
   _____

LESSON 5

Dealing with Anger

Teacher Notes

_____

_____

_____

_____

_____

_____

_____

_____

Purpose and Objectives

This lesson teaches students to understand their anger and to manage their anger proactively. In this lesson, students will

- List and describe the steps of an anger model
- Name and describe additional anger management skills
- Develop an awareness of personal anger triggers
- Apply anger management skills to situations

Materials Needed

- ☐ Supplements 5.1–5.5 (online download and handout)
- ☐ Supplement 5.6 (online download)
- ☐ Supplement 5.7 (online download and handout)
- ☐ Supplement 5.8 (homework handout)
- ☐ Optional: Locate a video depicting anger from onset to management for Introduction section

Running Short on Time?

Suggested stopping points: end of Activity C and Closure activity.

Instructor Reflection

Anger takes some management for everyone. Even the calmest of individuals must use strategies to manage his or her encounters with anger, sometimes without even knowing it.

In preparation for this lesson, think about your own relationship with anger. Which anger management techniques work well for you and which don't? Consider how your management techniques vary depending on the situation you are in. Consider the things that made you angry when you were the age your students are now and how those things have changed with time. As you present today's lesson, keep in mind for yourself and for your students that an important key to managing anger is understanding how anger operates in a general way and for you personally.

Review

🕒 **2–3 MINS.** Review the ideas (listed below) that were discussed in Lesson 4: Understanding Other People's Emotions.

- It is important to consider how other people may feel in certain situations.
- Not everyone shows emotions in the same way.
- It is important to consider other people's perspectives.
- We can sometimes use clues to understand how a person may be feeling.
- It helps to show empathy when you are interacting with someone who is in a difficult situation.

Sample Script

Recently, we learned about understanding other people's emotions. We talked about how important it is to consider how other people feel in certain situations. We talked about ways to determine how they might feel by looking for clues or cues or by asking them, if that is appropriate. We also discussed that not everyone shows emotions in the same way. We talked about how these skills can help us empathize with others and better understand possible reasons why people do what they do.

Introduction

🕒 **2–3 MINS.** Introduce the lesson. If you have any materials (video clips or skits), feel free to use them to introduce the topic of anger. Then lead students in a focusing activity.

Sample Script

Today, we will be thinking about anger management so that we can be better prepared the next time we feel ourselves getting angry. Being prepared and knowing what we are feeling helps us make helpful choices or decisions before we get so angry that we can't think clearly.

Mindfulness-Based Focusing Activity

🕐 2 MINS.

Sample Script

Before we get started with today's lesson, let's practice focusing our minds and calming our bodies. Like before, close your eyes or leave your eyes open and look at a point on the floor or on your desk. Rest your hands comfortably on your desk or in your lap. Today we will take a few moments to notice what we are feeling. First, pay attention to your breathing, the feeling of the air going in through your nose and out through your mouth. [Pause for 3 breaths.] [Note: The remainder of this script is meant to be read at a slow pace, to allow students time to notice each body part described.] *Now, feel your feet on the floor. Notice how the bottoms of your feet feel.* [Pause.] *Now, move your attention to your legs. Notice your calves, then your shins.* [Pause.] *Notice your knees and the backs of your knees.* [Pause.] *Now, notice the tops and backs of your legs. Whatever you notice is okay.* [Pause.] *Move your attention to your stomach, then your back. Notice how your stomach moves when you breathe.* [Pause.] *Notice your arms. Feel your fingers, then your wrists.* [Pause.] *Now pay attention to your elbows, the tops of your arms, and your shoulders.* [Pause.] *Notice your neck, then your head. Pay attention to your ears, cheeks, mouth, nose, eyes, and forehead. Maybe you notice air going in and out of your nose.* [Pause.] *Now, move your focus to your breath. Let's take two breaths together.* [Pause.] *When you finish letting out the second breath, slowly open your eyes. We are ready to move on to our lesson.*

Key Terms and Definitions

🕐 2–3 MINS. Use Supplement 5.1 as a handout to define the key terms that will be used in this lesson.

Sample Script

Here are some important ideas that we will be discussing related to dealing with anger. We'll define the words and discuss examples to understand what they mean. Can anyone think of any other words we use to describe anger?

Anger Has a Purpose

🕐 10 MINS. Anger is a natural and necessary emotion. Our anger usually signals us to take notice of a situation. Anger can sometimes be a signal to us that there is a problem to solve.

Sample Script

Even though we've probably all already had experiences that have taught us that anger can sometimes get us into trouble, it's important for us to remember that anger can also be a signal that there is a problem that needs to be solved or a decision that needs to be made. As we've discussed in previous lessons, all of our emotions are there for a reason, and even anger can help us understand more about the situation we're in.

Activity A: Using Anger to Problem Solve

 10 MINS. Use Supplement 5.2 as a handout to discuss the concept of using anger to lead to problem solving. Review the scenarios in the table. Allow students to respond independently or work in groups to talk about their emotional reaction to each situation and to respond to the scenarios by providing their potential reactions, decision-making questions, and possible responses.

Sample Script

Let's look at a couple of situations where you could possibly become angry, even if these situations don't really make you mad. Think about the emotional reaction someone may have if this was something that really bothers him or her. What could this person do, or what questions could he or she ask to figure out what to do? Then, let's talk about some of this person's options. Raise your hand when you have something to say.

Other Emotions Can Combine to Feel Like Anger

⏱ 10 MINS. Anger can sometimes be the result of a mixture of other upsetting emotions.

Sample Script

Sometimes, we can feel angry and not know why, even after we've looked carefully for the problem. In some of those cases, it could be that we are feeling a mixture of other upsetting feelings. There are some feelings that are pretty sneaky and can make us feel angry either by themselves or when they are mixed with other emotions. Some of these feelings are jealousy, fear, embarrassment/ shame, sadness, disappointment, frustration, irritation, hunger, failure, rejection, and being offended/hurt feelings.

Activity B: Identifying and Labeling Sneaky Emotions

⏱ 10 MINS. Facilitate a brief discussion about emotions that sometimes feel like anger or that can make you feel angry.

Sample Script

Has there ever been a time where you got angry and it turned out that what you were really feeling was some other emotion or even a combination of emotions? This is when emotions can be sneaky, because you think you are feeling one way, but in fact it could be a mixture of some other emotions. For example, if I see my best friend at a movie with someone else, I might feel angry at first. But, if I look closely at what I am feeling, I might notice other things like fear, sadness, and envy or jealousy over possibly losing this friend.

Raise your hand if you can recall a time when you got angry but later realized that what you were feeling was really based on a different emotion that made you feel angry.

Anger Can Be Difficult to Manage

⏱ 13 MINS. Convey the idea that anger can sometimes be hard to manage and that unmanaged anger for some people can lead to aggression or unhelpful choices.

Sample Script

Even though anger is a normal emotion with a role to play in our lives, anger can sometimes feel so strong that it can be hard to manage. And anger can look different in different people. For many people, it's difficult to make our brains think of any good ideas or choices when we're feeling intense anger. If we don't practice how to manage our anger before we get angry, our brain might lock out the good ideas that could be helpful to us and leave us with only a few choices, which may not be the best choices. Things like violence, threats, shouting, saying or writing rude or hurtful things, and ignoring others are some of the choices that we typically consider when we're really angry—if we're not aware of how to react in a helpful or healthy way.

Today, I'd like you to think about yourself when you're angry. Think about the way you feel, the choices you tend to make, and what you're thinking, and see if you can identify anything about your anger that you might need to improve—BEFORE the next time you're angry. The next two activities are for you to do alone to think a little more about your own anger patterns.

Note: It is implied that students understand why violence, threats, shouting, saying or writing (online posts or texts) rude or hurtful things, and ignoring others may not be the best choices. It may be beneficial to discuss with your students why these are problematic even though they may see these behaviors online, on TV and in movies, in video games, in their homes, and in the community.

Activity C: Analyzing Choices

⏱ 12 MINS. Walk your students through Supplements 5.3 and 5.4. Supplement 5.3 is intended to get students thinking and talking about the specific things that tend to "push their buttons." Depending on the makeup of your group, encourage self-reflection and independent work, or offer a safe means of sharing points to discuss. One of the learning points from this exercise (if done as a group) is that different people can get upset by different things.

Supplement 5.4 is intended to get students thinking about their own anger patterns and to identify areas that can be improved. Allow students to take and score their tests and to discuss their results. If your environment might not allow for students to share comfortably on the topic of their own anger, consider using this as an opportunity for a general discussion across the concepts.

Understanding Anger: An Anger Model

 5 MINS. Use Supplement 5.5 as a handout to introduce the anger model and Supplement 5.6 to walk through a scenario. As you walk through the scenario in Supplement 5.6, ask students to identify the different parts of the scenario as they relate to this anger model. Consider dividing your students into groups to discuss the consequences of each potential decision and/or behavior.

Sample Script

Anger usually has a few steps to it, even though a lot of times the steps get mixed together and you can't see them. [Point to the model in Supplement 5.5.] There's usually a trigger or event, an emotional reaction, a decision about how to behave and an associated action, and then a consequence. We will look at example situations and consider consequences of each behavior. Okay, let's look at the first example of Marcella and how she got angry. [Read through Marcella's scenario. Ask the follow-up questions.]

Developing Anger Management Skills

 15 MINS. Use Supplement 5.7 as a handout to introduce skills that can be used to cope with anger. Also use Supplement 5.7 with your students to briefly talk through the strategies that follow.

Sample Script

The way we handle our anger depends a lot on the situation we're in, who we're with, and what we hope to get out of the situation. Often, we handle anger differently when we're in a comfortable or familiar setting than when we're in an uncomfortable or unfamiliar setting. Let's take a look at some strategies here. [Read through the strategies listed in the supplement and allow a discussion of each one.]

Applying Anger Management Strategies

10 MINS. Encourage a discussion about triggers and using effective anger management strategies. Ask your students to volunteer triggers they may have developed from Supplement 5.3, then work together or in small groups to develop positive scenarios that incorporate strategies that could assist in preempting or correcting the situation. Encourage students to use these strategies in real-life situations when the triggers occur.

Sample Script

Can you think of any triggers that make you really angry and have led you to have an angry outburst in the past? Or perhaps certain situations cause you to avoid your anger instead of manage it? Let's think about ways we can use the anger management strategies we've learned by talking about a few things that really annoy us. Take a second and then raise your hand if you want to tell me about something that serves to "trigger" your anger. I'll write it on this list and then we can talk about it [in our groups]. [Optional: Some possible triggers if no one wants to share their triggers are cutting in line; play that leads to someone getting hurt; assuming the teacher treated you unfairly with the assignment grading.]

Putting It All Together

🕐 **5–10 MINS.** Use the following activity to practice the concepts discussed in this lesson.

Sample Script

Let's practice what we've learned by putting it all together.

This can be done in large or small groups.

Sample Script

Tell me what you remember about these points.

- Is all anger bad?
- Once you're very angry, is it easy to control your emotions or difficult to control your emotions?
- What other emotions can sometimes disguise themselves as anger?
- Why do we sometimes make unhealthy or unhelpful choices when we're angry?
- Did you learn anything new about your anger triggers and how you cope?
- What are some anger management strategies?

Closure

🕐 **2–3 MINS.** Close the lesson using a brief breathing activity and a reflection on the lesson content.

Sample Script

Let's take a moment to regroup. Close your eyes. Feel your feet on the floor. Counting to 3, take a breath in slowly. Inhale [Pause.] *and exhale counting to 4.* [Pause.] *One more time, inhale* [Pause.] *and exhale.* [Pause.] *Take a moment to think about something you learned today that was important to you and you really liked.* [Note to instructor: Pause for a moment to allow time for reflection.] *Counting to 3, take one more deep breath in slowly* [Pause.] *and exhale, counting to 4.* [Pause.]

Tips for Transfer Training and Homework

Use the ideas and activities in the following section to practice this lesson's content with your students at other times during the week. Also, remember to precorrect, remind, and reinforce concepts from this lesson whenever possible across settings.

Additional Activities

- Support students who may face some of their triggers (lunch, during passing, difficult assignments) by suggesting anger management strategies whenever possible. For example, if a student frequently gets into conflict with peers during lunch, first identify some strategies from Supplement 5.7 that could work for him or her. Then, before lunch, remind the student to use the strategies.

- Post the list of anger management strategies (Supplement 5.7 or another version that you like) in a visible location, and encourage students to think about the consequences associated with their actions, either before or after using the strategies.

- During the school day, point out any positive anger management strategies used by characters in fictional and nonfictional materials.

Homework Handout

Pass out the homework handout, Supplement 5.8, Anger Management Worksheet, and explain the instructions. Students describe an experience where someone was angry and they apply that situation to the anger model. Then, discuss anger management skills that could be used. Students may find it helpful to use Supplement 5.7 when doing this assignment.

Key Terms and Definitions

Anger

This is a powerful emotion of extreme unhappiness and dislike toward someone or something when you feel threatened or harmed.

Example: I feel angry when someone uses my things but doesn't return them or returns them broken.

Aggression

This is using hurtful words or inappropriate physical behaviors toward people or things.

Examples: Hitting, screaming, breaking things, kicking, and slamming doors can be signs of aggression. Sometimes, even things people write can be considered aggressive, such as online bullying.

Anger management

Having an understanding of your anger triggers and how you tend to react when you are angry will help you manage anger.

Example: Choosing appropriate/helpful behaviors when you are angry is the key to anger management.

(Emotional) reaction

An action or a feeling after some event, an emotional reaction is the most immediate response.

Example: My parent asks me where I've been and I stiffen in fear because I'm worried about what will happen to me when I say I was with my friends instead of at baseball practice.

Response

This is the information you provide when someone asks a question.

Example: Someone asks me where I've been and I answer in words or in some other way (e.g., pointing).

What Problem Does My Anger Want Me to Solve?

Situation where you feel angry	Example emotional reactions	Decision-making questions	Possible responses
Another student in class always blurts out the answers before you get a chance to figure it out for yourself.	You want to tell him, "Shut up," even though you know that will get you into trouble.	Does he know he does it?	Find a way to approach him.
	You want to stop trying to figure out the answer.	What can I do ahead of time?	Talk to the teacher about it.
	You want to cry.	What can I do instead to prevent myself from feeling frustrated when he does blurt out answers?	Study harder and try to be faster than him.
Someone vandalized some art you had displayed at school.	You want to cry.	How can I help the teacher make displayed art more secure?	Provide a recommendation to the teacher.
	You want to accuse someone.		Ask to have your art removed.
	You think your art wasn't all that good, so it probably deserved to be ruined.		

Here are some more scenarios to think through:

1. Some people were roughhousing or playing around in line and caused you to drop your phone and it broke.

2. Two other students have asked to start volunteering at the front desk. Until now, you had been the only one who was interested, but now it's become popular and you have to sign up on a waiting list to get your preferred time.

How Much Does This Bother You?

Read through the following items and decide how much each one would bother you. Use the scale below to decide which one best describes your feeling.

> a. This doesn't bother me at all. All I feel is _____.
> b. This doesn't bother me much.
> c. This only bothers me sometimes.
> d. This bothers me frequently, but I handle it well, and mostly no one knows.
> e. This bothers me frequently, and I get very angry.
> f. This always bothers me, and sometimes I've gotten into trouble for my anger about it.

1. Having to stop a fun activity to do something serious

   (a) _____ (b) (c) (d) (e) (f)

2. Getting bad grades

   (a) _____ (b) (c) (d) (e) (f)

3. Being teased by my friends

   (a) _____ (b) (c) (d) (e) (f)

4. Being teased by people I don't really know

   (a) _____ (b) (c) (d) (e) (f)

5. Getting privileges taken away

   (a) _____ (b) (c) (d) (e) (f)

6. Being compared to my older brother or sister or to other people in my class

   (a) _____ (b) (c) (d) (e) (f)

7. Making mistakes

   (a) _____ (b) (c) (d) (e) (f)

8. Some other things that can really make me angry are

   _____

   _____

   _____

   _____

What Does MY Anger Look Like?

Read each of the items below and decide how closely it describes your anger. When you have finished, count how many of each score you have. Did you have lots of 3s? Did you get low scores for Questions 2 and 3? When you think about your answers, what does it tell you about your anger? Is there anything you would change about the way you get angry?

Use the slider scale below each question to answer.

0   Yes, this is true.
1   This mostly describes me.
2   This is only sometimes true.
3   No, this is not true for me.

1. It takes me a while to get angry after something happens.

2. I tend to get quiet and distant when I'm angry. I mostly think angry and sad thoughts, but I don't do much of anything.

3. I tend to blame myself for things that make me angry.

4. I usually return to a better mood pretty quickly after being angry.

(continued)

5. I usually forget about the incident soon after it is over.

| 0
True | 0 ———————— 1 ———————— 2 ———————— 3 | 3
No. I tend to hold grudges. |

6. If I do something that I feel bad about while I'm angry, I usually apologize easily.

| 0
True | 0 ———————— 1 ———————— 2 ———————— 3 | 3
No. I usually don't apologize for what I said or did when I was angry. |

7. I don't get angry that often.

| 0
True | 0 ———————— 1 ———————— 2 ———————— 3 | 3
No. I get angry a lot. |

8. I can usually explain clearly what made me angry.

| 0
True | 0 ———————— 1 ———————— 2 ———————— 3 | 3
No. I'm not always sure what made me angry. |

9. I'm usually satisfied with how I handle situations that make me angry.

| 0
True | 0 ———————— 1 ———————— 2 ———————— 3 | 3
No. Sometimes when I look back it doesn't make sense that I got that mad. |

Some other ways I may behave when I'm angry are

_____

_____

_____

_____

Anger Model

Trigger	Emotional reaction	Action	Consequence
The event or situation that can cause a person to feel a particular emotion like anger	The emotion you have because of the situation; sometimes the emotion you have right away may be different from the emotion you have after you've thought about it.	What you decide to do when you realize that a particular situation is making you angry	What happens as a result of what you decided or did

Marcella's Problem

Scenario	Part of anger model?
Yesterday, Marcella was struggling with a problem that she felt she couldn't talk to anybody about, but her best friend convinced her to tell him and promised he would keep it secret. Marcella just overheard two people talking about it!	
Marcella feels her stomach twist. She knows that the only person who could have told them is her best friend.	

Decision/action	Consequence
At first, Marcella considers not talking to her friend anymore to make sure this never happens again.	
After a while, she decides to just find him and ask him if he did tell anyone and why.	
What should Marcella do if he admits that he did tell someone else?	

117

Anger Management Skills and Strategies

Strategy	Description
Notice and acknowledge that you feel anger.	Simply notice what anger feels like in your body. You are a human being, and it's normal and expected to feel anger. Tell yourself, "Oh, I'm feeling angry. Okay."
Ask yourself why you're angry (problem solve).	See if you can determine a problem to be solved. See if there are any sneaky emotions leading you to feel angry.
Use if-then statements to consider the consequences.	As you are deciding what to do, ask yourself, "If I do _____, then what will happen?"
Count up to or down from 10.	Quietly count up to or backward from 10 in your mind. This could give you just enough think time to make sure your first idea is a good idea.
Listen to another person.	Really listen to someone, either a friend or the person with whom you're upset. Use empathy to better understand why that person might be doing what he or she is/was doing.
Focus on your breathing.	Concentrate on breathing deeply in through your nose and out through your mouth so that your stomach moves. Breathing this way can often help people who are angry begin to calm down. For a few minutes, just breathe and feel the anger in your body. Do this without getting lost in your thoughts or running stories about the situation.
Take a walk or step away.	Walking away from a situation that is making you angry can sometimes prevent you from reacting too quickly and can give you some time to think clearly about choices you can make.
Give yourself good advice (self-talk).	Give yourself advice such as, "Stop and breathe deeply for a few minutes before you decide what to do" or "Remember to take his or her perspective and use empathy." Use positive self-talk.
Look for the humor.	If there is no danger, picture the situation as a scene in a comedy and see if you can laugh at yourself. Be sure not to make fun of someone else.

Anger Management Worksheet

Name (optional)_____

Directions: Describe a recent situation that you might have witnessed or been a part of that involved someone becoming angry. You can change the names of people that you would prefer not to talk about. This could have been a TV show. Be sure to include each step of the anger model in your description.

Trigger: _____

_____

Emotional reaction: _____

_____

Decision and action: _____

_____

Consequence: _____

_____

Directions: Using the anger management skills you have learned, indicate the skills that could have been used in the situation you described, and discuss how they could have been used. (Use Supplement 5.4 as a guide for identifying anger management skills.)

_____

_____

_____

LESSON 6

Clear Thinking 1

SEL Competencies Addressed in This Lesson

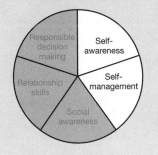

Teacher Notes

Purpose and Objectives

This lesson teaches students an awareness and understanding of common thinking traps. In this lesson, students will

- Understand the influence of thoughts on emotions and behaviors

- Develop an awareness of their own thoughts

- Identify common thinking traps that affect behavior, thoughts, and emotions

Materials Needed

☐ Supplements 6.1–6.2 (online download)

☐ Supplements 6.3–6.4 (online download and handout)

☐ Supplement 6.5 (online download)

☐ Supplements 6.6–6.7 (online download and handout)

☐ Supplement 6.8 (homework handout)

☐ Optional props (dark glasses, binoculars, and fortune cookie)

☐ Activity C sheet (volume slider)

Running Short on Time?

Suggested stopping points: end of Activity B and Closure activity.

Instructor Reflection

This lesson identifies thought patterns that can lead to overly pessimistic thinking and hinder well-being. In this program, these thoughts are called "thinking traps." We all fall victim to thinking traps sometimes. At times, thinking traps help us deal with our situation in the moment or help us feel better about the situation in the short term, without really dealing with the problem or helping us see alternative or more realistic perspectives. To help you prepare for this lesson, see if you can identify some of the thinking traps in this lesson. Have you noticed these thinking traps in your own life? If so, what were the consequences? Did they affect your emotional state, your behaviors, and your interactions with others?

Review

 5 MINS. Review the ideas (listed below) that were discussed in Lesson 5: Dealing with Anger.

- Anger is a necessary and a natural reaction.

- There are different ways to deal with angry feelings.

- Refer to the steps of the anger model.

- There are healthy strategies for expressing anger.

Sample Script

During our last meeting, we talked about ways to deal with your anger—what it looks like, what we do or say when we feel angry, and healthy ways of dealing with anger. We have a lot of choices for how we respond when we feel angry. We learned that, a lot of times, it helps to take a moment to think about our angry feelings before we do anything about them.

Introduction

 5 MINS. Introduce the lesson. Lead students in a focusing activity. Then, show students Supplement 6.1 and discuss how people have emotions and thoughts and how we can sometimes fall into thinking traps.

Sample Script

Today, we're going to learn about the thoughts we have when we experience emotions.

Mindfulness-Based Focusing Activity

 3 MINS. *Let's begin with an activity to settle our bodies and practice focusing our minds. Close your eyes or look at a point in front of you on the floor or on your desk.*

Rest your hands comfortably on your desk or in your lap. Feel your feet on the floor or your hands as they rest. First, pay attention to your breathing for three breaths. [Pause] During this activity, you may notice that your mind wanders when you are trying to pay attention to one thing. It's okay and normal that your thoughts wander. For the next minute or two, focus on your breath. When you notice your attention wandering to your thoughts, you can say to yourself, "Oh, I'm thinking" and then bring your attention back to your breath. [Allow students about 2 minutes to practice.] Now, let's take two breaths together. [Pause.] When you finish letting out the second breath, slowly open your eyes. Now that we've observed our breathing and thoughts, we are ready to move on to our lesson.

Introduction (Continued)

Show Supplement 6.1 first, followed by Supplement 6.2. This activity illustrates that how we think about a situation can affect our emotions and behaviors.

Sample Script

[Show Supplement 6.1.] *This is a picture of a snake. Imagine holding this snake in your hands. You can feel the weight of its body and cool skin on your hands. Notice your thoughts. What thoughts do you have when you imagine holding this snake?* [Ask students to share their thoughts, and seek a range of answers. They might find it interesting and wonder what kind of snake it is. Or they might recall memories about snakes.] *Now, notice your feelings. What feelings do you have?* [Ask students to share their feelings, and seek a range of answers. They might feel excited, scared, or disgusted. Then, lead them to make connections between their thoughts and feelings.] *If I have bad memories about snakes or I don't like the way they look, then I might feel disgusted or repulsed by the thought of holding the snake. However, if I find them interesting, I may feel excited or happy to hold the snake.* [Show Supplement 6.2.] *This is a person who studies snakes. How might she feel to hold the snake?* [Allow some speculation about how the scientist might feel.] *This is like everything in life! How we think about something can affect how we feel about it. Today, we will learn how our thoughts can affect our emotions and how we behave. In this lesson, we'll learn ways to be more aware of our thoughts and identify thoughts that might not be very helpful or healthy for us.*

Key Terms and Definitions

 5 MINS. Use the Supplement 6.3 handout to define the key terms that will be used in this lesson.

Sample Script

Here are some important terms that will help us understand how our thoughts are connected to our emotions and behaviors. We'll define the words and discuss examples to understand what they mean.

Thoughts Associated with Emotions

🕐 5–10 MINS. Use Supplement 6.4 as a visual aid. You can use the supplement as a handout or use the board to write down thoughts. Recognizing our thoughts helps us understand our emotions.

Sample Script

When we feel emotions, we have thoughts that go with those emotions. Sometimes, we don't even notice what we are thinking and feeling because it happens so quickly, or we get used to certain feelings and thoughts. Or our thoughts and feelings can be an automatic reaction based on experiences we've had in the past. It's important to pay attention to both our feelings and our thoughts. With awareness and practice, we can get really good at noticing our thoughts and feelings. Then we can better understand how they can affect the way we act. This understanding can help us feel better, make better friendships, and enjoy our lives more!

Activity A: Thoughts Associated with Emotions

🕐 5 MINS. Using Supplement 6.4 as a visual aid, ask for volunteers to share three to five thoughts and emotions. An example is provided in the sample script. To help your students understand this connection, you might share an example from your own life. Using Supplement 6.4, model your thoughts, self-talk, and feelings. You can use the board to write down student responses and draw connections between the thought and the emotion.

Sample Script

Let's take a closer look at this. Think of a time when you felt embarrassed or awkward. What kinds of thoughts did you have? What kind of self-talk did you have? Did your thoughts and self-talk lead you to feel more embarrassed or more awkward? Or your thoughts might have led you to feel another emotion, like anger. Maybe your thoughts helped calm you down and manage intense emotions. Who would like to share another example?

Identifying Thinking Traps

🕐 15 MINS. Use Supplement 6.5 as a visual aid. Sometimes, the way in which we think about a situation is not always accurate and can lead to a trap.

Sample Script

Thinking traps are thoughts or patterns of thoughts that are either inaccurate or unrealistic interpretations of events. They can trap us and make us feel even worse or make the situation worse. They can lead us to feel like this person you see here, stuck in a trap! But, if we better understand these thinking traps, we can affect the way we feel about something. We can also change the way we react to something. Today, we will discuss eight common thinking traps.

Activity B: Identifying Thinking Traps 1

5 MINS. Use Supplement 6.6 as a handout to guide students in an explanation of common thinking traps. Consider using one of the examples from Activity A to begin the discussion. Provide students with the opportunity to ask questions for each thinking trap.

Sample Script

Sometimes, these thinking traps feel like they happen without us even noticing them until we're right in the middle, or stuck. But if we practice noticing these traps, we can get better at spotting them early, before we get too stuck. Let's look at the different thinking traps we might fall into from time to time.

Activity C: Identifying Thinking Traps 2

5 MINS. Use Supplement 6.7 as a handout and the optional props (e.g., dark glasses) to discuss the eight situations. Ask students to identify which thinking trap is being demonstrated by referring to the Common Thinking Traps handout (Supplement 6.6). Read each situation aloud, and encourage students to follow along on the overhead. After reading each situation, ask, "Which of the thinking traps is occurring in this story?" If students identify more than one thinking trap, lead them to the best answer, but also explain that we can get stuck in more than one trap at a time. Provide feedback as needed.

Note: If your students are struggling, provide other examples that are directly relevant to them. Alternatively, ask them to come up with examples of their own.

Sample Script

Let's talk more about thinking traps. In your handout, there are example situations and we will identify the thinking trap in each situation. For example, Marcella made a little mistake in math class. She thought this little mistake was a HUGE deal. Class, what thinking trap is it if I feel like a small mistake is a big problem? [Binocular vision: You may choose to use the binoculars.] *But Marcella didn't recognize that it was a trap, so she was still stuck! At the end of the class, she felt like the WHOLE class went HORRIBLY. She ignored the good things that happened. She ignored what she did well! Class, what thinking trap is it if I see only the bad things about something?* [Dark glasses: You may choose to put on the dark glasses.] *Yes, Marcella got stuck in dark glasses ALL day. As she was getting ready for bed, she thought, "Tomorrow's math class will be horrible, too." Class, what thinking trap is it if I predict something without enough evidence?* [Fortune telling: You may choose to bring out your fortune cookie.]

So you see? If I didn't realize my thoughts were a trap, and I believed them, they could cause me to feel grumpy for days! How do you think the thinking traps of binocular vision, dark glasses, and fortune telling [show props] *affected how Marcella acted with her friends that day? Her family? How do you think she acted in math class the next day?*

Putting It All Together

5–10 MINS. Use the following activity to practice the concepts discussed in this lesson.

Sample Script

Let's practice what we've learned by putting it all together.

This activity uses the Supplement 6.8 homework handout and can be completed in small groups. If using small groups, have each group identify a note taker and a leader; the rest of the members are helpers. The members in the group can take turns being leaders and note takers until everyone has a chance being a leader and a note taker. The leader identifies a situation where he or she got stuck in a thinking trap. Leaders can also use situations they saw on television of someone stuck in a thinking trap. For each thinking trap, the helpers ask the leaders the following eight questions. The note taker records the answers.

1. What was the situation? What happened?

2. What were your emotions and physical feelings?

3. Was the emotion comfortable, uncomfortable, or both?

4. Where was the emotion on the slider?

5. What were your thoughts and self-talk?

6. What was your reaction?

7. What thinking trap were you stuck in?

8. Did your situation get better or worse?

Closure

2 MINS. Close the lesson using a brief breathing activity and a reflection on the lesson content.

Sample Script

Let's take a moment to regroup. Close your eyes and rest your hands in your lap. Feel your feet on the floor. Relax the muscles in your body and face. Relax and soften your stomach muscles. Counting to 3, take a breath in slowly. Inhale the air down into your lungs. Feel your chest and stomach expand like a balloon. [Pause.] *Now, exhale, counting to 4. Feel your chest and stomach collapse as all the air exits your body.* [Pause.] *Again, inhale deep into your lungs so that your stomach expands* [Pause.] *and exhale.* [Pause.] *Take a moment to think about something you learned today that was important to you or you really liked.* [Note to instructor: Pause for a moment to allow time for reflection.] *Counting to 3, take one more deep breath in slowly* [Pause.] *and exhale counting to 4.* [Pause.]

Tips for Transfer Training and Homework

Use the ideas and activities in the following section to practice this lesson's content with your students at other times during the day. Also remember to precorrect, remind, and reinforce concepts from this lesson in activities throughout the school week and to encourage students to use the skills taught in this lesson across settings including home, the bus, the cafeteria, and the community.

Additional Activities

- Ask students to be on the lookout for evidence of thinking traps they see on television shows or in books they may be interested in.

- Ask students to journal and record their thoughts and self-talk for a day or several days. Ask them to identify patterns and traps. Use the supplements in this lesson as guides.

- Have students make flash cards with the thinking traps and images on one side and example scenarios on the other side.

Homework Handout

Pass out Supplement 6.8, Practice Situations Worksheet, and explain the instructions. Students will list situations where they got caught up in a thinking trap or they saw someone on TV get caught in a thinking trap. They will identify the thinking trap.

Picture of a Snake

Picture of a Herpetologist

Key Terms and Definitions

Thoughts

These are ideas or opinions in the mind.

Example: The thoughts we have about something can affect how we feel about it and how we react to a situation. If I think something will be fun, like a bike ride, I am likely to feel more comfortable about it and seek it out. If I think something will be boring or too difficult, I may not feel comfortable about it and I may avoid it.

Self-talk

The things we say to ourselves, self-talk can be negative, positive, or neutral.

Example: Self-talk can be helpful or encouraging (e.g., "I can do this!") or discouraging (e.g., "I can't believe I said that. That was a dumb thing to say").

Thinking traps

These are thoughts or patterns of thoughts that are either inaccurate or unrealistic judgments or interpretations of events.

Example: "My sister is always messing up. She can't do anything right." This is inaccurate and an unrealistic interpretation. Just like no one is perfect, no one messes *everything* up.

Picture of a Thought Bubble

131

Picture of a Man Trapped in a Hole

Common Thinking Traps

Binocular vision

Looking at things in a way that makes them seem bigger or smaller than they really are

Example: You have a small pimple on your face. You feel like that's all people see when they look at you.

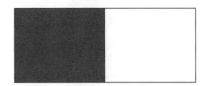

Black-and-white thinking

Looking at things in only extreme or opposite ways (e.g., thinking of things as being good or bad, never or always, all or none, friend or enemy)

Example: You had one fight with your good friend. Now you think, "We always fight. She hates me."

Dark glasses

Thinking about only the negative parts of things

Example: You met with your teacher. Your teacher said many good things about you. He also said your writing needs improvement. Now, you think all his comments were bad.

Fortune telling

Making predictions about what will happen in the future without enough evidence

Example: You don't talk to the new student in class because you think she will not like you.

(continued)

Making it personal

Blaming yourself for things that are not your fault or thinking things are about you when they are not

Example: Your friend is irritable today. You think it's because she's upset with you even though you can't think of any reason that would make her angry at you today.

Blame game

Blaming others for things that are your responsibility

Example: You didn't follow the rules, so your parents took your music away as punishment. You think it's your parents' fault because they don't like you.

All alone

Thinking you have problems that no one else understands

Example: Your parents can't afford to buy you the pair of shoes you want. You think no one else has money problems in their family.

Broad brush

Judging something based on one experience with it

Example: You met one person from another country, and you thought that person was rude. Now, you think all the people from that country are rude.

Example Situations

1. Michael's parents are getting a divorce. He thinks that this is all his fault because he has been getting into trouble lately.

2. Farah's teacher suggested that she run for class president. She decided not to run because she knew that no one would vote for her.

3. Marcella got a bad grade on a quiz. Now she thinks that she is the worst student in the class.

4. Ahmad's soccer coach gave him a lot of praise and encouragement in soccer practice. As Ahmad was leaving practice, the coach mentioned that Ahmad should practice his dribbling skills at home. Ahmad was upset about how poorly he played at practice.

5. Ling was grounded for not cleaning her room. She thought to herself, "I am always the bad kid. My sister Kimmy is always the good kid."

6. Latisha got in trouble because she shoved another student in the hallway. She doesn't think she should be in trouble because the other student gave her a mean look.

7. Caroline lost her favorite pet. She feels like no one else knows what it's like to lose something they care about.

8. Scott tried a Mexican dish once and thought it was too spicy, so he didn't like it. Now he thinks all Mexican food is too spicy.

Practice Situations Worksheet

Name (optional) _____

Directions: List four situations where you got stuck in a thinking trap. For each trap, write down the emotion you experienced; where on the volume slider your emotion was; if the emotion was comfortable, uncomfortable, or both; what the thought was; and the name of the thinking trap. You can also use situations you saw on television of someone stuck in a thinking trap.

Situation	What was your (or the person's) emotion?	What did it (might it) feel like? Comfortable, uncomfortable, or both?	Where on the slider was your (or the person's) emotion?	What was your (or the person's) thinking and self-talk?	What type of thinking trap did you (or the person) get stuck in?
1.					
2.					
3.					
4.					

Emotions Volume Slider

LESSON 7

Clear Thinking 2

SEL Competencies Addressed in This Lesson

Purpose and Objectives

This lesson provides students with the skills to evaluate thought patterns, consider alternative views, and reframe thinking traps. In this lesson, students will

- Develop the ability to notice or observe thoughts

- Understand the importance of identifying thinking traps early, before they accumulate or become ingrained patterns

- Discriminate healthy thought patterns that promote resilience from thought patterns that may be less helpful and hinder social and emotional growth

- Learn and apply techniques to reframe thinking traps

Teacher Notes

Materials Needed

☐ (Optional) Props for thinking traps: Binoculars, dark glasses, and fortune cookie

☐ Supplements 7.1–7.2 (online download)

☐ Supplements 7.3–7.4 (online download and handout)

☐ Supplement 7.5 (online download)

☐ Supplements 7.6–7.9 (online download and handout)

☐ Ruler or object used to measure (for Supplement 7.7)

☐ Supplement 7.10: Reframing Thinking Traps (homework handout)

Running Short on Time?

Suggested stopping points: end of Activity B and Closure activity.

Instructor Reflection

The Clear Thinking 2 lesson teaches students to evaluate their thought patterns and reframe thinking traps. Consider the unhealthy or less-than-helpful thought patterns you may have identified from your own life in the previous reflection section. How did they affect your emotional state? Did they gain momentum and get worse? Did you act on them? At the time, did you recognize that the thought pattern was a trap? If so, did you avoid getting ensnared in the thoughts by objectively reframing the thoughts and allowing them to pass by? If not, how might you reframe similar traps in the future?

Review

 2–3 MINS. Review the ideas (listed below) that were discussed in Lesson 6: Clear Thinking 1.

- Thinking about our thoughts

- Different thinking traps: binocular vision, dark glasses, black-and-white thinking, fortune telling, making it personal, the blame game, all alone, broad brush (Use Supplement 7.1 to review the thinking traps.)

- The connection between our thoughts and our emotions that produces thinking traps

Sample Script

During our last meeting, we talked about different thinking traps. By identifying thinking traps, we can keep them from becoming bigger problems that could affect the way we feel and the way we act. Also, avoiding getting caught up in traps can help us think clearly, get out of a bad situation, or make a situation better.

Introduction

 2–5 MINS. Introduce the lesson. Lead students in a focusing activity. Using Supplement 7.2, lead students through the introductory script. Consider using or showing the props—binoculars, fortune cookie, and dark glasses—to enhance the introductory discussion.

Sample Script

We all fall into thinking traps sometimes, so it's important to know when we are in one and how to get out.

Mindfulness-Based Focusing Activity

3 MINS. **Sample Script**

Let's begin with an activity to settle our bodies and practice focusing our minds. Close your eyes or look at a point in front of you on the floor or on your desk.

Rest your hands comfortably on your desk or in your lap. Feel your feet on the floor or your hands as they rest. First, pay attention to your breathing for three breaths [Pause.] Now, turn your attention to your thoughts. Do you notice that you can have a lot of thoughts in a very short time and they can jump all over the place? Thoughts are like clouds in the sky. They change shape all the time. Let's pay attention to our thoughts for a minute or two. Like a scientist watching clouds, notice the thoughts and when they change. Notice if there is a type of thought that keeps coming back. [Allow students 1–2 minutes to practice.] Now, let's take two breaths together. [Pause.] When you finish letting out the second breath, slowly open your eyes. Now that we've paid attention to our thoughts, we are ready to move on to our lesson.

Introduction (Continued)

Sample Script

If we don't realize we've made an error in the way we are thinking about something, our thoughts can keep getting worse and worse as time goes on. One wrong thought can lead us to another wrong thought, and everything can move quickly while it's getting worse along the way! This is kind of like a snowball rolling down a hill and collecting more and more snow and getting bigger and bigger as it goes. When this happens [Show Supplement 7.1.], things can feel worse than they actually are. Remember Marcella, who made a mistake in math class and got stuck in the binocular vision thinking trap? [Show binoculars.] She thought this little mistake was a HUGE deal. She didn't recognize that she was stuck in this trap and it made her gloomy all day. She was wearing dark glasses. [Show dark glasses.] At the end of the day, she was stuck in the fortune-telling trap. [Show fortune cookie.] She was so upset that she predicted that the next day would be horrible, too. One thought can lead to another and another and pretty soon we are REALLY stuck.

In today's lesson, we will learn how to avoid getting stuck in thinking traps, how to spot when we are getting caught in a thinking trap, and what to do if we do get caught in a thinking trap. Today, we will learn how to consider different ways of thinking about things. Also, we will learn that just because we think something doesn't mean it's true or that we need to act on it. We could simply identify the thinking trap for what it is—a trap!

Key Terms and Definitions

 5 MINS.   Use Supplement 7.3 as a handout to define the key terms that will be used in this lesson.

Sample Script

Here are some important terms that will help us understand ways to see traps and to consider other ways of thinking. We'll define the words and discuss examples to understand what they mean.

Recognizing Thinking Traps

5 MINS.

We can recognize thinking traps by examining our thoughts and by looking for the evidence that supports or does not support them. Use Supplements 7.4 and 7.5 to illustrate and discuss emotional intensity and evidence.

Sample Script

How do we know when we're stuck in a thinking trap? When we think about our thoughts and our self-talk like we do with our emotional volume slider [Show Supplement 7.4.] and realize that we are having strong, uncomfortable emotions about a thing or things that haven't happened yet except in our heads, we could be in a trap. Remember how we figured out how to tell how other people might be thinking and feeling by looking for clues if we couldn't ask? Well, we can be our own thought detectives [Show Supplement 7.5.] like in this picture showing a detective looking for more information. When we are feeling down, worried, anxious, or angry, we can use evidence to find out if we are in a thinking trap. Evidence is information or clues that can help us find out if something is true or realistic or not. When you look closely for evidence about certain thoughts, you will find that some thoughts are true because they are based on something realistic. For example, you may have worried or anxious thoughts about failing a test. [Show Supplement 7.4 to identify an intense feeling.] Is it realistic to think you might fail a test __if you did not study__? [Class responds, "Yes."] So, even though you feel uncomfortable, that's not really a trap because your emotions are telling you to study next time, right? But what about if you HAVE studied everything the teacher told you and practiced and prepared thoroughly but you're still having thoughts like, "I'm going to fail this test!" Is that a realistic thought? [Probably not.] You might be caught in a thinking trap. Can anyone tell me what the trap might be called if we are predicting the future without first looking for good evidence? [Fortune telling.]

Activity A: Looking for Evidence to Find Thinking Traps

5 MINS.

Use Supplement 7.5 as a handout to discuss using evidence to examine our thoughts. Help students understand the process of identifying a thinking trap using evidence to determine if the thought is realistic. Review each situation, asking the following questions:

- What is the thought?

- What is the evidence?

- How do I know that it's true or realistic?

Sample Script

We tend to think our thoughts are the truth, but sometimes they're just thoughts that we made up from other thoughts. Sometimes, our thoughts are worrying or planning thoughts. Sometimes, our thoughts judge or criticize ourselves or others. Sometimes, we have random thoughts that we can simply let pass by like the clouds in the sky.

Let's practice evaluating our thoughts by looking for evidence. Sometimes, evidence supports our thoughts, and sometimes it doesn't. That's how we can figure out if we're in a thinking trap. Remember, we talked about looking for evidence or clues to help us understand how other people might feel. We can do the same with ourselves!

Using Evidence to Find and Reframe Thinking Traps

🕑 **25 MINS.** In a large group, use Supplement 7.6 as a handout to demonstrate that there may be different ways of looking at the same situation.

Activity B: Finding Evidence

🕑 **5 MINS.** Ask students to get out a ruler or other object for measuring purposes. Sometimes, emotions can interfere with clear thinking and problem solving. We can use evidence to begin to change how we think about a situation, and that can change our emotions and our reactions to the situation. Let your students know that once they find evidence that they may be in a thinking trap, they can begin working to reframe the thoughts.

Sample Script

Did you know we can change the way we think about a situation by using evidence? Remember, just because we have a thought, that doesn't mean it is true! Sometimes, strong emotions like anger can keep us from thinking clearly. Sometimes, we just don't have all the facts.

Our brains can play tricks on us in lots of different ways and convince us that something is true even when it's not. For example, when we first look at these pictures, we may think the first middle circle is larger. But let's examine the evidence to find out whether this is true. [Use a ruler or small object to measure the middle circle.] What did you find? Right, they are the same size even though they look different! Sometimes, just like this, our thoughts and self-talk can lead us to believe things that aren't necessarily true. Sometimes, our emotions are so strong, they affect our thoughts in such a way that we aren't able to problem solve very well. If we know this about our thoughts, we can avoid getting too caught up in them when things start to feel uncomfortable. Instead, we can look for evidence to consider different ways of thinking about things.

Remember from our last lesson that Ling was grounded for not cleaning her room. She thought to herself, "I am always the bad kid. My sister Kimmy is always the good kid." How does she know she might be in a trap? [Elicit responses that suggest that the use of words like always or never often lead us into traps.] *What can she do? She can look for evidence that shows that she does many things well, too. She could also look for evidence that her sister Kimmy makes mistakes sometimes, too. "Well, I guess Kimmy makes mistakes just like me." Class, what thinking trap was Ling stuck in?* [Black-and-white thinking.] *Yes, Ling now sees the trap for what it is and thinks, "No one is always good or bad. In fact, Kimmy and I do a lot of things well, but we both make mistakes, too. I was thinking in black and white." After examining the evidence, and seeing things more clearly, Ling feels better and can climb out of that trap!*

Activity C: Reframing Using Evidence

5 MINS. Use Supplement 7.7 to guide students through the process of using evidence to consider different perspectives or ways of thinking or reframing. Reframing means looking at things differently or from another perspective. As a result of reframing, you may feel differently about a situation and often you can get out of a thinking trap. Read the examples aloud.

Sample Script

Sometimes, when we find we are in a trap, the evidence can help us to look at something from a different angle and consider other ways of thinking about things. This is called reframing. Reframing is a way of looking at something differently—from a different perspective. Think about the circles we just looked at. The first middle circle just seems bigger because of how it is framed by the other circles. We can reframe things in life, too. For example, we could look at a situation that isn't going well as if it is a problem. Or, we could reframe it and see it as a challenge or an opportunity to problem solve.

For example, if I'm told I didn't make the basketball team, I might think about that as a sign that I'm no good and I should give up. Or, if I feel strongly about playing basketball, I could think about that as a challenge to get even better. In fact, some famous basketball players got really good doing just that! It's exciting to think how reframing can give us more power over our own lives. We can choose how to think about things and then how we react to them! Here is how it would look if we wrote it down. In your handout, there are some example situations. Let's take a look. [Show and discuss Supplement 7.7.]

Activity D: Reframing Thinking Traps

15 MINS. Use Supplement 7.8 and the following list of questions to discuss how to use methods of reframing. Encourage students to think about times they suspected they were caught in a thinking trap. If your students are having difficulty providing examples, start the discussion by providing some examples from your own life or examples that are relevant to your students. The examples they come up with will be used for discussion. Once a list of scenarios is generated, facilitate a discussion. Ask the following questions:

1. What was the thought?

2. What evidence did you have that tells you it might be a thinking trap?

3. Was it a thinking trap?

4. What was the thinking trap?

5. How could it be reframed?

Sample Script

Let's practice using evidence to find thinking traps and reframing our thoughts using our own examples.

Putting It All Together

5-10 MINS. Use the following activity to practice the concepts discussed in this lesson. Ask students to take out their homework assignment or the Putting It All Together activity from Lesson 6, and use Supplement 7.9 as a handout. In small groups, students will work to see how identifying thinking traps and reframing can be useful in everyday situations. If there is time, ask for volunteers from the class to role-play some of the examples.

Sample Script

Let's practice what we've learned by putting it all together. When should we use evidence to examine our thoughts? We can think about our emotions by using an imagined slider. We can use this image in our minds to figure out how close we might be to being in a trap. If our emotions are medium and getting higher, and we feel uncomfortable, it's time to check and see if perhaps we're just caught in a thinking trap. Or, if we notice we are thinking similar uncomfortable thoughts over and over again, it could be a trap. We can use these clues to start looking for evidence behind our thoughts. Then, we use our facts or our evidence to spot a thinking trap. If we think it is a trap, we can try to reframe the thought by seeing if there is a different way to think about it or a different explanation for it. We are going to use the activity [or homework] *you did last time when we talked about how to identify thinking traps. This way, we can use our own examples to practice reframing.*

In your small groups, identify a note taker and a facilitator or leader like we did last time. The rest of the group members are helpers. Go around your group and take turns being facilitators or leaders and note takers. The leader identifies a situation when he or she got stuck in a thinking trap. The helpers suggest ways to reframe the thinking trap. The note taker records the answers to the questions.

Closure

🕐 2 MINS. Close the lesson using a brief breathing activity and a reflection on the lesson content.

Sample Script

Let's take a moment to regroup. Close your eyes and rest your hands in your lap. Feel your feet on the floor. Relax the muscles in your body and face. Relax and soften your stomach muscles. Counting to 3, take a breath in slowly. Inhale the air down into your lungs. Feel your chest and stomach expand like a balloon. [Pause.] *Now, exhale, counting to 4. Feel your chest and stomach collapse as all the air exits your body.* [Pause.] *Again, inhale deep into your lungs so that your stomach expands* [Pause.] *and exhale* [Pause.] *Take a moment to think about something you learned today that was important to you or you really liked.* [Note to instructor: pause for a moment to allow time for reflection.] *Counting to 3, take one more deep breath in slowly* [Pause.] *and exhale counting to 4.* [Pause.]

Tips for Transfer Training and Homework

Use the ideas and activities in the following section to practice this lesson's content with your students at other times during the day. Also remember to precorrect, remind, and reinforce concepts from this lesson in activities throughout the school week and to encourage students to use the skills taught in this lesson across settings including home, the bus, the cafeteria, and the community.

Additional Activities

- Create a class poster (e.g., Mr. Juan's class doesn't get stuck in traps!) with the thinking trap icons and sample scenarios from students' lives.

- Flip that thought! Provide scenarios that students can reframe, such as the difficult situation that is reframed as a challenge. Make a "before" and "after" reframing list. In the discussion, talk about ways thoughts, feelings, and behaviors might be different in the before and after scenarios.

- Create or modify an existing board game to include using evidence to identify thinking traps, reframing, and avoiding thinking traps (extra moves) and getting caught in thinking traps and allowing them to snowball (losing a turn or moving backward).

Homework Handout

Pass out the homework handout, Supplement 7.10, Reframing Thinking Traps. Explain how to fill in the columns. Encourage students to identify at least two events for the chart. Remind the students not to identify whom they are referring to in the homework.

Thinking Traps

Binocular vision
Looking at things in a way that makes them seem bigger than they really are

Example: You're invited to a beach party. It will be lots of fun, but you don't want to have to wear a bathing suit and that is *all* you can think of.

Black-and-white thinking
Looking at things in only extreme or opposite ways (e.g., thinking of things as being good or bad, never or always, all or none, friend or enemy)

Example: You feel irritated because you think your friend never makes mistakes. You feel like you are always the one who messes up.

Dark glasses
Thinking about only the negative parts of things

Example: You don't like school. When you think about it, all you can think of is the mistakes you make and the problems you have with your teacher.

Fortune telling
Making predictions about what will happen in the future without enough evidence

Example: You didn't do well on an art project. Now you think you will not do well in art in high school.

Making it personal
Blaming yourself for things that are not your fault or making things about you when they are not

Example: Your basketball team lost an important game. You think you let everyone down, and you feel like it's your fault.

Blame game
Blaming others for things that are your responsibility

Example: You waited until the night before a group project was due to work on the project. They couldn't help you get the materials you needed, and you got a bad grade. You're angry with your group members.

All alone
Thinking you have problems that no one else understands

Example: You have difficulty making friends. You think you are the only one who has difficulty with this.

Broad brush
Judging something based on one experience with it

Example: You tried soccer and found it to be difficult. Now you think that you are bad at all sports.

Picture of a Snowball

Key Terms and Definitions

Evidence

Clues that help you find out if something is true or realistic, evidence can give you information to help you solve a problem. We can use evidence to help us figure out if our thoughts and self-talk are realistic or logical or if they are distorted.

Example: Using the scientific method, a scientist uses evidence to help solve a problem. Detectives use evidence, like fingerprints, to solve a crime.

Reframing

This is looking at things differently or seeing things from another perspective; using reframing, you can change the way you think and feel about things.

Example: We can use reframing to see a difficult situation as a challenge rather than a problem.

Emotions Volume Slider

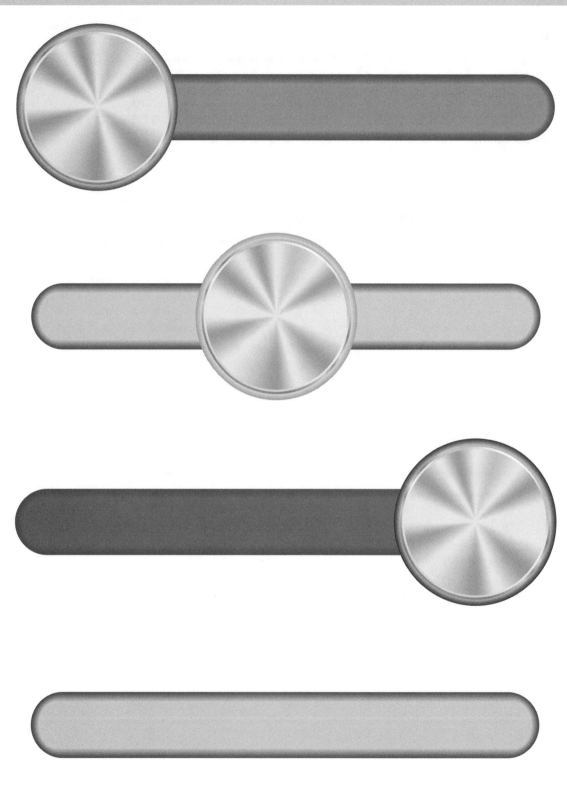

Picture of Looking for Evidence

Looking for Evidence to Reframe

Evidence for or Against

Thought	What is the evidence?		Is it realistic?
A	**For?**	**Against?**	
My friend never chooses me when it's time to choose sides for dodge ball. He hates me.	Over the past week, whenever we've played dodge ball, Michael has not chosen me for his team.	He comes over to my house on the weekends. He laughs at my jokes. He is really serious about dodge ball. I'm not.	If he hated me, he probably would not want to spend any time with me or even talk to me.
B	**For?**	**Against?**	
I am such an awful dancer. I will never make the dance team. I'm never good at anything.	All of the other students are catching on to the dance steps. I keep falling. I have failed both tryouts.	I cannot predict the future. I can't be good at everything, and there are other things that I am better at.	The team leader has some very specific requirements for someone who makes the team, and, so far, I have not been able to do them. It is reasonable to expect that I might not make the dance team this time around. There are other activities I can join instead.

Reframing Thinking Traps Examples

What was my thought?	What thinking trap did I get stuck in?	What is a more realistic way of thinking about it (reframe)?
My friend never chooses me when it's time to choose sides for dodge ball. He hates me.	Black-and-white thinking	Michael probably knows that I don't really like to play dodge ball, so he picks other people who like to play.
I am such an awful dancer. I will never make the dance team.	Fortune telling	If I don't make the dance team, I still have other things I can do.
Everything at home is bad.	Dark glasses	Some things at home seem bad right now, but there are some good things, too.
It's awful that I fight so much with my dad.	Binocular vision	Most of the time I don't fight with my dad, just sometimes.

Reframing Thinking Traps Using Evidence

What was the thought?	What is the evidence (for or against)?	Was there a thinking trap (yes or no)?	What was the thinking trap?	What is a more realistic way of thinking about it (reframing)?

Reframing Thinking Traps Worksheet

Name (optional) _____

Directions: Identify two situations in your life right now where you might be doing some unhelpful thinking that you would like to change. Use the questions at the top of the chart to help you identify the thoughts and reframe these thoughts.

What was the thought?	Was there a thinking trap (yes or no)?	What was the thinking trap?	What is a more realistic way of thinking about it?	If it was a trap, how could I prevent getting stuck next time?

LESSON 8

Solving People Problems

SEL Competencies Addressed in This Lesson

Responsible decision making / Self-awareness / Self-management / Social awareness / Relationship skills

Teacher Notes

Purpose and Objectives

This lesson provides students with ways to have healthy, positive relationships with others by making responsible, respectful, and realistic decisions when confronted with a social conflict. In this lesson, students will

- Learn ways to be aware of one's actions and maintain a healthy attitude

- Distinguish between helpful and unhelpful decision-making strategies to resolve conflict

- Identify and apply the steps of a problem-solving model to resolve conflicts

Materials Needed

☐ Supplement 8.1 (online download)

☐ Supplements 8.2–8.4 (online download and handout)

☐ Supplement 8.5 (homework handout)

Running Short on Time?

Suggested stopping points: end of Activity A and Closure activity. When continuing the lesson, begin with the Mindfulness-Based Focusing Activity found in the Introduction section and the introduction to the four-step problem-solving model.

Instructor Reflection

Disagreements are a natural part of life, so it is important to consider how we handle them. Take a few minutes to reflect on the conflicts you've had with others in the past and the actions you took to try to solve the problem. It may be helpful to write down a few notes to help you process this information. Thinking about your past conflicts, did you act quickly or take your time? Did you listen? Did you use effective communication skills? Did you look for information to better understand the situation? Did you consider a variety of solutions or look at potential outcomes to various actions? Did you notice an urge to act or retreat from the conflict? How did you feel about your behavior toward the other person? What roadblocks did you have in solving the conflict? Did your actions improve the situation?

Review

⏱ 2 MINS. Review the ideas (listed below) that were discussed in Lesson 7: Clear Thinking 2.

- Recognizing thought patterns

- Distinguishing healthy thought patterns that promote resilience and thought patterns that may hinder emotional well-being

- Eight thinking traps (binocular vision, black-and-white thinking, dark glasses, fortune telling, making it personal, blame game, all alone, broad brush)

- Using evidence to reframe thinking traps

Sample Script

During our last meeting, we discussed measuring the intensity of our emotions using an intensity scale, considering that intense or uncomfortable emotions may suggest that we are in a thinking trap, and using evidence to reframe thinking traps.

Introduction

⏱ 5–8 MINS. Introduce the lesson. Lead students in a focusing activity. Show students Supplement 8.1 as an introductory activity, and discuss what is happening in the pictures and how it is important to reflect on how both parties may feel as well as potential solutions.

Sample Script

Today, we will talk about ways to make responsible, respectful, and realistic decisions when confronted with a social conflict. We all have conflict or disagreements from time to time. Sometimes, it can be difficult to find agreement in a way that is reasonable, fair, and acceptable to everyone.

Mindfulness-Based Focusing Activity

Sample Script

⏱ 2 MINS. *Let's practice settling our bodies and focusing our minds. Close your eyes or look at a point on the floor or on your desk. Rest your hands comfortably. Feel your feet on the floor or your hands as they rest. Notice your breathing for three breaths. [Pause for 3 breaths.] Now, think about a person who has been nice to you or you know cares about you. Can you picture them in your mind? Think about what this person has done for you or said to you that was kind. [Pause.] Notice how you feel when you think of this person. You might feel grateful or thankful that you have him or her in your life. You might feel like smiling. [Pause.] You can think kind thoughts toward this person by saying to yourself, "I am wishing you happiness" or "I am wishing you good health." Use your own words and say them to yourself while you think about the kindness this person showed you. We'll do this for about a minute. [Pause.] Now, let's take two breaths together. [Pause.] When you finish letting out the second breath, slowly open your eyes. We are ready to move on to our lesson.*

Introduction (Continued)

 1 MIN.

Show Supplement 8.1, which shows pictures of two people arguing. Choose Picture A or B for discussion. If there is another opportunity to discuss this topic, you can use the other picture for discussion.

Sample Script

What is happening in this picture between these two individuals? Some things that we want to think about while looking at this picture are what they are arguing about; what the end result might be based on what this picture shows; do they seem calm; when they walk away, do you think they'll feel like their emotions or needs were heard and met? When we are in a situation with another person and we are not getting along or don't agree, it is important to stop and think about how we are feeling, how the other person is feeling, and how we are reacting. Remember, in earlier lessons we talked about being aware of our emotions, how our emotions can affect our ability to make helpful choices, and the importance of taking the perspective of another person. We will come back to this picture again and talk about how we can resolve the problem in a way that is acceptable for everyone. Today, we will talk about a skill called problem solving or conflict resolution. This is an important skill to practice so that we can be prepared to make responsible and realistic decisions when we are in conflict with another person. Being able to stop and consider ways we can manage our emotions is important so that the conflict gets resolved in a way that is agreeable and shows respect for everyone involved.

Key Terms and Definitions

 5 MINS.

Use Supplement 8.2 as a handout to define the key terms that will be used in this lesson.

Sample Script

Here are some important terms that will help us understand problem solving or conflict resolution. We'll define the words and also discuss examples to understand what they mean.

Maintaining a Responsible and Respectful Attitude During Conflict

🕐 **5–8 MINS.** Convey that everyone approaches conflict and views situations differently, but it's important that we make responsible decisions and show respect for ourselves and others in our behaviors.

- Everyone is different. Everyone will not always think, act, or feel the same way in a situation. (Refer back to the lesson on understanding other people's feelings to help deepen understanding.)

- Your attitude (e.g., being optimistic or pessimistic) can affect how you respond in a disagreement and your ability to be responsible and respectful toward others.

- You can have multiple thoughts and feelings and emotions at varying levels of intensity in a conflict (refer to the volume slider as needed).

Sample Script:

Thoughts, emotions, and attitude will vary depending on the situation we're in or the person or persons we are disagreeing with. This is okay. There isn't just one feeling, thought, or attitude or one way of doing something. But no matter the level of our emotions, remaining respectful and responsible can help us make choices and decisions that are helpful in the long term. Sometimes, when we feel angry or frustrated, we can react immediately or act without thinking of the consequences. We can say or do something that we regret or that makes the situation worse. We can be either pessimistic (someone who sees the worst or most unfavorable aspect of a situation) or optimistic (someone who is hopeful or sees a favorable aspect of a situation) in our attitudes. Let's think back to the picture we saw earlier when we started the lesson about the two individuals experiencing a conflict. Remember the questions I asked you to keep in mind? Think about them as we are going through this lesson.

Activity A: Being Respectful, Responsible, and Aware of Our Attitudes in Communication and Listening

🕐 **5 MINS.** Students will engage in a discussion about activities they enjoy with a partner or small group while practicing communication skills through listening and asking questions. Model active listening and respectful communication such as, "Thank you for sharing that! It sounds like you really enjoy [activity]" or "I liked how you showed interest and respect by listening, looking at the person, and asking questions." Encourage students to show respectful and responsible behaviors by offering compliments to those who have shared. Be aware of students' attitudes and physical demonstrations of listening. (*Note:* Consider cultural norms for attentive and active listening.) Then, have students discuss a school situation in which peers may have had a conflict. Ask students how they can use helpful communication skills in such conflicts.

Sample Script

Let's explore how we can use communication skills through listening and asking questions. Being respectful and responsible while being aware of our attitude are essential to good communication and listening skills. For example, someone approaching conflict with a negative attitude versus someone approaching a situation with a more optimistic attitude can affect the choices that are made to resolve the situation. Now, I'd like us to discuss a topic that we might all have different attitudes about [e.g., what we each like to do for fun or on the weekends]. Sometimes, when a person really enjoys something, he or she will use words like "This is epic!" You might disagree and say so. It doesn't mean that you are intending to cause a conflict by saying what you think, but it is just a way of sharing a perspective. Let's see if we can have a conversation about things that we enjoy that are different among us, and we can practice communication skills by listening and asking open-ended questions like, "What do you like about that activity?" When you have finished talking in your small group, we are going to share some of the words or actions that you noticed your classmates using during the discussion that conveyed respect for differing views. Then, with your partner, come up with situations at school that may cause conflict between individuals, and discuss how respectful communication skills can be used.

A Closer Look at Key Terms and Definitions: Conflict

5 MINS.   Use Supplement 8.1 to review the key points listed below. Then, ask students to discuss ways in which they would resolve that conflict.

- Not all conflicts are bad. They can be neutral or good. Conflicts can help us understand how we feel about a situation and that not everyone may feel the same way, which is normal.

- Conflicts are inherent in the human experience, and we can learn from conflicts.

- Conflict does not have to end with a "winner" and a "loser." The aim is to end the conflict with all people feeling respected and reasonably satisfied with the outcome.

- Conflict can range in intensity level depending on the situation, setting, and individuals involved. For example, a school conflict with a peer during a group project can look very different from a conflict with a parent at home who has taken away your weekend privileges.

Sample Script

Conflicts or disagreements can be uncomfortable, but they are not necessarily bad. They are a natural part of life and they even help us learn strategies to problem solve. In fact, they can be opportunities to learn about oneself and another person's perspective. Disagreements do not have to end with one person being right and one person being wrong. Sometimes, there is no particular right or wrong answer to the issue. Conflicts can be resolved by respecting other people's views, agreeing to disagree, or compromising. Conflict resolution strategies can help solve our problems or disagreements one step at a time. For example, think about the picture I showed you earlier with the individuals arguing. [Refer to Supplement 8.1, Picture A or B.] Make up a few ideas about what could have been happening between these people to cause them to experience such intense emotions. Let's think about what you would do to resolve this situation if you were involved in that conflict.

Twist: Would the individuals have the same conflict or react in the same way if they were in class or if someone got physically hurt in that situation?

Options to Conflict Resolution: What Can I Do?

🕐 **5–10 MINS.** There are many options to solving conflicts.

Sample Script

There are many respectful, responsible, and realistic ways to resolve conflicts. In this context, realistic means that the decision makes sense for the situation. For example, Sergei and his best friend like the same girl and both are interested in asking her to the school dance. Sergei suggests that he saw her first because they are in the same math period, so he should get to ask her to the dance. However, Sergei's friend feels that he should get to ask her. Is Sergei being respectful, responsible, and realistic? Now, we're going to talk about helpful options for solving conflict, such as in Sergei's situation.

Activity B: Conflict Resolution

🕐 **5 MINS.**

Use Supplement 8.3 as a handout to discuss different options for conflict resolution. Have students review the list of options in Supplement 8.3 and share and discuss in small groups when these options might be used. You can post the list in your classroom for a visual reminder.

Sample Script

When you are in a social situation that is difficult or uncomfortable, that is beginning to escalate into a conflict, it helps to look at the situation as if you were a third person observing it and ask yourself these questions: What is the issue exactly? What does person A need, and what does person B need? What are the options to resolve this conflict? Here are some options to keep in mind that can help you. [Show and review the list of options in Supplement 8.3.] Can anyone share if they've used any of these? Did it work to resolve your conflict?

Four-Step Problem-Solving Model: Introduction

🕐 1 MIN.   The problem-solving model is a way to attempt to resolve disagreements one step at a time. Conflicts are challenging, and it takes patience and creativity to use problem-solving strategies! Sometimes, thinking traps, thinking only of ourselves, or not being able to take others' perspectives can hinder effective problem solving and keep us from achieving a workable compromise.

Sample Script

Sometimes, conflicts can seem confusing and impossible to resolve because people involved may be angry; their emotional intensity may be "high" on the volume slider. Intense emotions make it difficult to figure out the exact nature of the conflict, and it may make you want to just not deal with it at all or to give the other person the silent treatment. Ignoring conflicts may seem to work in the moment, but in the long run, the problem is not being dealt with in a helpful, honest way. Instead of dealing with the issue, you are just pushing it aside. For example, if you don't do your laundry and it piles up more and more, it will become overwhelming and will take more of your time to wash. We will learn how to look at a problem in small steps, particularly when the situation may be really frustrating or seem confusing. By doing this, we can be better prepared to make helpful decisions and come to a solution that is agreeable to everyone.

Four-Step Problem-Solving Model

🕐 20 MINS.   Use Supplement 8.4 as a handout to discuss the steps to problem solving. Remind students that they can reference this table to help them remember the steps.

Sample Script

There are four steps we can use to solve a problem. We're going to practice these steps with example situations. Using the steps will help us come to a helpful solution. It can be difficult to use this problem-solving model in the heat of a moment or in the midst of a conflict—when our emotions are high on the volume slider. By practicing the steps when we are not feeling strong emotions, we will be better prepared to use these steps when we may not be thinking as clearly.

You will also learn about showing empathy and how to compromise when it is appropriate. In some situations, you may try different solutions and nothing is working right away; in these cases, you may sometimes have to be patient and politely say, "I hear what you are saying. Maybe we can talk about this another time and try again to solve the problem?" Or sometimes, if everyone doesn't know about the four steps to problem solving, it can turn into a bigger argument. Be patient and open-minded to different perspectives and strategies. Here are the four steps in the problem-solving model and a visual picture to help you remember.

Activity C: Problem-Solving Application

 10 MINS. Use Supplement 8.4 again to apply the four-step problem-solving model to the example situations. There are three situations listed below the sample script. Choose two of the three situations to do at this time. Read the situation samples aloud. Remind students to use Supplement 8.3 to reference possible ways to solve the problem. As a whole group, complete the first situation you choose. The next situation can be with a partner or in a small group. The third situation is provided in the event that you have a need to repeat the exercise with the same group and/or to provide variety for future classes. A "twist" is included at the end of the scenario to provide students with a deeper level of thinking and utilization of problem-solving skills.

> ### Sample Script
>
> *Now that we've talked about the steps, let's go through some example situations and see how we would apply these steps. I will read the first situation and we will discuss the steps together as a class. We will write our thoughts in the middle column under Situation 1. For Situation 2, you will partner with the person next to you (or get into small groups), go through the problem-solving model, and write down your ideas in the Situation 2 column.*

Situation 1

- Problem: You and your classmate are partnered up to do a science project. The two of you disagree on how to do the project.

- *Twist:* You know that your classmate is really good at science.

Situation 2

- Problem: Your friend has a crush on the same person you do. You notice that they have been talking to each other more often and you hear that the other person make also like your friend.

- *Twist:* You know that sometimes you tend to be jealous of others.

Situation 3

- Problem: You were told by a few classmates that your close friend is spreading rumors about you at school or online. You feel that people are giving you looks, and now you are furious at your friend.

- *Twist:* You had made prior arrangements with your friend to come over to your house for dinner and hang out.

Activity D: Discuss Examples and Nonexamples of Problem Solving

10 MINS. Begin with the Example Problem below to discuss the ways in which a conflict might be solved. Review the six problem-solving scenarios listed below to facilitate this discussion, and ask students to evaluate whether the scenario is an example or nonexample of a helpful way to solve a problem. You may also use other current and realistic conflicts that may be particularly relevant to your students. Remember, the problem-solving skills students just discussed may be inappropriate in some situations (e.g., in a life-threatening situation, a discussion with a potentially dangerous individual may not be safe).

Sample Script

Let's discuss examples of problem-solving strategies—what to do and what not to do. First, let's go back to the situation earlier in the pictures of the students arguing. [See Supplement 8.1.] I will read aloud some strategies, and you tell me if they are examples (helpful) or nonexamples (unhelpful). Examples are the strategies we want to do or should do. Nonexamples are what we don't want to do or want to avoid. Then, I'd like for you to share with a partner your own situations and the strategies you have used in conflicts. Think about situations at school, at home, or in your community.

Example problem: Begin with the introductory situation to illustrate: the students arguing with each other over some possible rumors spread at school or posted online. Choose some of the problem-solving strategies listed below (Problem-Solving Scenarios 1–6), and prompt students with the question, "Is this an example of problem solving or a nonexample of problem solving?" For the items that are nonexamples of problem solving, ask students how they would use problem-solving skills to resolve the conflict.

Problem-solving scenario 1 (example): The students identify the problem, say what they want to happen, and discuss outcomes to different solutions. One of the solutions was to be honest with each other and express what bothers them. They agree on this solution and shake hands.

Problem-solving scenario 2 (nonexample): The students argue and interrupt each other, and one person gets close to the other person's face.

Problem-solving scenario 3 (nonexample): The students identify the problem, say what they each want to happen in the situation, and each list and discuss a few potential solutions. They can't agree on any of the solutions, and they decide to ignore each other or hold a grudge.

Problem-solving scenario 4 (nonexample): The students identify the problem, but they're each so interested in describing what they want to happen that they don't really listen to what the other person wants. The students are arguing over each other and raising their voices, and each says that he or she will get other students to dislike the other, bringing third parties into the argument.

Problem-solving scenario 5 (example): The students identify the problem, say what they each want to happen, and each list and discuss a few potential solutions. One of the solutions is to agree to use evidence and agree that spreading rumors is disrespectful.

Problem-solving scenario 6 (nonexample): The principal gets involved, calms the students down, and tells the students to see a counselor. As the two students walk away, they use a few last rude words and hand gestures to continue the fight a little longer.

Putting It All Together

🕐 **5 MINS.** Use the following activity to practice the concepts discussed in this lesson.

Sample Script

Let's practice what we've learned by putting it all together.

In small groups or as a class, use the following questions to ask students to share the lesson's talking points.

- What are examples for the terms *responsible, respectful, attitude, conflict/ problem, communication, resolution, resolve,* and *problem solving/conflict resolution?*

- What are some strategies for dealing with conflict?

- Can you describe the four-step problem-solving model?

- Why is being responsible, respectful, and realistic; taking perspectives; using communication skills; and thinking about choices important to conflict resolution?

Closure

🕐 **2 MINS.** Close the lesson using a short breathing activity and a reflection on the lesson content.

Sample Script

Let's take a moment to regroup. Close your eyes and rest your hands in your lap. Feel your feet on the floor. Relax the muscles in your body and face. Relax and soften your stomach muscles. Counting to 3, take a deep breath in slowly. Inhale the air down into your lungs. Feel your chest and stomach expand like a balloon. [Pause.] *Now, exhale, counting to 4. Feel your chest and stomach collapse as all the air exits your body.* [Pause.] *Again, inhale deep into your lungs so that your stomach expands* [Pause.] *and exhale.* [Pause.] *Take a moment to think about something you learned today that was important to you or you really liked.* [Note to instructor: Pause for a moment to allow time for reflection.] *Counting to 3, take one more deep breath in slowly* [Pause.] *and exhale, counting to 4.* [Pause.]

Tips for Transfer Training and Homework

Use the ideas and activities in the following section to practice this lesson's content with your students at other times during the day. Also, remember to precorrect, remind, and reinforce concepts from this lesson in activities throughout the school week and to encourage students to use the skills taught in this lesson across settings including home, the bus, and the cafeteria.

Additional Activities

- Here are some suggested books:

  How to Stop Arguing: Dealing With Stress, Anger, Rejection, Conflict, Fighting, and Difficult People by Amber Rain

  The Fear of Conflict Treatment: How to Overcome Your Fear of Conflict and Express Yourself With Confidence for Life by Allan Green

  Eight Keys by Suzanne LaFleur

- Have students make a list of conflicts and identify if any of the strategies were used. Then, have students identify how they showed respect to another person through their communication strategies (e.g., looking, listening, talking).

- Have students ask family members or neighbors to describe conflicts they've experienced. Discuss how the steps to conflict resolution could have helped.

Homework Handout

Pass out Supplement 8.5, Using a Problem-Solving Model to Resolve Conflicts. Explain to students that they will use the problem-solving model to work through a past or current problem situation and provide a new resolution for the problem.

Pictures of Two Students Arguing

Picture A

Picture B

Key Terms and Definitions

Responsible

This is making choices that are considerate of yourself and others, being able to choose right from wrong, following through with your word or promise, and being dependable.

Example: The students found a wallet with some cash in it. Instead of taking the money or keeping the wallet, they decide to turn it in to the office.

Example: The students disagree about who made the winning basketball shot, but they decide that it doesn't matter who made the last shot as long as their team won.

Attitude

This is the way you choose to think about things and how those thoughts are reflected in your behaviors toward a situation or a problem.

Example: While working on a group project with a student with whom he does not always get along, Timothy knew he would have to change his attitude because he was beginning to act disrespectfully.

Conflict

This is a disagreement or something that doesn't match or work well together.

Example: The students had a conflict when they could not agree on how to start the project.

Problem solving/conflict resolution

This is a way of dealing with a problem in a helpful or constructive manner and finding some way to reach an agreement.

Example: The students used conflict resolution to decide who would drive to the party.

Communication

This is expressing oneself effectively after listening to the other person's perspective while respecting the rights and beliefs of others.

Example: The student used communication in the group to discuss a science topic that she had been researching for a few months, but she also listened to comments from her peers.

Resolution

This is the process of (trying to) settle the conflict or find a solution.

Example: After disagreeing about who would be the lead presenter in a group project, the two students decided on a resolution of each taking turns talking.

Resolve

This is reaching a decision or finding a solution.

Example: The students were able to resolve their disagreement by finding a possible solution and deciding to try it.

Respectful

Showing consideration or thoughtfulness is being respectful.

Example: The students were respectful toward the chaperones on their field trip to the science conference.

Conflict Resolution: What Can I Do?

Compromise

One or both people agree to give up a little of what they originally wanted but are okay with it in order to resolve the conflict.

Agreement

Both individuals decide on a resolution or plan.

Agree to disagree

Both people decide this is something they will likely not agree on, and they will accept this fact. Having differing perspectives is okay!

Friendly rivalry/leave it to chance

People decide to play a game to resolve the conflict or just not do anything and see how things turn out.

Seeking guidance from an adult

You can ask an objective outside party, someone you trust who can help give responsible suggestions.

Making a deal

Both people agree to do one thing in exchange for something else (e.g., "If I do this, will you do that?").

A Four-Step Problem-Solving Model for Conflict Resolution

Four-step problem-solving model	Situation 1 example	Situation 2 example
1. **Identify the problem:** What are you arguing about? • Have the other person state his or her wants and feelings. • Describe how you feel. • Read the other person's body language. • Summarize both people's wants and feelings and what they suggest. Is there a disagreement?		
2. **Develop a plan (solutions):** List some of the ways you can solve the problem. Each person should generate at least two solutions. • Is someone willing to compromise? • It is important to be open minded and respectful instead of being spiteful or sarcastic during this brainstorming of ideas step. • Which way seems the most reasonable, responsible, and respectful for those involved?		
3. **Evaluate the plan:** Determine whether the plan will work. • What would happen if. . .? • Would it be safe and fair? • How would everyone feel? • Does it work for all involved? • Is it a win–win situation? • Is the plan realistic and does it help make the situation better?		
4. **Implement the plan:** Everyone agrees to try the plan.		

Merrell's Strong Kids—Grades 6–8: A Social and Emotional Learning Curriculum, Second Edition,
by Dianna Carrizales-Engelmann, Laura L. Feuerborn, Barbara A. Gueldner, and Oanh K. Tran.

Using a Problem-Solving Model to Resolve Conflicts

Name (optional) _____

Directions: Think of a problem or conflict you had with a person in the past for which you wish you had done something differently. How did you handle it? How could you have handled it differently? Use the problem-solving steps you learned today and provide a new ending to this problem or conflict. Refer to Supplement 8.3 for ideas on alternatives to conflict.

Four-step problem-solving model	Situation
1. **Identify the problem:** What are you arguing about?	
2. **Develop a plan (solutions):** List some of the ways you can solve this problem. Each person should generate at least two solutions.	
3. **Evaluate the plan:** Determine whether the plan will work.	
4. **Implement the plan:** All parties agree to the plan.	

LESSON 9

Letting Go of Stress

SEL Competencies Addressed in This Lesson

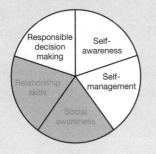

Responsible decision making

Self-awareness

Relationship skills

Self-management

Social awareness

Teacher Notes

Purpose and Objectives

This lesson provides students with the skills to understand the different kinds of stress and its effects and ways to proactively cope with stress. In this lesson, students will

- Identify helpful and unhelpful stress and stress triggers

- Understand the effects stress can have on our emotional and physical well-being

- Learn the difference between realistic (achievable) and unrealistic (unachievable) expectations on ourselves that may produce stress

- Learn relaxation and coping techniques to reduce stress

- Learn how to choose helpful ways to manage and release stress

Materials Needed

☐ Supplement 9.1 (online download)

☐ Supplements 9.2–9.5 (online download and handout)

☐ Supplement 9.6 (homework handout)

Running Short on Time?

Suggested stopping points: end of Activity B and Closure activity. When continuing the lesson, begin with the Mindfulness-Based Focusing Activity found in the Introduction section and Activity C.

Instructor Reflection

Stress is a normal part of life. It can occur when there are difficulties in our lives; it can also occur when there are good things happening, such as a job promotion, a wedding, and travel. How we perceive it and deal with it, the intensity of the stress we experience, and the kinds of expectations that we place on ourselves can all affect stress level. Helpful stress encourages us to work harder or smarter at tasks, and unhelpful stress slows us down and acts as a barrier to accomplishing tasks. When stress occurs, there are positive ways to manage it. What types of stress have you experienced that affected you in a positive way? What types of stress did you find difficult to manage or affected you negatively? Were your expectations for yourself or the situation realistic or unrealistic? Think about what you did to manage your stress. Was it a temporary fix or did it work for you in the long term?

Review

🕐 2–3 MINS. Review the ideas (listed below) that were discussed in Lesson 8: Solving People Problems.

- Importance of being responsible, respectful, and realistic; taking perspectives; using communication and listening skills; and thinking about choices in conflict management

- Options for resolving conflict

- Four-step problem-solving model to resolve conflict

- Examples and nonexamples of conflict resolution

Sample Script

During our last meeting, we discussed ways to solve problems during conflicts. We talked about being responsible, respectful, and realistic; taking perspectives; and using communication and listening skills during conflict with others. We also talked about ways we can solve problems and make healthy choices in times of conflict. We also discussed the four-step problem-solving model and examples and nonexamples of conflict resolution.

Introduction

🕐 10 MINS. Introduce the lesson. Lead students in a focusing activity. Show Supplement 9.1 as a start-up activity, and discuss how emotions and thoughts may be different in each picture and how different situations may evoke different feelings.

Sample Script

Today, we will talk about stress. Stress can affect our physical and emotional health, so we will learn to distinguish the kind of stress that can help us from the kind of stress that doesn't help us and can even slow us down. We need to know ways to cope with stress so we can stay healthy and be able to do the things we need to do every day.

Mindfulness-Based Focusing Activity

 2 MINS.

Sample Script

Let's practice settling our bodies and focusing our minds. Close your eyes or look at a point on the floor or on your desk. Rest your hands comfortably. Feel your feet on the floor or your hands as they rest. Pay attention to your breathing for three breaths. [Pause for three breaths.] *Today's lesson will talk about ways we can take good care of ourselves. One thing we can do is be kind to ourselves. Sometimes, we focus on the mistakes we make or we feel like we're not good enough. Just like we thought of kind thoughts to send to another person the last time we met, we can send kind thoughts to ourselves. You might say to yourself, "I am wishing myself happiness." Take a moment to think of something kind to say to yourself and say it silently and with a little smile. We'll do this for about a minute.* [Pause for 1 minute.] *Now, let's take two breaths together.* [Pause.] *When you finish letting out the second breath, slowly open your eyes. We are ready to move on to our lesson.*

Introduction (Continued)

 8 MINS.

Sample Script

Let's take a look at these pictures. What do you think these kids are think-ing or feeling? How can you tell? [Take a moment and review each picture in Supplement 9.1 individually.] *Now, look closely. Do you notice anything common in these pictures? Despite the fact that these people may have different feelings and thoughts, all might be feeling stress. Stress is the way your body gets you ready to face challenges and positive situations with attention, energy, and strength. Stress can be caused by feeling worried or anxious, like getting into an argument with a friend. You can also feel stress if something good is happening, like going on a vacation with your family or your team going to the playoffs. It's exciting but also stressful because there's a lot of pressure and plans to make. A little bit of stress can give you the motivation to get things done. This is considered healthy or help-ful stress. But there can be problems when your level of stress feels overwhelming and you have a hard time dealing with it. Think about a volume slider as a stress intensity scale. Sometimes if it's higher than usual, it might suggest a great level of stress. For example, the volume slider may be high when you're feeling sick to your stomach or having a headache when you feel stress. When you're feeling stressed, you may not sleep or eat well or even think or remember things very well. Stress is part of being human, and it can help us or it can get in the way of achieving our goals. In this lesson, we will learn some ways to manage our stress. Keep in mind the pictures we saw. Perhaps put yourself in these situations and imagine where your stress falls on an intensity scale. We will come back to this later in the lesson.*

Key Terms and Definitions

5 MINS. Use Supplement 9.2 as a handout to define the key terms that will be used in this lesson. Then, discuss the concepts in the table (at the bottom of the slide/handout) regarding commons signs of stress that affect different areas of daily functioning.

Sample Script

Here are some important words or ideas that will help us understand stress and what it may look like. We'll define the words and discuss examples to understand what they mean. [After going through the definitions, review the concepts in the table. Then ask about which signs of stress students have experienced.] Here are some signs of stress in four different areas. Can you think of any other signs that can go in this table? Write your responses on your handout so that you can remember all the signs.

Effects of Stress on Body, Emotions, and Behavior

10 MINS. Stress affects your body, emotions, and behavior. Too much stress or feeling stressed for a long period of time has been associated with health problems.

Sample Script

Stress not only affects your thoughts, emotions, mind, and behavior, but it can also affect your health. Sometimes, you may think you are sick because of a headache or because you can't sleep or eat, but stress could be part of the problem. Let's consider a car dashboard. There are different signs and lights that flash when you start the car. Sometimes certain lights stay on to warn you that something is wrong with the car and you have to take it into the mechanic to get it checked out and fixed so you can drive safely. Your body can give you signals kind of like a dashboard. It gives you feelings and sensations to get your attention so you can focus on things that may be affecting you in other ways. On the car, the warning light on the dashboard is telling you to "stop and pay close attention to how the car is driving." If you know about some of the signs of stress and are aware of yourself and how you react to situations, you can start to manage stress in a helpful way. Stress affects people of all ages, and it can interfere with your relationships and your ability to focus and do well in school, at work, or in life.

Activity A: Stress Symptoms and Sample Situations

9 MINS. Use Supplement 9.3 as a handout to facilitate a discussion (in either large or small groups) about the ways in which your body, emotions, thoughts, and behaviors may show stress symptoms. Read the situations aloud, or students can read them in small groups. Discuss the scenarios and how stress may be exhibited in different people and situations. Ask students to discuss/write their reactions under each column to explain how they might feel. Students should be

able to relate to some of the signs of stress and see that other students may feel differently in stressful situations. Consider modifying the situations to make them even more relevant to your students' current situations.

Sample Script

There are some situations that would make almost anyone feel relaxed, and other situations that make many feel stressed. For example, going to the movies with your friends may make you feel good and relaxed. Having to make a speech in front of a large group of people on a topic that you do not enjoy may make you feel stressed. Sometimes, people can feel more stress about a particular situation because of their attitude or the way they are thinking about the situation— like when they have unrealistic or unhealthy expectations of themselves. They may be caught in thinking traps, they might be having a bad day, or they might not feel confident in what they are doing. Sometimes, stress comes as a result of feeling unprepared or uncomfortable in a situation that you have no choice about enduring. At times, stress comes from a feeling of not being able to escape from that situation or from other situations that require more from us than we are able or willing to give in that moment. Some people even experience stress as a physiological response that they can't easily identify, like the stress associated with being in an enclosed space. [Allow time for discussion in either whole group or small groups.]

Stress Triggers and Healthy and Unhealthy Coping Strategies

🕑 20–30 MINS. Identifying healthy ways of coping and the triggers that make us stressed will lead to better awareness and more effective coping strategies.

Sample Script

We can find ways to cope with our stress that are helpful and healthy. We can also figure out the specific triggers that may make us feel stressed. First, we'll start by talking about coping strategies.

Activity B: Healthy and Unhealthy Coping Strategies

🕑 10–15 MINS. Generate specific ways students can relax or find positive solutions when they are experiencing or anticipating stress. Encourage them to share what they have used in the past or might try. Write ideas suggested by the students on the board, even those you may consider unhelpful (e.g., alcohol, drugs, over- or undereating). Be prepared to name ways these methods could cause more trouble in the future (e.g., addiction, poor judgment with decision making, problems in relationships, physical illness, increases in risky behavior, accidents). Be prepared to refer students to appropriate school resources if students need help with these issues for themselves or their friends and family. If students do not mention any solutions, refer to the examples in the table below. The next step will be to evaluate them as helpful/healthy or unhelpful/unhealthy ways to deal with stress and discuss whether the outcomes would be desirable in the long term.

If students bring up alcohol or drug use, emphasize the legalities and health risks involved in both the short and long run, and encourage these students to talk with a trusted adult (e.g., parent, school personnel). Also, consider discussing that these maladaptive coping strategies are temporary ways to escape. They do not address the cause of the stress but only confound the problem.

Sample Script

Let's talk about some of the ways we manage our stress. What are some things you could do when you're feeling stress or when you know you're about to get into a stressful situation? Think of things that you've done when you felt stressed or overwhelmed about a situation. I'll write them up on the board, and we'll discuss them. After we make our list, I would like volunteers to come up and put a plus sign next to the examples that are helpful or healthy, and a minus sign next to the ones that are unhelpful or unhealthy. Healthy ways of coping with stress are helpful in the long term, whereas unhealthy ways are only temporary escapes. In time, they can actually make things worse. We will discuss these choices and talk about their outcomes. Keep in mind that some examples can be both helpful and unhelpful. I want you to also keep in mind that whatever strategies you use, ask yourself these questions, "Will this cause me more stress in the long run?" and "Will this help me feel better or work harder?"

Here are examples of (+) helpful/healthy and (-) unhelpful/unhealthy ways of dealing with stress:

(+) Helpful/healthy ways	(-) Unhelpful/unhealthy ways	Both helpful and unhelpful ways
(+) Talk about the problem with friends or family.	(-) Use alcohol or other drugs.	(+,-) Cry.
(+) Take a walk or hike outside.	(-) Eat a whole cake by yourself.	(+,-) Scream in the bathroom.
(+) Do physical activity (e.g., yoga, martial arts, skateboarding, dancing, swimming).	(-) Sleep all day.	(+/-) Remove yourself from the situation for an extended period of time.
(+) Count to 10 to give yourself time to think.	(-) Get angry at your family or friends.	
(+) See a medical provider to see if there is help available.	(-) Tell yourself that you are the worst person in the world.	
(+) Face the source of your fears (e.g., if having to do a speech, practice beforehand to build comfort).	(-) Procrastinate by playing video games.	
(+) Choose healthy foods.	(-) Distract yourself by going on the computer, surfing the Internet, or chatting with your friends for an amount of time that gets in the way of household or school responsibilities.	

(+) Talk to a friend, a family member, or a clergy member.	(-) Stop exercising.	
(+) Practice deep breathing and meditating.	(-) Chew on pencils, paper, or other objects.	
(+) Draw or make other art work.	(-) Smoke cigarettes.	
(+) Imagine a calm place or resting in a peaceful place in nature.		
(+) Refer to my *Strong Kids* training and think about strategies I learned.		
(+) Engage in a hobby such as reading, crafts, or playing sports.		
(+) Keep a journal.		

Activity C: Personal Triggers and Stress Identification

 10–15 MINS. Use Supplement 9.4 as a handout and have students, in small groups, discuss, role play, and respond to the following questions about their personal stress: 1) What was your body feeling? 2) What thoughts, emotions, and behaviors did you have? 3) What was the level of your emotions on the intensity scale? 4) How did you reframe thinking traps? 5) Did you have realistic expectations and strive for excellence, or did you expect perfection? 6) How did you cope? 7) How did it work? Allow time for students to complete the handout, and then come together for a class discussion. Facilitate a discussion on the pressure that we may put on ourselves when we expect to be perfect at something, and how they might cause stress. Emphasize that it is okay if students do not feel stress or do not know how stress affects their body.

Sample Script

We've talked about stress and how it may affect your body, thoughts, emotions, and behavior, and we've discussed healthy and unhealthy ways to deal with stress. Now, I would like you to get with a partner and discuss stress in your lives, using the worksheet to write down your thoughts. First, make a list of the things or triggers that can lead to stress. Remember, different things can make people feel more or less stressed, and stress can be visualized on a scale of intensity. Sometimes, stress is created by thinking traps, such as black-and-white thinking, or when we expect too much from ourselves or we expect to be perfect at something. There's no right or wrong thing to put on your list. Rank order the items you've listed so that you have an idea of the different things that cause you more or less stress. Then, choose the stressor that you ranked first—the one that stresses you the most. Talk about how you felt and what you did in that situation. Then, in the body diagram, identify and put an X if you know what part of your body felt the stress. Some people may feel their stress in their neck, their back, their jaw, their stomach, or multiple places in their body. Some people may not notice stress in their body. That's okay; everyone is different. Talk about your emotions, thoughts, and behaviors that told you about your stress. Finally, talk about how you coped with your stress in that situation. Afterward, we will talk about our similarities and differences. Last, talk about ways you can prepare for the next time you expect to encounter your stress triggers.

Relaxation Techniques to Manage Stress

🕐 10 MINS. Relaxation techniques can be used to manage stress and help our bodies relax. These techniques to help relieve stress can be done anywhere.

Sample Script

Now that we've talked about stress, let's figure out ways to help our bodies relax, decrease tension, and feel better. We will try a relaxation exercise together. In the future, when you start to feel yourself getting stressed by noticing small symptoms, or if you identify a trigger, you can think back to this exercise. You can do this on your own, in a quiet place, or even when you are doing other things. At the end of the relaxation activity, I would like for you to quietly say something positive about yourself.

Activity D: Relaxation Exercise

🕐 5–10 MINS. Use Supplement 9.5 as a handout to describe a brief relaxation exercise. Relaxation exercises with deep breathing have benefits of improving health, decreasing stress, and improving overall emotional well-being. Two options are provided: abdominal breathing (Option 1) or muscle relaxation (Option 2). Choose one that is most appropriate for your students, and you can use the other option for another time. You may want to dim the lights and play relaxing music during either exercise.

Sample Script

We are going to do some relaxation exercises that include deep breathing or diaphragmatic breathing. This type of breathing helps with improving health by optimizing the immune system; reducing negative stress by reducing the stress hormone cortisol; improving mood, mental focus, and concentration; and boosting overall emotional well-being. The first relaxation exercise is called diaphragmatic breathing [Option 1]/muscle relaxation [Option 2]. We will try to [Option 1] focus on the movement of our stomachs for abdominal breathing or [Option 2] tighten and loosen our muscles for muscle relaxation. Let's get started.

Putting It All Together

🕐 5 MINS. Use the following activity to practice the concepts discussed in this lesson.

Sample Script

Let's practice what we've learned by putting it all together.

Review the concepts from this lesson that are listed below.

- Stress is a normal part of being human and it can be different for everyone.
- Identify common signs of stress.
- Identify how you feel when stressed.
- Identify your stress triggers.
- Identify realistic and unrealistic expectations for yourself.
- Identify helpful and unhelpful ways of reacting to stress.
- Apply relaxation exercise.

Sample Script

Today, we learned about stress and relaxation. Everyone feels stress differently and it varies from situation to situation. A little stress is normal and it can spur you to work harder. If you are super-relaxed and don't care about how things turn out, you may not be motivated to accomplish your goals or things that are challenging. Remember that there are different ways to deal with stress, which can either help or make things worse in the long run. Be careful of strategies that are temporary, because these strategies can trick you in the moment but make things worse in the long term. It can be helpful to make decisions about how you spend your time. Working too much and worrying too much can cause a lot of stress. On the other hand, if you're only dealing with school stuff or working and have no time to hang out with your family or friends or do fun activities, you can feel a lot of stress. Interestingly, doing too many activities that are fun can also cause stress if it causes you to fall behind in your school or work. To help you cope with stress before it becomes overwhelming, you can become more aware of your triggers; how you cope emotionally, mentally, and physically; and how stress management strategies are used. Also, you can use the relaxation exercise to lessen the feeling of stress.

Closure

🕐 2 MINS.   Close the lesson using a brief breathing activity and a reflection on the lesson content.

Sample Script

Let's take a moment to regroup. Close your eyes and rest your hands in your lap. Feel your feet on the floor. Relax the muscles in your body and face. Relax and soften your stomach muscles. Counting to 3, take a deep breath in slowly. Inhale the air down into your lungs. Feel your chest and stomach expand like a balloon. [Pause.] *Now, exhale, counting to 4. Feel your chest and stomach collapse as all the air exits your body.* [Pause.] *Again, inhale deep into your lungs so that your stomach expands* [Pause.] *and exhale.* [Pause.] *Take a moment to think about something you learned today that was important to you and you really liked.*

[Note to instructor: Pause for a moment to allow time for reflection.] *Counting to 3, take one more deep breath in slowly* [Pause.] *and exhale, counting to 4.* [Pause.]

Tips for Transfer Training and Homework

Use the ideas and activities in the following section to practice this lesson's content with your students throughout the week to help reinforce the skills. Also, remember to precorrect, remind, and reinforce concepts from this lesson in activities throughout the school week and to encourage students to use the skills taught in this lesson across settings including home, the bus, and the cafeteria.

Additional Activities

- Here are some suggested books:

  Fighting Invisible Tigers: Stress Management for Teens (Revised and updated 3rd rdition) by Earl Hipp

  Too Stressed to Think? A Teen Guide to Staying Sane When Life Makes You Crazy by Annie Fox and Ruth Kirschner (eBook)

  What to Do When Good Enough Isn't Good Enough: The Real Deal on Perfectionism: A Guide for Kids by Thomas S. Greenspon

- Writing activities

  For older students, instruct them: "For the next four days, if you feel stress, take 15–20 minutes to write down your deepest feelings about an emotional challenge in life (past or current). See what happens if you take a few minutes to write down what is making you stress and then walk away. Think about these questions at the end of writing or at the end of walking away: 1) What are your thoughts and how did you feel? 2) How did you manage your stress? 3) Did it work?"

  For students who enjoy drawing, encourage them to keep a note pad in their backpack. Instruct them: "For one week, draw your thoughts and how you feel. Did you feel stress? How did you cope with your stress?"

Homework Handout

Pass out Supplement 9.6, Letting Go of Stress. Explain that students will write about situations where they felt stressed; they will choose strategies that work for them, plan for an anticipated stressor, and choose a relaxation technique.

Pictures of Stressful Situations

Studying for a test

Bullying

Trying out for a team

Giving a speech in class

Moving

New student in class

Key Terms and Definitions

Stress

A feeling of physical and/or emotional tension or pressure that is often related to being challenged to perform or react outside of your typical range of behaviors (outside of your "comfort zone"), this feeling can happen before, during, or after a difficult or exciting situation.

Example: You can feel stressed, worried, uncomfortable, or overwhelmed when you have too much to do or when you are trying to concentrate on something important and you feel distracted and nervous inside. Stress can also occur when there is uncertainty or if outcomes are unknown.

Excellence

Work diligently to reach goals that are ambitious yet realistic, learning from disappointments and setbacks, and persevering.

Example: You have a goal in mind and know it will take work to accomplish it. You understand that mistakes are part of the process of learning and growing, and you feel good about your effort.

Perfectionism

This is striving for flawlessness or exceptionally high performance standards.

Example: You feel as if you have to do everything right and you are not allowed to make a mistake. You often are concerned about what other people think of you. It may take you a very long time to finish a project because you re-do much of the work; you aren't quite satisfied, even after knowing the product you will hand in will likely get a good grade.

Helpful or healthy stress

This kind of stress helps us work harder to get what we want; it usually doesn't lead to feeling overwhelmed or exhausted.

Example: You may do a better job on your research project if the stress inspires you to prepare well before you have to present it to the class (e.g., healthy competition, positive anticipation of an event, personal goals).

Unhelpful or unhealthy stress

This kind of stress can interfere with accomplishing our goals and makes us feel upset more often than not.

Examples: You continue thinking about the research project so much, you become exceedingly worried to the point you feel sick and take time off, and you don't finish the project (e.g., deadlines that may be very difficult to meet, feeling unprepared, not knowing the outcome of something that may be life changing).

Situational triggers

This is something that can lead to stress.

Example: A particular activity (e.g., giving a speech), place (e.g., being at a family member's house where there is a lot of conflict), person/people (e.g., being with people you don't know

(continued)

or don't like), or personal expectation (e.g., having to do well on a test or you may get a lower grade for the semester). Triggers can vary from person to person and situation to situation. The situation is a source of tension that may heighten/increase your emotions and trigger stress.

Relaxation

This is a feeling of letting go of stress. You can do this by physically loosening tense muscles or finding other healthy ways to deal with the things that are bothering or overwhelming you.

Example: The test was so hard that doing some relaxation breathing was the only way to begin to relieve the tension. Deep breathing and taking a walk in nature are examples of healthy ways to relax.

Realistic/unrealistic expectations

These are expectations you have for yourself that can affect stress. Expectations can be too high (e.g., you expect too much from yourself) or too low (e.g., you expect too little from yourself). Realistic expectations are challenging yet achievable.

Example: Are the expectations you have doable for that situation (realistic), or are the expectations you have too far to reach or obtain (unrealistic), at least in the moment? Unrealistic expectations can add stress if they make you more overwhelmed.

Common signs of stress

Stress can affect your body (physical), how you think (thoughts), how you feel (emotions), and how you behave (behavior). There are different signs or cues that let you know that you are experiencing unhealthy stress. (Discuss the example symptoms in the table below.)

Example: Signs of stress

Thoughts	Emotions	Physical	Behavior
Worrying	Irritability or short temper	Aches and pains	Sleeping too much or too little
Anxious or racing thoughts	Feeling overwhelmed	Rapid heartbeat	Eating too much or too little
Thinking traps	Moodiness	Nausea, fatigue	Nervous habits (nail biting, pacing)
Difficulties concentrating	Unhappiness	Sensitive to sounds and noises	Procrastination

Stress Symptoms and Example Situations

Example situations	Physical (How might your body feel?)	Emotions, thoughts, behaviors (What thoughts, emotions, and behaviors may occur?)	Realistic or unrealistic expectations (Were expectations realistic or unrealistic?)	How stressful might this be for you? (What level of stress would you have?) How might you deal with this stress?
Situation 1 (Mark)				
Situation 2 (Sonia)				
Situation 3 (Jen)				
Situation 4 (José)				

Situation 1 (school example)

Mark forgot that he had a history test today, and he didn't study for it. The teacher passes out the test, and Mark sits and stares at his test. What are some helpful or healthy ways to deal with his stress? What are some unhelpful or unhealthy ways to deal with his stress?

Situation 2 (social example)

Sonia is new to her school and wants to attend the school dance. She hears her classmates talking about the event and who they will be going with. Sonia doesn't know any of her classmates yet. What are some helpful or healthy ways to deal with her stress? What are some unhelpful or unhealthy ways to deal with her stress?

Situation 3 (community example)

Jen is trying out for a play. Her friend tried out for the play last night and said that the director seemed really picky. What are some helpful or healthy ways to deal with her stress? What are some unhelpful or unhealthy ways to deal with her stress?

Situation 4 (home example)

At home, José sees his parents arguing with each other about work and taking care of the house. Sometimes, he even hears them arguing at night when he is in bed. What are some helpful or healthy ways to deal with his stress? What are some unhelpful or unhealthy ways to deal with his stress?

Personal Triggers and Stress Identification

1. Write down the things that cause you stress (triggers). Then, rank order your list. Now, circle the thing that makes you the most stressed.

   _____

   _____

2. Using the diagram below, put an *X* on the areas of your body where you feel stress.

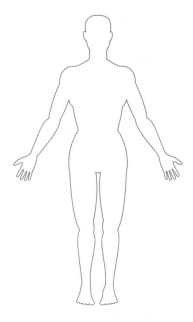

3. What emotions, thoughts, and behaviors did you have in that situation?

   _____

   _____

4. Where was the stress on the intensity scale?

   _____

   _____

5. Were your expectations realistic? Were you striving for excellence or getting caught in perfectionism?

   _____

   _____

6. How did you cope with your stress? Did you reframe thinking traps? Did it work in making your situation better?

   _____

   _____

7. What might you do to plan for the next time you encounter this trigger? What are some ways you could proactively manage your stress or manage it before it gets too intense?

   _____

   _____

Relaxation Techniques

Option 1: Abdominal breathing (optional: play relaxing music)

Sitting comfortably, notice how your body feels at rest. [Pause for 10 seconds.] *We will begin to do a breathing exercise. You have the option to put your hand on your stomach to feel how your body works to move air in and out in a way that can be relaxing. Like this.* [Model putting hand on own stomach.] *Now, while you focus on taking a breath in, let your stomach expand as you inhale. You may imagine filling up a balloon. Watch me.* [Model inhalation with stomach expanding.] *Now, as you let the air out and exhale, let your stomach fall back toward your spine, like this.* [Model exhalation with stomach moving back toward spine.] *You don't need to push the air out with a lot of force. Think of it as a nice, easy, natural cycle of relaxed and comfortable breathing. Try it a couple more times.* [Pause to allow practice.] *To keep a nice easy rhythm, you may want to count to 3 while you inhale, and count to 4 while you exhale. Keep your mind on gently breathing with your counting. Now, let yourself take about six relaxed breaths. Remember: Breathe in by letting your stomach expand out. Then naturally breathe out by letting your stomach come back in. Notice how you begin to relax and calm yourself with this gentle breathing. Enjoy the feeling.*

Option 2: Progressive muscle relaxation

- *Close your eyes. Take a few minutes to breathe in and out in slow, deep breaths.* [Pause for a few breaths.]

- *When you're ready, shift your attention to your right foot. Take a moment to focus on the way it feels.*

- *Slowly tense the muscles in your right foot, squeezing as tight as you can. Hold for a count of 10.* [Pause for 10 brisk counts. You may count aloud or instruct the class to count silently.]

- *Relax your right foot. Focus on the tension flowing away and the way your foot feels as it becomes limp and loose.*

- *Now, shift your attention to your left foot. Tense these muscles, squeezing tightly and hold for 10 counts.* [Pause for 10, brisk counts.] *Then, relax your left foot.*

- *We will focus on contracting and relaxing other muscles in your body. It may take some practice at first, but try not to tense muscles other than those I'm mentioning.*

- *Now focus on* [next body part, following the sequence below and using the language above]:

  1. Right foot
  2. Left foot
  3. Right calf
  4. Left calf
  5. Right thigh
  6. Left thigh

(continued)

7. Hips and buttocks
8. Stomach
9. Chest
10. Back
11. Right arm and hand
12. Left arm and hand
13. Neck and shoulders
14. Face

Now feel the weight of your whole, relaxed body, from the tips of your toes to the top of your head. You are ready to return to your day refreshed and relaxed.

Letting Go of Stress

Name (optional) _____

1. Write down times or situations in which you felt stress.

   _____

   _____

   _____

2. We talked about strategies that can help you deal with stress. Some are listed below. Check off one or two relaxation strategies you think you can try to use, or write in one that has worked for you.

   ☐ Talk to a trusted friend or adult.

   ☐ Exercise or take a walk in nature.

   ☐ Think positively about yourself and the situation; have healthy expectations.

   ☐ Address the situation one step at a time using the problem-solving model.

   ☐ Focus on your breathing and relaxing your muscles.

   ☐ Identify and reframe thinking traps.

   ☐ _____

3. This week when I _____

   (write in stressful situation), I will _____

   (write in relaxation technique).

4. After you have tried using one of the techniques you checked off above, write about how it worked for you. Did it work? What will you do next time in the same situation?

   ☐ It helped!

   _____

   _____

   ☐ I'll try something different next time.

   _____

   _____

LESSON 10

Positive Living

SEL Competencies Addressed in This Lesson

Teacher Notes

_____

_____

_____

_____

_____

_____

_____

_____

Purpose and Objectives

This lesson teaches students how to incorporate positive habits into their day-to-day lives. In this lesson, students will

• Understand the value associated with positive daily choices

• List some typical actions or behaviors that contribute to a healthy and positive lifestyle

• Distinguish between examples and nonexamples of positive life choices

Materials Needed

☐ Supplements 10.1–10.6 (online download and handout)

☐ Supplement 10.7 (homework handout)

Running Short on Time?

Suggested stopping points: end of Activity B and Closure activity.

Instructor Reflection

There is a fundamental relationship between our actions and our emotions. You have probably read somewhere that exercise can boost your mood and that stress can make you sick. There is also research that suggests other behaviors and acts such as gratitude, interacting with nature, and volunteering have powerful and positive impacts on mood and health. Before teaching this lesson, take a few minutes to reflect on experiences in which your behaviors positively influenced your

189

mood, your health, or how you felt. Think about your own immediate highs associated with behaviors like achieving (or exceeding!) goals, with exercising, or with doing something good for someone else. Also, think about the longer-lasting or delayed effects you've found from eating healthily and/or getting a good amount of sleep. During this lesson, you will be encouraging your students to strive for general well-being by cultivating positive living habits through daily choices.

Review

🕐 2–3 MINS.　Review the ideas (listed below) that were discussed in Lesson 9: Letting Go of Stress.

- Stress triggers
- Common stressors
- Healthy coping strategies and setting realistic expectations

Sample Script

During our last meeting, we discussed what stress triggers are and how to recognize some of the signs of stress. We talked about how to set realistic expectations for ourselves so we don't make ourselves so stressed out. We also practiced healthy coping strategies like deep breathing and relaxing our bodies.

Introduction

🕐 3–5 MINS.　Introduce the topic of positive living. Lead students in a focusing activity. Then, discuss the concept of positive living as a way of developing the habit of looking for the healthy and positive choices in all the things we do.

Sample Script

Today, we're going to talk about developing positive habits by looking for the healthy and positive choices in things we do every day. One of the easiest ways to keep a great attitude is to be on the lookout for choices we can make that lead us to feel more positive in lots of different ways.

Mindfulness-Based Focusing Activity

🕐 2 MINS.　### Sample Script

Before we begin, let's practice settling our bodies and focusing our minds. Close your eyes or leave your eyes open, looking at a point on the floor or on your desk. Rest your hands comfortably. Feel your feet on the floor. Notice your breathing, air going in through your nose and out through your mouth. [Pause for three breaths.] Now, picture in your mind a small tree or a flower waving in the breeze. Allow your upper body to slowly sway back and forth like the tree or the flower in the wind. Relax your body and notice what your body feels like when it's moving. Move as slowly and as little as you want to. You may notice that you have thoughts while you are swaying. That's okay. When you notice yourself thinking about something else, just bring your attention back to the feelings in your body as you sway. I'll tell you when to stop in about a minute. You can also stop when you are ready. [Pause to allow 1 minute of practice.] Let's stop swaying and take two breaths together. [Pause.] When you finish letting out the second breath, slowly open your eyes. We are ready to move on to our lesson.

Key Terms and Definitions

5 MINS. Use Supplement 10.1 as a handout to define the key terms that will be used in the lesson.

Sample Script

Here are some important terms that will help us understand the role of positive thinking and living. We'll define the words and discuss examples to understand what they mean.

What We Do Influences How We Feel

12 MINS. Things we do physically in our daily lives can influence our emotions, thoughts, and attitudes. Convey the following ideas:

- It is good to develop healthy habits related to things that have positive impact on our lives.

- Healthy habits are when we regularly do things that are good for us. This means we do them with enough frequency, effort, and attention to have a positive influence on our lives without it feeling like a burden or a stress to us. Even good things can be overdone.

- A positive lifestyle includes cultivating a positive attitude in all of life's daily activities: thinking, eating, playing, working, and interacting with others.

Sample Script

We can usually make choices in the things we do, like eating, playing, working, and being with other people, that can support a positive lifestyle and a positive attitude. Remember that in Lesson 8, Solving People Problems, we talked about the importance of attitude and how it can affect our interactions with others? Well, it can be the other way around, too. Your actions can affect how you think and feel. Positive actions can lead us to feel more energized, motivated, joyful, and connected to others. So let's talk about developing healthy habits, which means doing certain things with balance and moderation, just enough for them to help you, not too much or too little.

Activity A: Activities that Make Me Feel Good, Good About Myself, or Happy

🕒 10 MINS. Use Supplement 10.2 as a handout to facilitate a discussion for this activity. This supplement lists example activities. Encourage your students to provide additional examples. Use a white board or some other means of documentation to record students' responses in a way that everyone can see them. As you write, see if you can organize the students' suggestions into the four categories noted in Supplement 10.3: physical health, emotional and mental health, community connections, and family and social connections.

Sample Script

Let's take a look at some examples of activities we can do that can help us live a healthy life. We'll also make a list of our own examples. Can anyone think of examples of doing things that make you feel positive while you're doing them or maybe after you've done them?

How Often Is Too Often?

🕒 12 MINS. Continue to use Supplement 10.2 to discuss how some activities and actions can improve emotional and physical well-being in the short term, whereas some activities are great as positive and healthy habits for frequent, long-term use. Use the list of suggestions that the students provided in order to compare activities. Emphasize that even though certain activities may feel good in the short term (eating ice cream/treats, playing video games, using social media, talking on the phone, watching TV/movies, reading comic books), they should probably be sought out less frequently than activities that have longer-lasting positive boosts when those choices exist.

Sample Script

Let's think about some of these activities and actions that we've listed here. I decided to put them into different groups. For now, I want to make sure that we focus on the activities and actions that can develop into the kind of habits that make us healthier, stronger, kinder, or smarter in some way every time we do them. Now, we are going to identify activities in two ways: 1) things we enjoy because they make us feel good right away, but not necessarily for a long time; and 2) things that help us to become better and better every time we do them.

Activity B: How Often Should I Do This?

🕒 10 MINS. Divide the students into groups and use the activities that were generated by the students and recorded (or other activities of your own selection) for this activity. Ask students to decide whether the activity has more long-term or short-term impact. Ask students to decide if the activity should be a frequent or an occasional habit. Ask questions such as, "What could happen if we do this too much or not enough?" and "Is this something that should become a frequent habit or just an occasional activity?"

Sample Script

I'm going to give each of your groups the name of an activity, and I'd like you to work in your group to decide whether you think that activity should be a frequent habit—meaning something we do regularly—or just an occasional activity, and why.

Areas of Life that We Can Focus On

🕐 30 MINS. Sometimes, small adjustments in only one or two important areas of life can influence other parts of our lives.

Sample Script

Often, it only takes making small changes to make a big difference in our lives. Let's talk about some things we can do that can have a powerful impact.

Activity C: Healthy Habits

🕐 10 MINS. Use Supplement 10.3 as a handout along with the list your students created and/or the list provided below. Discuss the examples and suggestions provided in the different life areas that can influence general well-being.

- Eating healthy foods in the right amounts at the right times and for the right reasons

- Exercising regularly, but not too much

- Spending time in the outdoors, either doing activities or appreciating nature

- Helping others who are in need

- Being polite to others

- Helping around the house

- Engaging in quiet time/down time/meditation

- Getting enough sleep each night

- Looking for reasons to be grateful

- Taking responsibility for things that you should (stepping up)

Sample Script

Let's look at our list again and see if there is anything we've forgotten. [Use the list above to augment your list if necessary.] *Remember how I broke it into four categories.* [If you haven't already, conduct an activity to label the items on your list into the four categories: physical health, emotional and

mental health, community connections, and family and social connections.]
Let's talk about what kinds of healthy habits we expect to see in each of these areas.

Activity D: Seeing Healthy Choices Every Day

 10 MINS.   Use Supplements 10.4 and 10.5 as handouts (weekday and weekend routines), and encourage students to think about what they *routinely* do in any given day. Encourage students to look for opportunities to develop and support healthy choices in their day-to-day activities by incorporating healthy habits.

Choose one of the following options to conduct the next activity:

- Option 1: Divide your class into discussion groups in which individual students interview each other on different areas of their day using the questions provided or other questions that they improvise.

- Option 2: Lead the whole class through steps by asking the questions provided and/or by supplementing with additional questions to eliminate yes/no type answers; for example, "Do you have a choice about this?" "How would you change this?" "What specifically do you do in this area?"

- Option 3: Extract a subset of questions from across the day and collect "data" on the general habits of your class.

Sample Script

Now, let's look at the activities we do during the week and on the weekends. We'll use these examples to help us think of things we can do in our own lives.

Activity E: Helping Marcella Improve Her Day

 10 MINS.   Use Supplement 10.6 as a handout to work on the scenario as a class or by breaking the class into groups. Read the Scenario Script to introduce the scene. Students will examine the character's daily routine and make suggestions for changes that can be made toward healthy habits.

Sample Script

Let's practice looking at another student's daily routine to see if we have any ideas for how Marcella Llewelyn can have healthy habits.

Scenario Script

Marcella noticed that she didn't always feel great. She wasn't sick, but some days it took a lot of work for her to find reasons to be happy. She wasn't sure exactly what to do, so she decided to look for small things to change in her life every day. Can you help identify some of the things Marcella can change that might have a long-term positive effect on her life and that could help her feel more energized and motivated? Here's a hint: It may be best to skip some stages and return to them when you know more information about her day.

Putting It All Together

🕒 5-10 MINS. Use the following activity to practice the concepts discussed in this lesson.

Sample Script

Let's practice what we've learned by putting it all together.

Use the Supplement 10.3 handout again. Using the questions in the Sample Script, call on students to discuss the main ideas that were reviewed in this lesson.

Sample Script

We are going to review some of the main ideas discussed in today's lesson. Raise your hand if you know some of these ideas.

- *What is healthy or positive living about?*
- *What are some parts of healthy living?*
- *How can we feel better about ourselves?*

Closure

🕒 2 MINS. Close the lesson using a brief breathing activity and a reflection on the lesson content. At the end, prompt students to bring a photo of themselves at a younger age.

Sample Script

Let's take a moment to regroup. Close your eyes. Feel your feet on the floor. Counting to 3, take a breath in slowly. Inhale [Pause.] and exhale, counting to 4. [Pause.] One more time, inhale [Pause.] and exhale. [Pause.] Take a moment to think about something you learned today that was important to you and you really liked. [Note to instructor: Pause for a moment to allow time for reflection.] Counting to 3, take one more deep breath in slowly [Pause.] and exhale, counting to 4. [Pause.]

For next week's lesson (Lesson 11: Creating Strong and SMART Goals), one of the activities requires you to bring a picture of yourself at a younger age. It can be any age, but at least 2 years ago. If you don't have a picture of yourself, you can draw a picture of yourself at a younger age. Bring the picture to class for our next lesson. We will have a fun activity with it.

Tips for Transfer Training and Homework

Use the ideas and activities in the following section to practice this lesson's content with your students at other times during the day. Also, remember to precorrect, remind, and reinforce concepts from this lesson in activities throughout the school week and to encourage students to use the skills taught in this lesson across settings including home, the bus, and the cafeteria.

Additional Activities

- Encourage students to think about healthy choices every day by engaging in an activity called "Healthy Idea for the Day." Draw one of the healthy ideas from this lesson from a bag or box in which you've placed all the good ideas. Make whatever you pick into the healthy idea for the day. For example, if on Monday you select "Being Polite to Others," your students should look for opportunities to be polite that day, and so forth. Keep a visible log that tracks the activity for each day so that it can serve as a prompt during the day's other events.

- When students experience a moment of success after significant effort or difficult choices, point out the connection between the choices they made previously and the successes they are enjoying currently.

- When students demonstrate positive living behaviors such as biking to school, exercising, or eating healthy snacks, take a quiet moment to connect the dots to this lesson for the student.

Homework Handout

Pass out Supplement 10.7 and review the instructions. Explain that students will keep a journal for a week and look for situations that present choices. Encourage them to keep a record of when they deliberately make a choice because they believe it is the best choice for a positive lifestyle and attitude.

Key Terms and Definitions

Habit

A usual way of behaving, this is something that a person does often in a regular and repeated way.

Example: David makes a habit of calling his grandmother every Sunday night before bedtime.

Moderation

Choosing to avoid too much or too little of any one thing, behavior, or activity; and seeking balance in behaviors and actions is moderation.

Example: Even though Marcella really enjoys long-distance running, she knows that it's best not to run long distances every day because her body needs time to rest and repair after that level of activity.

Choice

This is the act of making a decision if there is more than one option from which to select.

Example: Ahmed has an hour between dinner and bedtime and he wants a good night's sleep. He decides to read a book instead of eating sweets or playing video games.

Feeling Good Activities

Physical activity

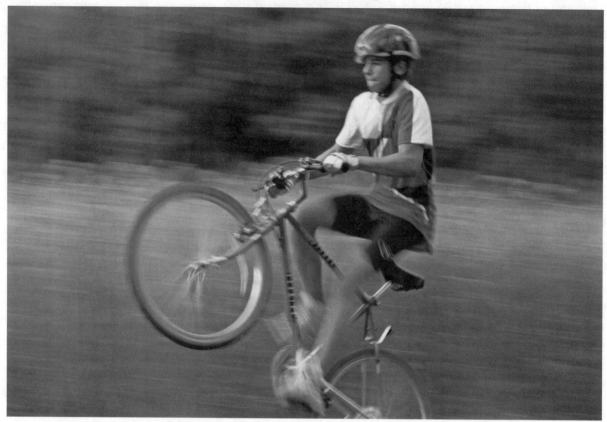

Swimming, running, riding a bike, hiking, skiing, skateboarding; playing football, soccer, baseball, hockey, volleyball; doing yoga

(continued)

Developing skills you enjoy

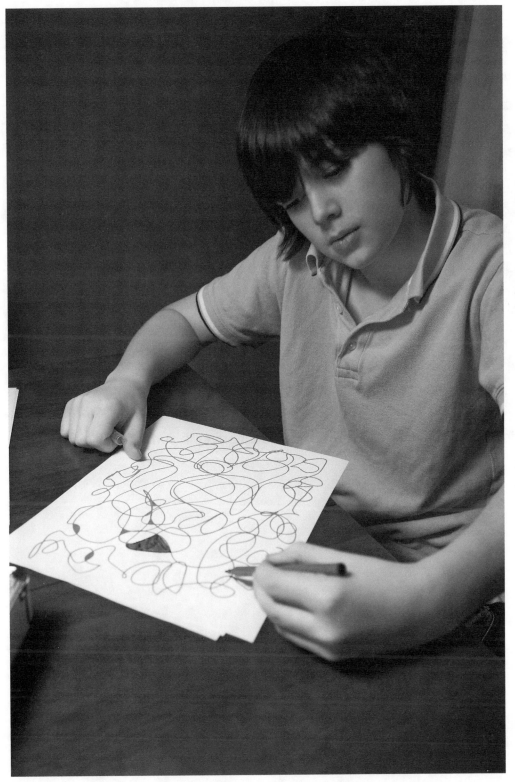

Cooking, sewing, drawing, playing an instrument

(continued)

Spending time outdoors

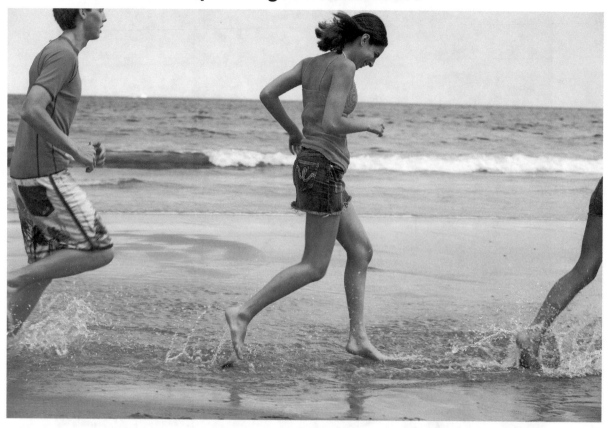

Gardening, hiking, going to the beach, vacationing in summer, enjoying spring break

(continued)

New or rare things

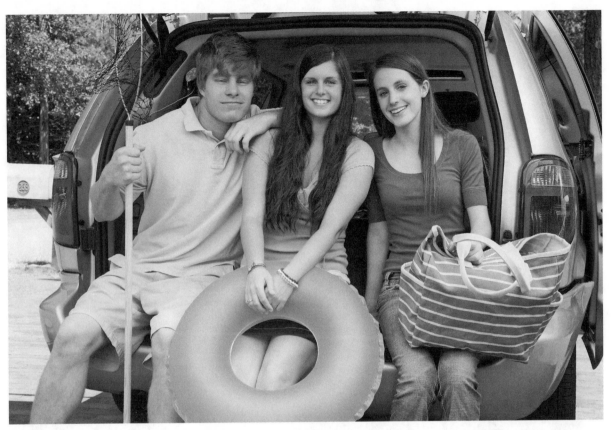

Traveling, going to see live theater

(continued)

Friends and family time

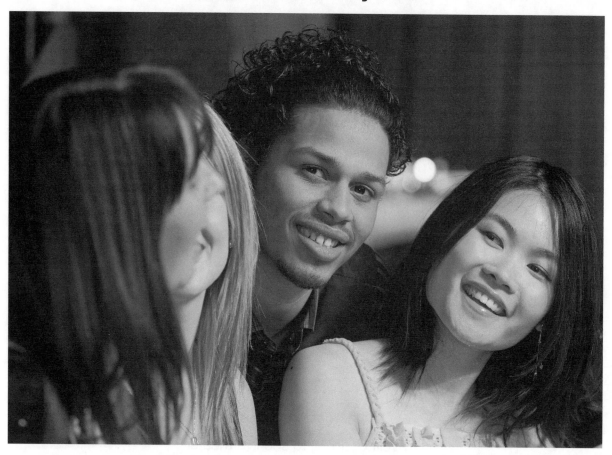

Helping parent/guardian around the house, spending time with a pet, visiting grandparent(s), volunteering, hanging out with a group of friends, hanging out with one special friend

(continued)

Recreation

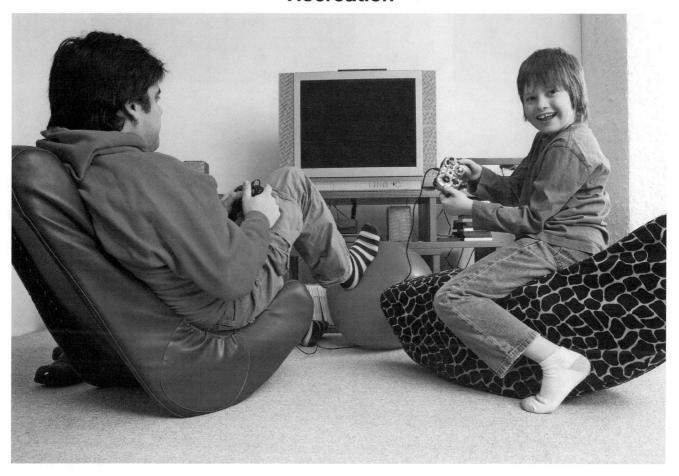

Watching a good movie, reading a good book, singing, learning skills you enjoy, listening to music, playing with friends, watching a comedy, playing video games

(continued)

Certain tastes and smells

Smelling flowers, tasting foods you enjoy

(continued)

Quiet time/time to rest your brain

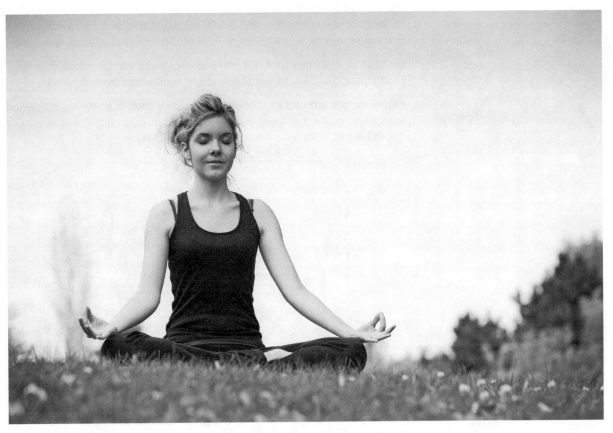

Resting, going to a place of worship, spending time alone, taking time to meditate or rest your brain

Healthy Habits

Physical health	Make healthy meal choices every day and eat treats responsibly. Eat lots of fruits and vegetables, and avoid sugary, fatty, and processed foods. Eat when you're actually hungry, and stop when your body tells you to.

Engage in activities that get you moving every day to make sure you are using your muscles to get them strong and keep them that way.

Get the right amount of sleep to allow your muscles to rest; adolescents should be getting at least 9.5 hours of sleep each night. For example, go to bed at 8:30 p.m. and wake up at 6:00 a.m.

From U.S. Department of Agriculture. (2016). *Choose my plate.* Retrieved from www.choosemyplate.gov.

Emotional and mental health	Spend some time outdoors.

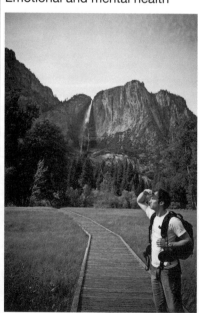

Make sure you get fresh air and an opportunity to step away from screens (computer and TV) and books (this could be combined with exercise).

Find time to enjoy silence and reframe thinking traps (this could be combined with your time outdoors).

Make goals: Learn how to do new things or get better at things.

Be optimistic: Expect good outcomes, and look for ways to ensure good outcomes when you can.

Refrain from comparing yourself to other people. Find reasons to be grateful for what you have.

(continued)

Community connections	Help other people when you can. Volunteer and do your part to play a role in something larger than yourself.
Family and social connections	Maintain healthy relationships. Interact positively and pleasantly with friends and family and people in your community (this can be combined with helping other people when you can). Refrain from gossip or talking about other people—either in person, on the phone, in texts, or online. Think about what other people need out of a situation as well as what you need out of a situation.

Weekday Habits and Routines

Time/activity	Habits and routines (PH, physical health; MH, mental health; CC, community connections; SC, school connections; FC, family connections)
Waking up and breakfast	Do you have enough time to eat a healthy meal and brush your teeth? (PH) Do you wake up easily, or is waking up on time a big struggle for you? (MH)
Getting to school	If you travel with others to school, are you kind and attentive? (CC) Do you get to school and to your classes on time? (SC)
Morning at school	Are you polite to your teachers and friends? (SC) Do you follow the rules? (SC) Are you able to pay attention? (SC)
Lunchtime	Do you make healthy meal choices? (PH) Do you eat only as much as you need? (PH) Do you chew with your mouth closed/finish chewing before talking? (CC) Do you eat at a thoughtful pace? (PH)
Afternoon at school	Do you pay attention to what the teacher says and follow directions? (SC) Do you ask questions if you don't understand? (SC) Do you complete your assignments? (SC) Do you help others when helping others is allowed? (CC/SC)
Afternoon/after school	Do you make it on time to meet your ride? (CC) Do you engage in any after-school activities that are healthy for your body and mind? (PH/MH) Do you make time for your homework/ask for help when you need it? (SC)
Evening/dinner	Do you help with dinner preparations and cleanup? (FC) Do you eat good portions and make healthy choices? (PH)
Bedtime	Do you make sure you do all of the things you need to do to get ready for bed without resisting or waiting to be told? (FC) Do you get to bed at the right time? (PH)

Weekend Habits and Routines

Time/activity	Habits and routines (PH, physical health; FC, family connections; CC, community connections; SC, school connections; MH, mental health)
Waking up and breakfast	Do you wake up at a good time so that you don't sleep in for more than 2 hours longer than during a school day? (FC)
	Do you eat a healthy breakfast and clean up after yourself? (PH)
Morning activities and events	Do you do chores around your house without being told? (FC)
	Do you do things in your community when you can? (CC)
Lunchtime	Do you eat a healthy lunch and clean up after yourself? (PH)
Afternoon activities and events	Do you find ways to get outdoors that can be helpful to your family or community? (PH/CC)
	Do you look for school assignments that may require you to make a trip to a store with your parents or to your local library so you can be prepared for your school days? (SC)
Events before dinner and evening activities	Do you get clean and calm before dinner? (FC)
	Do you offer to help or offer healthy suggestions for meals that you will eat? (FC/PH)
	Do you avoid playing video games and doing other online activities right before bedtime so you can sleep better?

Example Situation:
Helping Marcella Make Healthy Choices

Typical routine	What would you change and why?
Wake-up time: Marcella typically wakes up at 6:45 a.m.	
Getting dressed in the morning: Marcella typically takes a long time—sometimes more than 20 minutes—to find something to wear.	
Eating breakfast: Marcella usually eats a toaster pastry while watching a cartoon.	
Leaving the house: Marcella always leaves the house in a hurry and feels like she's forgetting something.	
On the way to school: Marcella takes the 7:30 a.m. bus and is usually sleepy. She doesn't talk to anyone and doesn't pay much attention to the other people on the bus.	
At school: Marcella tries really hard to listen to the teachers.	
At lunchtime: Marcella is very hungry by lunch, so she chooses lots of different food from the cafeteria and eats a lot.	
After lunch: Marcella talks with her friends before class.	
At home: Marcella goes straight to the fridge, finds a snack, and watches TV until someone tells her to stop.	
Before bed: Marcella is usually doing homework until bedtime and feels very stressed out as she's trying to fall asleep.	

What Did You Do
Toward Positive Living This Week?

Name (optional) _____

	Monday	Tuesday	Wednesday	Thursday	Friday	Saturday	Sunday
Morning at home							
Morning before lunch							
Lunchtime							
Afternoon activity							
Evening before dinner							
Dinnertime							
Bedtime							

LESSON 11

Creating Strong and SMART Goals

SEL Competencies Addressed in This Lesson

Responsible decision making

Self-awareness

Self-management

Relationship skills

Social awareness

Teacher Notes

_____

_____

_____

_____

_____

_____

_____

_____

Purpose and Objectives

This lesson teaches students the skill of goal setting and increasing positive activity as a means to a healthy life. In this lesson, students will

- Understand the importance of increasing and maintaining healthy activities

- Increase awareness of their own strengths and limitations

- Set SMART goals

- Monitor progress toward goals

- Develop perseverance in the goal attainment process

Materials Needed

☐ Supplement 11.1 (photographs or drawn pictures of each student at a younger age [2+ years ago])

☐ Supplements 11.2–11.3 (online download and handout)

☐ Supplements 11.4–11.6 (online download)

☐ Supplement 11.7 (homework handout)

☐ Green, red, and yellow colored pencils for Healthy Living Domains activity

Running Short on Time?

Suggested stopping points: end of Activity C and Closure activity.

Instructor Reflection

The Creating Strong and SMART Goals lesson teaches students to set goals to achieve a healthier, more resilient life. To prepare for this lesson, reflect on the times in your life that you have made personal goals (e.g., New Year's resolutions) or professional goals (e.g., getting a specialized license). Reflect on why you created the goals, and reflect on your progress toward these goals. If you have achieved your goals, what do you think contributed to your success? If you haven't achieved your goals yet, have you achieved part of the goal and what obstacles have you encountered so far? Now, consider an area in your life for which you could create a new goal or modify an existing goal. Do you see a way the strategies within this lesson can assist you in creating that goal and a plan for monitoring your progress?

Review

🕒 2–5 MINS. Review the ideas listed below that were discussed in Lesson 10: Positive Living.

- Finding ways to make healthy choices to improve positive living

- Making choices such as eating, playing, working, and being with people who love us, which can support a positive lifestyle and a positive attitude

- Doing things to help us feel better about ourselves

Sample Script

During our last meeting, we talked about how the things we do can influence the way we feel. We talked about how making healthy choices in all the things we do, like eating, playing, working, and being with other people who support us, can help us live a healthy lifestyle and have a positive attitude. We also talked about developing healthy habits in our everyday activities.

Introduction

🕒 10 MINS. Introduce the lesson. Lead students in a focusing activity. Introduce the concept of goal setting and creating an action plan to meet goals.

Sample Script

Today we will learn how to set goals and accomplish them. Setting and accomplishing goals is something that everyone can do to grow and to change things in our lives for the better. Doing this successfully is called goal attainment. Together, we will set goals for ourselves and create an action plan to make them happen.

Mindfulness-Based Focusing Activity

 2 MINS.

Sample Script

Let's begin with an activity to settle our bodies and practice focusing our minds. Close your eyes or look at a point in front of you on the floor or on your desk. Rest your hands comfortably on your desk or in your lap. Feel your feet on the floor or your hands as they rest. First, pay attention to your breathing for three breaths. [Pause.] Today, we will imagine the feelings we have when we're successful at something. Think of something you've done that made you feel good about yourself. [Pause.] Did you feel happy, proud, excited, or content? [Pause.] What does this emotion feel like right now? [Pause.] What are the thoughts that go with your feeling of success? Do you think, "I did it!"? Whatever emotion you experience, and however your body feels, is okay. Just notice those feelings. [Pause for about 30 seconds to allow practice.] Now, imagine yourself being successful at doing something new or reaching a goal. Notice what your body feels, the emotions you have, and your thoughts. [Pause for about 30 seconds to allow practice.] Now, let's take two breaths together. [Pause.] When you finish letting out the second breath, slowly open your eyes. We are ready to move on to our lesson.

Optional Activity: Your Younger Self

 5 MINS.

Start students on the Supplement 11.1 activity. This activity requires students to obtain a picture of themselves at a younger age. Some students might forget and others might not have a copy to bring in to class. If this is the case, students can close their eyes and imagine themselves, draw a picture, or list words to help them describe themselves as they were at this younger age (at least 2 years younger). As an alternative or supplement to the picture, you can have students bring in objects or things that were important to them at a younger age.

Sample Script

Now, take out your picture of yourself at a younger age and look at it. What were you like then? What were your thoughts like? How did you behave? How did you feel? How are you different today from the time when the picture was taken? Share your picture with someone sitting next to you. Each of you, take 1 minute to talk about how you were then and how you are different now. [Pause. Then, after the partner activity, allow some sharing out to the large group. Guide the discussion to focus on ways the students may have changed due to intentional and healthy changes in daily behaviors; e.g., increase in skills.] Some changes are physical and are caused by getting older. But other changes are caused by things we learn and things we choose to do from day to day. You might be better at some things than you were last year. How did that happen? Probably not by chance! We change because of what we learn, feel, think, and do every day. When you think about yourself in the _____ grade [name a grade or two above the students], you probably don't see yourself exactly the same way as you are today. How about now—do you see yourself any differently? Are there things about yourself that you are able to change—that will help you grow stronger, healthier, or smarter? What can you do today to be the person you want to be in [name the higher grade]? *Next week? Next year? That's what we're going to talk about today.*

Key Terms and Definitions

 5 MINS.　Use Supplement 11.2 as a handout to define the key terms that will be used in this lesson.

Sample Script

Here are some important terms that will help us understand healthy living and goal setting. We'll define the words and discuss examples to understand what they mean.

Healthy Living Domains

 15 MINS.　Use Supplement 11.3 as a handout to show students that there are many areas in our lives in which we can develop healthy habits. Students will need red, green, and yellow colored pencils.

Sample Script

These circles represent the areas of our lives where we can be healthy. We are going to talk in more detail about what we're doing in these areas.

Activity A: Healthy Living Domains

 5 MINS.　Continue with the Supplement 11.3 handout. Ask students to think about each domain and the activities they do for each and to record them on their worksheets. Examples may include getting enough sleep each night (physical health), eating healthy foods (physical health), getting outside in nature (emotional health), reframing thinking traps (emotional health), doing volunteer work (family and community), helping out a brother or sister (family and community), being present or attentive in class (school), and completing their homework (school).

Sample Script

We all have things we focus on a lot, and we all have other things we wish we paid more attention to. Here's an activity that will help us figure out the areas in our life where we focus most of our attention and the areas that could use more. Take out your Healthy Living Domains worksheet and fill in the blanks with what you do now to keep healthy in each domain. For example, in the physical health area, if you eat well and get enough sleep, you can put those in that area. If you help your brother or sister, you can put those activities in the family and community area. If you come to class prepared, you can put that in the school area. If you are keeping a journal, you can put that in the emotional health area, and if you volunteer in the community, you can put that in the family and community area. Then, use green to color the area with the most activities or those that are the easiest for you to do. Use yellow to color two areas you do some things in but you would like to do more. Last, use red to color the area with no activities or if you have things you'd like to start working on.

Relationships Among Healthy Living Domains

🕒 5 MINS.   Each healthy living domain has a relationship with the others. What we do in one domain affects the other domains.

Activity B: Interactions Among Healthy Living Domains

🕒 5 MINS.   Use the example in the Sample Script below, or another example to illustrate how making an improvement in one area of your life can affect other areas. The example in the script illustrates how changes in a physical domain can lead to changes within the school and emotional domains.

Sample Script

Did you know that if we make healthy choices in one area, they can affect other areas of your life too? Most times, what we do to improve one area of our life can affect other areas of our life. That's a bonus! Suppose Michael wants to improve his physical strength. He decides he wants to try out for the basketball team at school. If he achieved his goal by trying out, doing his best, and making the team, how could some of the other circles be affected?

Goal Setting: Introduction

🕒 5 MINS.   Goal setting is important to achieve what we want in life. There are ways to set goals that work well for us and other ways that do not work well.

Sample Script

Setting goals is important to achieve what we want in our lives, and the way we set our goals can affect whether or not we achieve them. We're going to talk about some examples of successful goal setting and other times where it did not go so well.

Activity C: Examples and Nonexamples of Goal Setting

🕒 5 MINS.   Use Supplement 11.4 and the example from Activity B (Michael) and discuss examples and nonexamples of goal setting and attainment.

Sample Script

Now let's talk about examples of goal setting—how the goal was set and how it went. Remember Michael? He wanted to improve his physical strength and try out for the basketball team. How do you think he got from the point where he was just thinking about the idea of physical strength to actually making it onto the team? How do you think he set his goal? Let's discuss what may have worked for him and what may not have worked for him.

Setting Specific, Measurable, Attainable, Relevant, and Timely (SMART) Goals

10 MINS. Use Supplement 11.5 to introduce students to SMART goals. Setting SMART goals is a descriptive approach designed to help people set more attainable goals.

Sample Script

Many people struggle to achieve their goals because they do not set SMART goals. Many people make the mistake of setting goals that are too broad or vague and unrealistic or unattainable. Not us! Today, we will learn to create SMART goals. SMART goals are specific, measurable, attainable, relevant, and timely objectives to help us achieve what we want. Let's talk more about what SMART stands for.

Activity D: Steps to Setting and Attaining Goals

5 MINS. Use Supplement 11.6 as a handout to review the four steps to setting and attaining goals. Use the examples provided below, modify them to fit the needs and interests of your students, or ask students to generate their own examples to individualize the content. As part of the discussion, introduce and dissect goals that do not meet the SMART criteria, such as having prettier eyes or making someone like you.

Sample Script

1. *Identify your goal area. Refer to your Healthy Living Domains worksheet [Supplement 11.3], and review the area you colored red. Identify a specific action in that area for which you would like to create a SMART goal. For example, if your physical area is colored red, and you are often tired, you may choose to create a goal to get better sleep.*

2. *Create a SMART goal. Create a goal that is specific, measurable, attainable, relevant, and timely. Using my example from before, I might create this goal: "By the end of this month, I will get at least 8–9 hours of sleep each night, at least 5 days a week."*

3. *Implement your plan. Write out a calendar. Tell someone you trust about your plan of action; it may turn out that someone you tell can play a role in helping you to get to your goal. Perhaps a friend has a similar goal and you can support one another. Perhaps your parents can help you implement your plan. Also, think about what could get in the way of your goal. Try to address*

possible obstacles early. Using my example, if I had a friend who stays late playing video games, I might need to ask him or her to leave earlier so I could get to sleep earlier.

4. *Check your progress. Is your plan working? Do you need to make changes? Are there other goals you want to start working on? Maybe you have identified obstacles that are getting in your way that you need to address. Maybe you feel so much better that you decide to try to get 8–9 hours of sleep every night. It can help to keep notes about our progress so we can see if our plan is working. With enough practice, many goals can become healthy life habits; we may not need to think about them quite so much.*

If you find you're not making progress toward your goal, the important thing is to not give up! It takes energy and effort to change old habits and behaviors, so if this is a worthy goal to strive for, we need to remember to have patience with ourselves. We can't expect to change overnight. We all face setbacks or make mistakes when striving toward new goals. Mistakes and setbacks can feel frustrating and make us feel like quitting. Actually, we can reframe this as thinking that these are opportunities to learn and grow. When you see you aren't making progress toward your goal, you can once again be a scientist and look for evidence that will help you figure out what went wrong. You can ask yourself: Was my goal a SMART goal? Maybe it was not specific. Maybe it wasn't attainable or it was unrealistic. Or, did something unexpected get in the way? If so, what can I do to avoid this next time? Are there things I can do or people I can talk to who can help me? How can I change my plan and try again?

Putting It All Together

 10 MINS. Use the following activity to practice the concepts discussed in this lesson. In small groups or individually, ask students to use their Healthy Living Domains worksheet (Supplement 11.3) to identify a goal area and generate their own SMART goals and action plan toward goal attainment. As necessary, prompt students through the steps. After a few minutes, ask if any students want to share their goals. If students do not want to share, that is okay. Continue sharing examples of steps and the overall process. Provide positive feedback for students who shared examples. Emphasize that goal setting and increasing positive activities are important as a means to a healthy life.

• Define SMART goals, goal setting, and goal attainment.

• List the steps to goal attainment.

Sample Script

Let's practice what we've learned by putting it all together. Today, we learned more about the activities we do and about how we might want to change them to live happier, healthier lives and be smarter. We learned to create SMART goals

*and learned a skill called goal attainment. I want you all to get really good at set-
ting and meeting goals so that it feels natural and easy. Let's practice by creating
our own SMART goals and action plans.*

Closure

🕐 2 MINS.   Close the lesson using a brief breathing activity and a reflection on the lesson
content.

Sample Script

*Let's take a moment to regroup. Close your eyes and rest your hands in your lap.
Feel your feet on the floor. Relax the muscles in your body and face. Relax and
soften your stomach muscles. Counting to 3, take a breath in slowly. Inhale the
air down into your lungs. Feel your chest and stomach expand like a balloon.*
[Pause.] *Now, exhale, counting to 4. Feel your chest and stomach collapse as all
the air exits your body.* [Pause.] *Again, inhale deep into your lungs so that your
stomach expands* [Pause.] *and exhale.* [Pause.] *Take a moment to think about
something you learned today that was important to you or you really liked.* [Note
to instructor: Pause for a moment to allow time for reflection.] *Counting to 3,
take one more deep breath in slowly* [Pause.] *and exhale, counting to 4.* [Pause.]

Tips for Transfer Training and Homework

Use the ideas and activities in the following section to practice this lesson's
content with your students at other times during the day. Also, remember
to precorrect, remind, and reinforce concepts from this lesson in activities
throughout the school week and to encourage students to use the skills taught
in this lesson across settings including home, the bus, the cafeteria, and the
community.

Additional Activities

- Letter: Ask students to write a letter to themselves with a SMART goal and
  the reasons why they made the goal. Have students hand them in. Then, at the
  end of the *Strong Kids* program (or at some later date as appropriate), return
  the letters to students and have them reevaluate their plans.

- Strength inventories: Hand out a sheet of paper with all the students' names
  on it to each child, so that each child has a list of all the students in their class.
  Ask students to write down a strength that they sincerely associate with each
  student in the class. We recommend that students record their names at the
  top of their lists to help instructors monitor for sarcastic or spiteful statements. When students are finished with their lists, collect and review the

statements, inventory the strengths, and share them so that students can see themselves and their strengths in a new way. We recommend reviewing what students have written about their peers before handing the comments back to the students.

- Resilience: Have students read books or watch videos that highlight perseverance and grit. Include famous people who showed determination in the face of challenges (e.g., Malala Yousafzai).

Homework Handout

Pass out Supplement 11.7, Personal Goal Organizer. Explain to students that they are to complete a personal goal organizer for home, school, and free time. Students will evaluate their SMART goals.

Your Younger Self

Key Terms and Definitions

Goals

These are specific objectives that you want to achieve.

Example: Goals can be short term, like completing an assignment, and they can be long term, like creating a new healthy living routine.

Goal setting

This is defining a goal and creating a plan of action to achieve that goal.

Example: I'd like to start going to bed 45 minutes earlier so I can get more sleep and feel better the next day. I'll start by going to bed 15 minutes earlier this week. Next week, I'll go to bed 30 minutes earlier.

Goal attainment

This is completing your action plan and achieving your goal. Goal attainment helps us feel more confident in our skills and abilities and helps us get what we want out of our lives.

Example: I am now going to bed 45 minutes earlier than I used to. I can tell it's a little easier to get up in the morning, and I'm focusing a little better during the day.

Healthy Living Domains

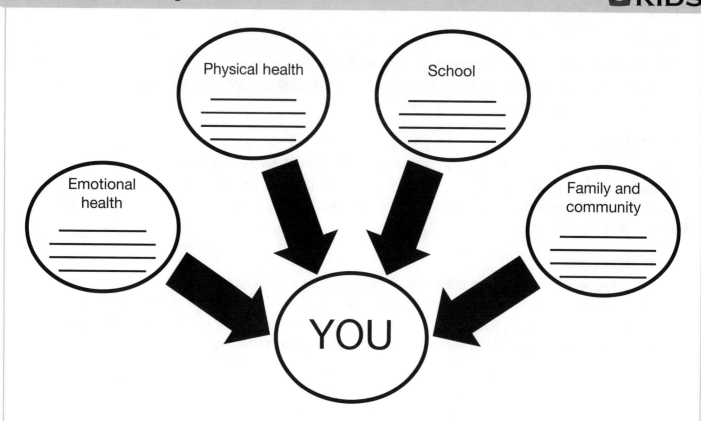

Examples and Nonexamples of Setting Goals

Situation 1 (nonexample—no goal and no action)

Michael daydreams every day about his life after making the team.

Situation 2 (nonexample—no goal and ineffective action)

Michael draws basketballs and famous ball players while in class.

Situation 3 (nonexample—partial goal and action)

Michael makes a goal to find out when tryouts or practices will take place.

Situation 4 (example)

To increase his chances that he'll make the team and to do his best, Michael makes a goal to spend at least 4 hours a week practicing until the day of tryouts.

Setting SMART Goals

Smart goals are *specific*. Specific goals speak about the exact part of something that we are going to address. "I'm going to be a nicer person," would become, "I'm going to be more open to different people by saying hello to someone new every day at lunch."

SMART goals are *measurable*. Measurable goals mean that we choose things that can be compared to how they used to be to see how much they have changed. "I'm going to be happier," would become, "I'm going to keep a gratitude journal and write down all the things that I am thankful for every morning, at least 5 days a week."

SMART goals are *attainable*. Attainable goals mean that the goal is something that could actually happen because of something you do. It can be a waste of our energy to be bothered by something we cannot change. "I'm going to get taller so I can play better volleyball" would have to change to "I'm going to practice at least three times a week to get better at volleyball."

SMART goals are *relevant*. Relevant goals connect with what we truly want and can lead to healthier, happier lives. Getting a higher score on a video game probably won't do much to help us with our goals of physical fitness and meeting new people, but setting a goal to get outside and connect with our friends more could help.

SMART goals are *timely*. We need a time frame to achieve our goals. "I am going to get stronger by running 3 miles" may be specific, measurable, attainable, and relevant, but there is no time frame. "I'm going to run 3 miles by 3 months from now" is a timely goal.

Steps to Setting and Attaining Goals

1. Identify your goal area from the healthy living domains: emotional health, physical health, school, and family and community.

2. Create your SMART goal: specific, measurable, attainable, relevant, and timely.

3. Implement your plan: Can someone help you? What might get in the way?

4. Check your progress: Are you on track to attain your goal? If not, investigate why. What changes do you need to make?

Merrell's Strong Kids—Grades 6–8: A Social and Emotional Learning Curriculum, Second Edition,
by Dianna Carrizales-Engelmann, Laura L. Feuerborn, Barbara A. Gueldner, and Oanh K. Tran.

Personal Goal Organizer

Name (optional) _____

Directions: Complete this personal goal organizer for your activities at home, in school, and during your free time.

	Home	School	Free time
My SMART goal			
Evaluate my goal	○ Specific ○ Measurable ○ Attainable ○ Relevant ○ Timely	○ Specific ○ Measurable ○ Attainable ○ Relevant ○ Timely	○ Specific ○ Measurable ○ Attainable ○ Relevant ○ Timely
Did I implement my plan?	☐ Yes ☐ No	☐ Yes ☐ No	☐ Yes ☐ No
Is my plan working?	☐ Yes. What goal can I work on now? _____ _____ _____ ☐ No. What changes can I make? _____ _____ _____	☐ Yes. What goal can I work on now? _____ _____ _____ ☐ No. What changes can I make? _____ _____ _____	☐ Yes. What goal can I work on now? _____ _____ _____ ☐ No. What changes can I make? _____ _____ _____
How did it make me feel?			

LESSON 12

Finishing UP!

Teacher Notes

_____

_____

_____

_____

_____

_____

_____

_____

_____

Purpose and Objectives

To provide students with a review of major concepts and skills in the *Strong Kids* curriculum. In this lesson, students will

1. Review Lessons 1–11 content

   - Comfortable and uncomfortable feelings and distinguishing healthy and unhealthy ways to express emotions

   - How thoughts, feelings, and behaviors are connected

   - The anger model and the problem-solving process

   - How to set and attain SMART goals

   - Common thinking traps and reframing them

   - Signs of stress and strategies for managing stress

   - Strategies for increasing habits for positive living

2. Develop an awareness of supports and safety networks.

   - Identify when students need more help and support.

   - Identify where to go for more help.

   - Identify support systems that contribute to school and life success.

3. Enhance an understanding of resilience and persistence.

   - Identify ways to persist in adversity.

   - Understand the importance of social and emotional learning to healthy decision making.

4. Participate in the posttest (optional).

   - Complete the posttest assessment (provide additional time if necessary).

Materials Needed

☐ Supplement 12.1 (online download and handout)

☐ Supplements 12.2–12.3 (handout)

☐ Color markers and poster board for Activity B

☐ *Strong Kids—Grades 6–8* Certificate of Achievement (optional certificate)

Running Short on Time?

Suggested stopping points: end of Activity A and the Closure activity. When continuing the lesson, begin with the Mindfulness-Based Focusing Activity found in the Introduction section, then Activity B.

Instructor Reflection

We have now come to the end of *Strong Kids—Grades 6–8*, and your students have gained essential skills for emotional, mental, social, and physical health. Think about the skills that you have taught your students throughout this program. How can you continue to reinforce these important skills so your students continue to practice them after the program ends? How can you encourage the development of these skills in your students' lives outside of this setting? Have you used any of these skills in your own life? If so, what experiences and outcomes did you observe? Did you learn anything about yourself, your strengths, and your weaknesses? What challenges in your professional or personal life might interfere with you reaching improved social, emotional, behavioral, social, and physical health? How might you address these challenges proactively? How can you prepare yourself to persist with your goals when you experience challenges? What goals do you have for yourself and your students moving forward? What steps can you take today to move forward and practice resilience when challenges come your way?

Note: If you have further concerns about how students may be coping with any social-emotional difficulties, consider talking to your administrator/ supervisor, school psychologist, or school counselor. It is important to be familiar with your school's/agency's mental health referral process and community resources.

Preparation

Prior to teaching the Finishing UP! lesson, it can be helpful to review Lessons 1–11 to refresh your memory. Be familiar with names of those people at your school/ agency who are there to support mental health concerns. Students will also be asked to identify resources and safety networks at the end of the lesson. As applicable, consider inviting your school's primary mental health practitioner (school psychologist, counselor, or other affiliated mental health provider) into your class to introduce him- or herself to your students.

Optional Posttest

If you conducted a pretest assessment before or during Lesson 1 and intend to conduct follow-up assessment of *Strong Kids—Grades 6–8* at the end of this lesson, you will need to reserve enough instructional time to do so. If you do not intend to conduct a follow-up assessment, extend the instruction portion of the lesson with review as needed. Refer to www.strongkidsresources.com for assessment recommendations. It is recommended that the same tests from the preassessment be used to determine the effects of students' participation in this curriculum.

Introduction

🕐 2–5 MINS. This is the final lesson of *Strong Kids—Grades 6–8*. This lesson reviews all of the skills learned over the past weeks while integrating these skills for emotional resilience. Students may complete a brief posttest to measure what they learned. Emphasize that the skills learned from the curriculum are vital to students' social and emotional health, and there will be opportunities to use these skills throughout their lives. Students will also engage in the final focusing activity of the program.

Sample Script

Today is our last lesson of the Strong Kids program and we will review all the important skills we've been talking about for the past few months. We started each lesson with an activity to help us get started on the lesson and focus our minds. We also discussed how to understand our emotions and those of the people around us, ways to take someone's perspective, how to show empathy and respect, the importance of taking responsibility, how to practice a positive attitude, how to reframe traps using evidence, ways to solve problems, how to set and attain goals, how to deal with anger and stress, and how to create healthier daily habits. These skills support us when we have to deal with adversity. They help us practice resilience and bounce back from problems we encounter in order to continue toward our goals. We will use some time today to talk about what to do and whom to talk to if we need help. We will talk about how to persevere toward our goals even when we stumble. We will end with setting a goal to keep practicing what we've learned so that we can continue to be emotionally and physically strong and healthy.

Mindfulness-Based Focusing Activity

🕐 2 MINS. **Sample Script**

Let's practice settling our bodies and focusing our minds. Close your eyes or look at a point on the floor or on your desk. Rest your hands comfortably. Feel your feet on the floor or your hands as they rest. Pay attention to your breathing for three breaths. [Pause for three breaths.] Let's take a moment to practice some of the focusing activities we've worked on. First, notice the sounds you hear in the room, near and far. [Pause for about 15 seconds.] Now, focus your attention on the feelings in your feet, legs, stomach, back, arms, shoulders, neck, and head. [Pause for about 15 seconds.] Next, with a curious and kind mind, pay attention to the emotions you are having. Notice how they feel. [Pause for about 15 seconds.] Now, focus on your thoughts. Notice how they change. [Pause for about 15 seconds.] Remember, whatever you are experiencing is okay. Now, let's focus on our breath for a minute. [Pause for 1 minute to allow practice.] Now, let's take two breaths together. [Pause.] When you finish letting out the second breath, slowly open your eyes.

Activity A: *Strong Kids* Lesson Review and Discussion Questions

11–14 MINS. Use Supplement 12.1 as a handout to guide this activity. Have students get into small groups to quickly review the lesson's main ideas. Then, have students share their thoughts regarding the discussion questions within their small groups. For each lesson, allow a leader to lead the discussion, then alternate to the next leader to lead the next lesson review. Continue to rotate for each lesson thereafter, allowing each student to be a leader. Allow 1–2 minutes for each lesson discussion. In order to keep things moving, you may wish to set a timer that rings every 60–90 seconds per lesson to remind students to move to the next lesson.

Sample Script

We have learned so much by doing this program, so it's important to discuss what you remember and how you will continue to use these important skills. In small groups, identify someone in the group to be the leader to review the topics and discussion questions for the first lesson. The leader will read the main ideas from each lesson from this handout. Then, the leader will briefly facilitate a discussion based on the questions listed. We will only have about a minute to review each lesson, so you will need to be focused and efficient in your discussion. I will let you know when to move to the next lesson review and discussion, then the next student leader leads the lesson review. Within your groups, you will rotate to allow all students to be leaders. [Depending on the number of students in small groups, some may be a leader multiple times.]

Note: Keep students in small groups for the next activity.

Using *Strong Kids* Skills to Persevere Through Adversity

15 MINS. Use Supplement 12.2 for this activity. Persevering through life's challenges helps to develop resilience. Encourage students to use the skills they've learned over the course of this program (e.g., positive thinking, coping strategies, making healthy choices) to persevere through adversity in creating a rap, song, poem, dance, and so forth.

Activity B: Design a Media Commercial and Emotional Resilience Slogan

🕐 40 MINS. Show Supplement 12.2 as an example of slogans. Students will get into small groups and develop a 2- to 3-minute media commercial advertising the importance of social-emotional development skills for student success. Allow students to write their scripts on paper; role play; act out scenes; develop a song or rap, a poem, a lyric, or a dance that is relevant to their commercial; and determine what they feel is important as a take-away message. Emphasize considering what skills are needed to deal with challenging situations. As part of the commercial, a resilience slogan will be developed to represent a saying or slogan that is memorable to the students in learning the *Strong Kids* program (show Supplement 12.2 for slogan examples). Allow students to use color markers and a poster board to create their slogan. Monitor the time to allow students to move through different parts of this activity (e.g., 10 minutes to think and discuss their ideas, 15 minutes to put their commercial together, 10 minutes to create their slogan poster). Then, come together and have groups volunteer to share their commercial and poster slogan (allow 10 minutes total for all sharing).

Sample Script

This activity will require you to work together and be creative in your ideas. Use your summary handout or any handouts you think would be helpful for your group. Within your group, you will develop a 2- to 3-minute media commercial about the importance of social and emotional learning. Use words and terms that you've learned and think about the activities that we've done to help you come up with a take-away message. Why should students know about becoming socially and emotionally strong? You are allowed to create a song, a rap, a poem, a dance, a lyric, a role-play scene, a riddle or rhyme, or a speech. Your commercial will be what your group feels is important to be successful in life. You will also create a slogan to represent your commercial. [Show Supplement 12.2 slogan examples.] Here are some example slogans for you to reference. You will be given a poster board and color markers to create your slogan. I will monitor the time and allow 10 minutes for group thinking and discussion, 15 minutes for putting together your commercial, and 10 minutes for creating the poster slogan. Afterward, we will come together and share our commercials. [Allow students time for any questions.]

Support Systems and Knowing When to Get Help

🕐 5 MINS. Students may require additional assistance and support when faced with life's challenges. Encourage them to be proactive by knowing to whom they can turn in advance of any crisis. Ensure that they are able to identify the school personnel, personal safety networks, and community organizations that can be helpful.

Sample Script

We will talk about how to know when we might need help and things you can do if you feel like you need more help or support. There are resources available, and knowing who they are now, before you have any need for them, will help improve your chances of getting help quickly if you ever need it.

Activity C: When to Seek Help

🕐 **2 MINS.** Explain to students that they have learned important skills during this program but that these skills may not be enough help for all of the possible problems they might have. They may require other adults to be involved or they may need professional help. Encourage a discussion of when to seek help. Emphasize awareness of their thoughts, emotions, and behaviors and the intensity of their problems by using the skills they have learned from *Strong Kids.* Encourage students to share their concerns with an adult they trust. In addition, encourage them to be aware of others' emotions and challenges so that they can suggest resources to their peers.

Sample Script

At times, a problem can be too much for us to handle on our own, and sometimes our emotional issues can turn into serious problems like anxiety or depression. If a problem ever gets serious, there are people you can turn to for help. A problem is serious when it gets in the way of you being able to do the things you like to do or you need to do, like having healthy relationships and getting your work done. So, if you feel like life is feeling really difficult, you're having a hard time knowing what to do, some of the not-so-good or unhelpful ideas are coming to mind, or nothing is working to make you feel better, this is when you want to ask an adult you trust for help. For example, if you don't get asked to the school dance or feel rejected by someone, and you are sad for days and cannot eat or sleep, or you don't want to leave the house, this is when you may want to talk to someone to help you feel better. It's also important for you to be aware of how your friends are feeling and what kinds of challenges they are going through. Remember, we talked about cues and paying attention to those cues so that you can be a support to others or encourage them to talk to someone. There are adults here at school who can help you and your classmates.

Activity D: List of Resources

🕐 **3 MINS.**

Use Supplement 12.3 as a handout. Have students think about and list the adults and other individuals they trust and can talk to at school, at home, and in the community. Help students generate names if they can't think of any (e.g., parent, other adult family members, a close adult friend or neighbor, clergy, principal, teacher, counselor, school psychologist). Have students also identify community resources or organizations that also can be helpful when needed. Be familiar with your school's mental health referral process in case students have questions or if you ever need to make a referral.

Sample Script

Use this handout to discuss and write down the adults in your life whom you trust and can go to for help. If you do not know anyone to contact, I will help you and give you some names of people who can support you. These people care about you and they want you to be well and help you to participate in life more fully. It is also important to know the resources within your community and identify them before you ever need them (e.g., clergy). Can someone share what other resources are in our community? [Allow time for sharing.] When you are in a situation and you need someone to talk to or you have problems, look at this handout. Keep it in a safe place so that you can use it when needed.

Optional Assessments

🕐 15–20 MINS. If you administered pretests from the *Strong Kids* web site during Lesson 1, now is the time to administer these tests again so that you can determine how effective *Strong Kids—Grades 6–8* was at increasing students' knowledge and enhancing their emotional resilience. It will take approximately 15–20 minutes to take these tests.

Putting It All Together

🕐 5 MINS. Reiterate the importance of perseverance and overcoming adversity. Encourage students to continue to reflect on the *Strong Kids* skills to help them through life's challenges. Use Supplement 12.1 to review any last comments or questions from the lesson discussion. Facilitate discussion on which *Strong Kids* skills can be used to build resilience. Allow time to hand out certificates for participation in *Strong Kids* if you choose to give certificates.

Sample Script

Let's practice what we've learned by putting it all together. Today, we reviewed everything we learned in this program and talked about emotional resilience and dealing with adversity. In the review activity we did earlier, are there any questions or comments about the key points from the lessons? [Allow time for students to share.] Believe it or not, we will continue to work on these skills throughout our entire lives. Some days will be better than others. But, by learning about and practicing the concepts in these lessons, you are preparing yourself to cope well and have a healthy and productive life. Which Strong Kids skills would be helpful to build resilience when challenges arise? [Allow time for students to share.] As we have worked through the program, we have shared stories with each other. Remember that stories are personal, and even though today is the last day of the lessons, we will remember not to share each other's stories with anyone outside of the group. By keeping other people's stories to yourself, you will be respecting others. Congratulations on finishing Strong Kids! Your skills have built up your emotional strength, and they will continue to be valuable as you become an adult. [Optional: Hand out Strong Kids Certificates.]

Closure

🕐 **2 MINS.**   Close the lesson using a brief breathing activity and a reflection on the lesson content.

Sample Script

Let's take a moment to regroup. Close your eyes and rest your hands in your lap. Feel your feet on the floor. Relax the muscles in your body and face. Relax and soften your stomach muscles. Counting to 3, take a deep breath in slowly. Inhale the air down into your lungs. Feel your chest and stomach expand like a balloon. [Pause.] *Now, exhale, counting to 4. Feel your chest and stomach collapse as all the air exits your body.* [Pause.] *Again, inhale deep into your lungs so that your stomach expands* [Pause.] *and exhale.* [Pause.] *Take a moment to think about something you learned today that was important to you.* [Note to instructor: Pause for a moment to allow time for reflection.] *Counting to 3, take one more deep breath in slowly* [Pause.] *and exhale, counting to 4.* [Pause.]

Tips for Transfer Training

Use the ideas and activities in the following section to practice the *Strong Kids* content with your students after completing the program. Also, remember to precorrect, remind, and reinforce concepts from the lessons in activities throughout the school week, and encourage students to use the skills taught in this lesson across settings including home, the bus, in the cafeteria, and in the community.

Additional Activities

- Have students create a dream board of pictures or a word collage of their dreams and the ways the skills learned in this program can help them achieve their dreams, goals, and aspirations.

- Have students perform research or an Internet search on community resources that are available in their area. They could interview the school psychologist or school social worker.

- Have students make school posters on emotional resilience and showcase them at an assembly or hang them in the office/hallway.

- Have students write a letter to the people in their support circle and explain how these people can help them. Encourage students to share their letter(s) with those individuals.

Strong Kids Lesson Review and Discussion Questions

Lesson 1: About *Strong Kids:* Emotional Strength Training (introduction to the program, learning the rules of the group, and beginning to learn about emotions)

- Key terms: resilience, adversity, and perseverance

- We all have emotions, every day, and everywhere we are. Emotions are like signals that tell us something about our situation.

- There are different emotions that we all have, and we can experience more than one emotion at the same time (refer to list of emotions/faces).

Discussion questions

1. What emotions have you noticed and learned about by participating in this program?

2. Provide an example situation that brought out an emotion. How did you recognize your emotion?

Lessons 2 and 3: Understanding Your Emotions 1 and 2 (there are physical feelings that go along with our emotions; there are thoughts and behaviors or actions that go along with our emotions)

- Key terms: emotions, thoughts, behaviors, action, respect/respectful, disrespect/disrespectful, physical feelings, comfortable, uncomfortable, emotional intensity, resilience, adversity, and perseverance

- Emotions can be physical and are linked to thoughts, feelings, and behaviors.

- Emotions can range from comfortable (happy, excited) to uncomfortable (worried, frustrated), and we can gauge these emotions on an intensity scale.

- We can respond to emotions in helpful ways to match our situation and our social needs.

Discussion questions

1. What emotions feel comfortable to you, and what emotions feel uncomfortable? What emotions feel both comfortable and uncomfortable?

2. How might you express emotions at home? In the cafeteria? With friends? With a teacher?

(continued)

Lesson 4: Understanding Other People's Emotions (noticing other people's perspectives and showing empathy)

- Key terms: empathy, sympathy, social clues, and perspective
- We can learn how to notice other people's feelings, how to try to understand other people's feelings better, and how to begin to see a situation from another person's perspective.

Discussion questions

1. What can you look for to give you clues about how someone might be feeling?
2. What kinds of information can help you take another person's perspective?

Lesson 5: Dealing with Anger (identify and manage angry emotions)

- Key terms: anger, aggression, anger management, perspective/point of view, response, and reaction
- Anger is a natural emotion that we all have, and it can be the result of a mixture of other upsetting emotions.
- When anger is unmanaged, it can lead to some not-so-good decisions, from holding it in to showing aggression.

Discussion questions

1. Do you think all people experience anger in the same way?
2. What are some helpful anger management strategies? Have you used any of these strategies? Which strategies worked best for you?

Lesson 6: Clear Thinking 1 (identify when our thoughts get stuck in thinking traps)

- Key terms: thoughts, self-talk, emotions, reactions, and thinking traps
- Thoughts influence emotions and behaviors.
- It is helpful to develop an awareness of our own thoughts and identify common thinking traps.

Discussion questions

1. What are thinking traps, and why is it important to be aware of them?
2. How are thoughts, emotions, and behavior related?

Lesson 7: Clear Thinking 2 (strategies we can use to think about other perspectives in a situation)

- Key terms: evidence and reframing
- We can develop the ability to notice or observe our thoughts.
- We can learn how to spot thinking traps, get out of them early, and keep them from snowballing by reframing.

(continued)

Discussion questions

1. Think of a time when you or someone you know was stuck in a thinking trap. How did you know it was a thinking trap? What was the evidence? Did it snowball or grow and become a bigger trap?

2. Did you or the person reframe the thinking trap to get unstuck? If so, how? If not, how could you or the person have reframed it to get unstuck earlier?

Lesson 8: Solving People Problems (ways to solve problems and get along with others)

- Key terms: responsible, attitude, conflict, problem solving/conflict resolution, resolution, and resolve

- Conflict is an unavoidable part of life, so it's important to know how to deal with it effectively.

- We can use the four-step problem-solving model and examples and nonexamples of problem solving.

- We can make responsible and respectful choices in solving conflicts with others.

Discussion questions

1. Conflict is a natural part of life, but sometimes we try to avoid it. Other times we might overreact. How have you handled conflict, and how could you apply the four-step problem-solving model to the situation?

2. How might showing empathy or taking another person's perspective help you when you are in conflict with another person?

Lesson 9: Letting Go of Stress (strategies we can use to deal with stress in our lives)

- Key terms: stress, helpful or healthy stress, unhelpful or unhealthy stress, situational triggers, relaxation, realistic or unrealistic expectations, and common signs of stress

- There are ways to identify healthy and unhealthy stress and stress triggers before you feel stressed out.

- We can learn the difference between helpful and unhelpful options and techniques for managing stress, and we can learn to tell realistic from unrealistic expectations.

Discussion questions

1. What are your triggers and signs of stress in your life?

2. What are some strategies for managing stress early on, before getting too stressed out?

(continued)

Lesson 10: Positive Living (things we can do to live a positive and healthy life)

- Key terms: habit, moderation, attitude, and choice
- Our behaviors and actions can contribute to a healthy and positive lifestyle in the long term.
- We can learn the differences between examples (helpful) and nonexamples (unhelpful) of life choices that can affect our lives at home, at school, and in the community.

Discussion questions

1. What are some activities or actions that energize us, motivate us, and make us happier in the long term?

2. What are some healthy living activities that you do now and healthier habits that you can create?

Lesson 11: Setting Strong and SMART Goals (setting goals and doing things that will help us lead a healthy life)

SMART Goals

S Specific

M Measurable

A Attainable

R Relevant

T Timely

- Key terms: goals, goal setting, goal attainment, and healthy living
- It is important to increase and maintain positive activities.
- Set SMART goals and monitor your progress.

Discussion questions

1. What are SMART goals?

2. What are some ways we can identify areas of our lives in need of SMART goals?

3. How can we improve the chances that we will attain our goals?

Resilience Example Slogans

Believe that you can

yes you can!

STAY STRONG AND BELIEVE IN YOURSELF

KEEP CALM AND HAVE RESILIENCE

Helping Resources Handout

List the important resources that you can turn to if you need some help or someone to talk to. Include their phone numbers, too. If you do not have their numbers, try to obtain them within the next week or so. Having this information readily available can be very helpful. After you've completed this form, keep it in a safe place so that you can get to it when/if needed.

When I need help or someone to talk to, I will contact one of these people:

This person at home supports me and I can talk to him/her for help: _____
_____

This friend supports me and I can talk to him/her for help: _____
_____

This adult at school supports me and I can talk to him/her for help: _____
_____

This person in the community supports me and I can talk to him/her for help: _____
_____

This is an organization/community resource in my area that I can go to for help: _____
_____

Remember that your school administrators, counselors, and teachers will know what to do or to whom you can talk if you need help.

Certificate of Achievement

Strong Kids—Grades 6–8 Certificate of Achievement

Awarded to

_____

for participating in
The *Strong Kids* Curriculum

**Resilience and emotional knowledge
are the keys to success!**

Instructor _____

Date _____

SECTION III

Appendices

Strong Kids Knowledge Test for Students in Grades 6-8

INSTRUCTIONS FOR TEACHERS/GROUP LEADERS

The *Strong Kids* Knowledge Test is a 20-item assessment tool designed to measure students' knowledge of social and emotional concepts and coping strategies; it is based on content from the curriculum. The Knowledge Test may be used to measure how effective *Strong Kids—Grades 6–8* is in increasing students' knowledge of social-emotional concepts and coping strategies. If you choose to use the Knowledge Test as a pre- and posttest measure, you should administer it before the first lesson (Lesson 1) and again after the last lesson (Lesson 12). Most students can complete the entire Knowledge Test in about 20 minutes. Some students (especially younger students and those students with reading problems) may have difficulty understanding the Knowledge Test and may require assistance (e.g., having the teacher read the items out loud or be available to answer questions about specific words) in completing it.

HOW TO SCORE THE KNOWLEDGE TEST

An answer key is included for the Knowledge Test. The key lists the correct answers for each of the 20 items, along with the lesson from which the question was drawn. To score students' tests, compare the students' actual answers to those in the key and place an *X* or other mark by every answer that is incorrect. Each item that has a correct answer should be given 1 point, and the final tally of correct answers can be converted into a percentage of correct responses. For example, if a student correctly answered 17 of 20 questions, his or her raw score would be 17 and the percentage correct would be 85%.

HOW TO USE THE TEST SCORES

To compare posttest scores to pretest scores, subtract the pretest total score from the posttest total score for each of the two tests. The difference reflects how much change occurred from the beginning to the end of the curriculum. Ideally, participation in *Strong Kids—Grades 6–8* will result in an increase in knowledge from pretest to posttest (i.e., the posttest scores will be greater than the pretest scores).

Strong Kids Knowledge Test for Students in Grades 6–8

PRETEST _____ POSTTEST _____

Name _____ Grade _____ Age _____

School _____ Today's date _____

On the next few pages, you will be asked to answer questions to see how much you know about feelings, thoughts, and behaviors. Read each question carefully and choose what you think is the *best* answer to each question. You may not know the answers to all the questions and you may not have heard some of the words before, but try your best. You will not be graded on your answers. If you have any questions, please ask your teacher.

TRUE or FALSE

Read each sentence. If you think it is true or mostly true, circle the word *True*. If you think it is false or mostly false, circle the word *False*.

1. True   False   Clenched fists and trembling or shaking hands can be signals that tell us to stop and use strategies to problem solve through a situation.

2. True   False   Emotions feel the same for everyone.

3. True   False   Stress can be caused by comparing yourself to other people because you think they're doing better than you.

4. True   False   The way we show how we feel can change depending on who we are with or where we are.

5. True   False   Feeling uncomfortable is normal and to be expected.

6. True   False   There are physical feelings or sensations that often happen when we have emotions.

MULTIPLE CHOICE

Circle the letter that goes along with the *best* answer for each question.

7. An example of an emotion that feels uncomfortable for most people is
    a. Hopeful
    b. Frustrated
    c. Curious
    d. Excited

8. What is an emotion?
    a. A thought you have about a situation
    b. Your inner voice inside your head
    c. A memory you have about something that happened to you
    d. A feeling that tells you something about a situation

(continued)

9. Self-talk can be a way to calm down after you get angry. Helpful self-talk might include telling yourself

   a. I don't deserve this

   b. I should get angry when something like this happens

   c. I can work through this

   d. I hope I never see this person ever again

10. Which of the following statements *best* describes empathy?

    a. Knowing how you are feeling

    b. Not knowing why another person is feeling sad

    c. Understanding how another person may be feeling based on your own similar experiences

    d. Wanting another person to feel better soon

11. Your thoughts can become traps when

    a. You see things in a way that is unhelpful or keeps you stuck

    b. You see both the good and bad in each situation

    c. You think something different from your friend

    d. You think about how another person might feel

12. Reframing is a way to

    a. Make new friends

    b. Think about how you can ignore the situation

    c. Think about a situation differently

    d. Make sure someone gets in trouble for what he or she has done

13. Why would you want to know how someone else is feeling?

    a. So you can leave that person alone when he or she is angry

    b. To better understand and support that person

    c. To tell other people about that person

    d. To act the same when you are together

14. Conflict resolution is *best* described as

    a. Discussing a problem until there is a winner and a loser

    b. Arguing with another person until he or she sees your point and gives in

    c. Problem solving so you can reach an agreement that is respectful and responsible for all involved

    d. Talking about the problem until something changes the other person's mind

(continued)

15. Which of the following is a *positive* or *helpful* way to handle being anxious when you have to show a bad grade to someone like your parent (or guardian)?

    a. Tell him or her why you are anxious and that you will work harder next time.

    b. Hide your grade and hope he or she will forget about it.

    c. Be sad and angry with yourself and stay in your room.

    d. Say that your grades were bad because other kids at school distracted you.

16. Which of the following is a helpful way to deal with a problem when you are feeling stressed?

    a. Cry somewhere quietly.

    b. Talk about the problem with someone you trust, such as a friend or teacher.

    c. Throw things around.

    d. Ignore the problem.

17. Which of the following is a helpful way to handle your emotions in class when your neighbor's talking begins to annoy you?

    a. Yell at that person and tell him or her to stop.

    b. Call out to the teacher about the student.

    c. Stare at the person until he or she knows you're annoyed.

    d. Stop and breathe deeply.

18. If you're feeling tired and low in energy, and you're having a hard time enjoying yourself even though things are mostly fine in your life, you could try

    a. Eating healthy meals

    b. Getting more sleep

    c. Spending time outdoors

    d. Spending time with friends

    e. Any of the above

19. An important step toward achieving goals is knowing how to set them. Which of the following is *not* an important part of a SMART goal?

    a. Specific

    b. Timely

    c. Abstract

    d. Measurable

20. Your friend seems upset. You want to show your friend that you care about what he or she is feeling. The most helpful way to do this is to

    a. Talk about something completely different that happened to you to change the subject

    b. Listen and show that you are paying attention

    c. Talk about something else

    d. Look away and don't say anything

Strong Kids Knowledge Test for Students in Grades 6–8 Answer Key

Correct answers for each of the 20 items are listed below. The *Strong Kids* lesson to which the question corresponds is indicated in parentheses.

1. T (Lesson 2)
2. F (Lesson 1)
3. T (Lesson 9)
4. T (Lesson 8)
5. T (Lesson 2)
6. T (Lesson 3)
7. b (Lesson 2)
8. d (Lesson 1)
9. c (Lesson 6)
10. c (Lesson 4)
11. a (Lesson 6)
12. c (Lesson 7)
13. b (Lesson 4)
14. c (Lesson 8)
15. a (Lesson 3)
16. b (Lesson 9)
17. d (Lesson 5)
18. e (Lesson 10)
19. c (Lesson 11)
20. b (Lesson 4)

Basic Fidelity Checklist

INSTRUCTIONS For each section, check the box if the lesson component was completed. If no items were implemented, check "Not" for not implemented. If some items were implemented, but not all, check "Partial" for partially implemented. If all items were implemented, check "Full" for fully implemented. In the Notes column, record the reason(s) for incomplete implementation of the component. In the Lesson Notes row, describe conditions that may have affected the fidelity for the lesson overall. Include any modifications made to the lessons.

Lesson Component	Level of Implementation			Notes
LESSON 1	Start time:		End time:	
Introduction	☐ Not	☐ Partial	☐ Full	
Pretest	☐ Not	☐ Partial	☐ Full	
Focusing Activity	☐ Not	☐ Partial	☐ Full	
Lesson Topics	☐ Not	☐ Partial	☐ Full	
Key Terms	☐ Not	☐ Partial	☐ Full	
Activity A	☐ Not	☐ Partial	☐ Full	
Activity B	☐ Not	☐ Partial	☐ Full	
Putting It All Together	☐ Not	☐ Partial	☐ Full	
Closure	☐ Not	☐ Partial	☐ Full	

Lesson notes:

Lesson Component	Level of Implementation			Notes
LESSON 2	Start time:		End time:	
Review	☐ Not	☐ Partial	☐ Full	
Introduction	☐ Not	☐ Partial	☐ Full	
Focusing Activity	☐ Not	☐ Partial	☐ Full	
Key Terms	☐ Not	☐ Partial	☐ Full	
Activity A	☐ Not	☐ Partial	☐ Full	
Activity B	☐ Not	☐ Partial	☐ Full	
Activity C	☐ Not	☐ Partial	☐ Full	
Putting It All Together	☐ Not	☐ Partial	☐ Full	
Closure	☐ Not	☐ Partial	☐ Full	

Lesson notes:

(continued)

Lesson Component	Level of Implementation			Notes
LESSON 3	Start time:		End time:	
Review	☐ Not	☐ Partial	☐ Full	
Introduction	☐ Not	☐ Partial	☐ Full	
Focusing Activity	☐ Not	☐ Partial	☐ Full	
Key Terms	☐ Not	☐ Partial	☐ Full	
Activity A	☐ Not	☐ Partial	☐ Full	
Activity B	☐ Not	☐ Partial	☐ Full	
Activity C	☐ Not	☐ Partial	☐ Full	
Activity D	☐ Not	☐ Partial	☐ Full	
Putting It All Together	☐ Not	☐ Partial	☐ Full	
Closure	☐ Not	☐ Partial	☐ Full	

Lesson notes:

Lesson Component	Level of Implementation			Notes
LESSON 4	Start time:		End time:	
Review	☐ Not	☐ Partial	☐ Full	
Introduction	☐ Not	☐ Partial	☐ Full	
Focusing Activity	☐ Not	☐ Partial	☐ Full	
Key Terms	☐ Not	☐ Partial	☐ Full	
Activity A	☐ Not	☐ Partial	☐ Full	
Activity B	☐ Not	☐ Partial	☐ Full	
Activity C	☐ Not	☐ Partial	☐ Full	
Activity D	☐ Not	☐ Partial	☐ Full	
Putting It All Together	☐ Not	☐ Partial	☐ Full	
Closure	☐ Not	☐ Partial	☐ Full	

Lesson notes:

(continued)

Lesson Component	Level of Implementation			Notes

LESSON 5

Start time: End time:

Lesson Component	Level of Implementation			Notes
Review	☐ Not	☐ Partial	☐ Full	
Introduction	☐ Not	☐ Partial	☐ Full	
Focusing Activity	☐ Not	☐ Partial	☐ Full	
Key Terms	☐ Not	☐ Partial	☐ Full	
Activity A	☐ Not	☐ Partial	☐ Full	
Activity B	☐ Not	☐ Partial	☐ Full	
Activity C	☐ Not	☐ Partial	☐ Full	
Putting It All Together	☐ Not	☐ Partial	☐ Full	
Closure	☐ Not	☐ Partial	☐ Full	

Lesson notes:

LESSON 6

Start time: End time:

Lesson Component	Level of Implementation			Notes
Review	☐ Not	☐ Partial	☐ Full	
Introduction	☐ Not	☐ Partial	☐ Full	
Focusing Activity	☐ Not	☐ Partial	☐ Full	
Key Terms	☐ Not	☐ Partial	☐ Full	
Activity A	☐ Not	☐ Partial	☐ Full	
Activity B	☐ Not	☐ Partial	☐ Full	
Activity C	☐ Not	☐ Partial	☐ Full	
Putting It All Together	☐ Not	☐ Partial	☐ Full	
Closure	☐ Not	☐ Partial	☐ Full	

Lesson notes:

(continued)

Basic Fidelity Checklist *(continued)*

Lesson Component	Level of Implementation			Notes
LESSON 7 Start time:			End time:	
Review	☐ Not	☐ Partial	☐ Full	
Introduction	☐ Not	☐ Partial	☐ Full	
Focusing Activity	☐ Not	☐ Partial	☐ Full	
Key Terms	☐ Not	☐ Partial	☐ Full	
Activity A	☐ Not	☐ Partial	☐ Full	
Activity B	☐ Not	☐ Partial	☐ Full	
Activity C	☐ Not	☐ Partial	☐ Full	
Activity D	☐ Not	☐ Partial	☐ Full	
Putting It All Together	☐ Not	☐ Partial	☐ Full	
Closure	☐ Not	☐ Partial	☐ Full	

Lesson notes:

Lesson Component	Level of Implementation			Notes
LESSON 8 Start time:			End time:	
Review	☐ Not	☐ Partial	☐ Full	
Introduction	☐ Not	☐ Partial	☐ Full	
Focusing Activity	☐ Not	☐ Partial	☐ Full	
Key Terms	☐ Not	☐ Partial	☐ Full	
Activity A	☐ Not	☐ Partial	☐ Full	
Activity B	☐ Not	☐ Partial	☐ Full	
Activity C	☐ Not	☐ Partial	☐ Full	
Activity D	☐ Not	☐ Partial	☐ Full	
Putting It All Together	☐ Not	☐ Partial	☐ Full	
Closure	☐ Not	☐ Partial	☐ Full	

Lesson notes:

(continued)